PENGUIN BOOKS

UNRAVELLING THE NATION: SECTARIAN CONFLICT AND
INDIA'S SECULAR IDENTITY

Kaushik Basu is Professor of Economics at Cornell University and the
Delhi School of Economics. He did his Ph.D from the London School of
Economics and was Distinguished Visitor there in 1993.

Sanjay Subrahmanyam is Professor of Economic History at the Delhi School
of Economics, and Director d'é'tudes at the Ecoles des Hautes Etudes en
Sciences Sociales, Paris. He is the author of the forthcoming *Vasco da
Gama: Career and Legend.*

Unravelling the Nation

Sectarian Conflict and India's Secular Identity

edited by

Kaushik Basu

and

Sanjay Subrahmanyam

- G. BALACHANDRAN • ALAKA M. BASU
- VEENA DAS • SUDHIR KAKAR
- AMARTYA SEN

PENGUIN BOOKS

An imprint of Penguin Random House

PENGUIN BOOKS

USA | Canada | UK | Ireland | Australia
New Zealand | India | South Africa | China | Singapore

Penguin Books is part of the Penguin Random House group of companies
whose addresses can be found at global.penguinrandomhouse.com

Published by Penguin Random House India Pvt. Ltd
4th Floor, Capital Tower 1, MG Road,
Gurugram 122 002, Haryana, India

Penguin
Random House
India

First published by Penguin Books India 1996

10 9 8 7 6 5 4 3

'The Construction of a New Hindu Identity' by Sudhir Kakar appeared earlier in
his book The Colours of Violence, Viking Penguin India, 1995 and is
reprinted by permission of the publishers.

ISBN 9780140257588

Typeset in Times New Roman by PP LASER PRINTERS, New Delhi

Printed at Manipal Technologies Limited, India

www.penguin.co.in

CONTRIBUTORS

G. Balachandran is Reader in Economics at the Delhi School of Economics. He has published widely on British financial policy in late colonial India and is currently doing research on Indian maritime labour.

Alaka M. Basu is Senior Research Associate at Cornell University. She has written extensively on issues related to the demographic transition and is currently working on the politics of fertility decline. She is the author of *Culture, the Status of Women and Demographic Behaviour* (1992).

Kaushik Basu has written papers and lectured in the areas of development studies, game theory, the problem of basic needs in South Asia and political economy. He is the author of *The Less Developed Economy* (1984).

Veena Das is Professor of Sociology at the Delhi School of Economics. She has contributed to theories of myth and history, collective violence and anthropology of health and disease. She is the author of *Structure and Cognition* (1977) and of *Critical Events* (1995) and editor of *Mirrors of Violence* (1991).

Sudhir Kakar is a psychoanalyst in New Delhi who works in the fields of cultural psychology and the psychology of religion. His latest book is *The Colours of Violence* published by Viking Penguin in India and University of Chicago Press in the USA.

Amartya Sen is Lamont University Professor and Professor of Economics and Philosophy at Harvard University. He has published widely in the areas of economic theory, development and moral philosophy. He is the author of *Collective Choice and Social Welfare* (1970) and *Poverty and Famines* (1981).

Sanjay Subrahmanyam has published widely on the history and economic history of South Asia, the Indian Ocean and the Iberian world in the early modern period.

ACKNOWLEDGEMENTS

This book emerged out of a project on *Nationalism and Political Security* supported by the Common Security Forum at the Centre for History and Economics, King's College, University of Cambridge in cooperation with The Harvard Center for Population and Development Studies. We are grateful to the Common Security Forum not ony for the financial support but also for organizational help at various stages of this project. For comments and suggestions on the manuscript we owe special thanks to Emma Rothschild. Research assistance for this work was provided by Rimjhim Aggarwal and Arghya Ghosh. We also acknowledge institutional and secretarial support from the Centre for Development Economics at the Delhi School of Economics. Finally, we would like to thank Rimjhim Aggarwal, Sunil Khilnani and Anne Malcolm for comments on specific chapters.

Kaushik Basu
Sanjay Subrahamanyam

For K.N. Raj
in admiration for his integrity and human concerns

CONTENTS

CONTENTS

Introduction

Kaushik Basu and Sanjay Subrahmanyam

THIS BOOK comprises a set of essays written around the problems and conflicts that inhere in notions of community, nation and nationalism in South Asia, and more particularly India, as seen from the perspective of the closing years of the twentieth century. By all accounts, whether one uses conventional quantitative measures of rates of growth of GNP, population, per capita income, and international trade in goods and services, or more complex qualitative ones, the century has been one of dramatic change globally. Its very first years witnessed the invention of the aeroplane (and the first mechanical flight, by Orville Wright, in 1903), which captured the optimistic idea of the closing of physical distances between peoples and nations; many were hopeful that metaphorically speaking too, distances would be narrowed as a consequence. Yet, early on in its career, the aeroplane demonstrated its other aspect, and was used as a weapon of destruction in a struggle between nations and empires, and thus contributed its part to the carnage of the First World War. Arguably, the same could be said of wireless communication, where Marconi's major breakthrough corresponded closely, chronologically speaking, with that of the Wrights. If then, as Michael Adas has noted, the years leading up to the First World War were characterized by a technological optimism, and linked to forms of universalistic humanism, the subsequent years failed signally to bring about changes in the direction that had been predicted. Rather than leading to the triumph of universalism and humanism, this century has repeatedly emphasized difference, separateness and – in the process – nationalism.

We may develop this paradox a little further. Let us recall that from the rubble of the Great War there emerged what to many observers, not only convinced Marxists like M.N. Roy and Ho Chi Minh, but rather more uncertain Socialists from Bernard Shaw to Jawaharlal Nehru, appeared to be the key positive event of the century, namely the October Revolution in Russia. Besides, the war equally helped to accelerate the disintegration of two of the imperial political formations that had survived from an earlier age, the Austro-Hungarian (Habsburg) Empire and the Ottoman Empire, whose adversarial relationship had once, in the sixteenth century, been the key to European politics. Now, as the century comes to an end, it begins to appear that matters have come full circle, as the Soviet Union – the unkempt child of the Russian Revolution – seems to have become unviable politically and economically. Some observers have taken to comparing the former Soviet Union to an empire, conveniently forgetting that its demise has also meant the destruction of a particular model of the large, complex, nation-state, and thus the uncertain beginning to a new phase of history, rather than the 'End of History'.

How does the end of the twentieth century compare to its beginning, from the viewpoint of nation-building? The rhetoric that accompanied the formation of new nations at the close of the First World War was based largely on the identification of nation with ethnicity, and both of these were seen as largely unproblematic notions at the time. To be sure, some of the nation-states formed out of the Ottoman Empire in West Asia and in the Balkans had premises other than purely ethnic ones; but the broad tendency was nevertheless towards ethnocentred fragmentation. It is now quite clear that a certain amount of rather brutal 'ethnic cleansing' equally accompanied this process, as we know from the Armenian example, for instance. In sharp contrast, the Soviet Union persisted as an example of a very large, multi-ethnic, multi-cultural state structure, even if the glue that held it together turns out to have been Russian chauvinism rather than federal or collective decision-making. In turn, the ambitious, and deeply traumatic, attempts to relocate whole populations in order to delink ethnicity and region, are characteristic of the Soviet belief that summary solutions could be applied to such artefacts of 'false consciousness' as religion and ethnic identity.

In the wave of decolonization that followed the Second World War, and which ran into the early nineteen-sixties (or the mid-seventies, if one prefers to stress the southern and south-central African cases of Zimbabwe, Mozambique and Angola), these two opposing tendencies are once more to be seen in tandem. On the one hand, the leaning towards political fragmentation, and the formation of small (even tiny) nations based on religious identity, ethnicity (however defined), or language, on the other the persistence of some relatively large, multi-ethnic, pluri-cultural, religiously diverse nation states, of which India is clearly an important (perhaps, today, even the most important) example. The trajectory of India as a nation-state is thus not only important in itself; it is also the crucial test case for whether relatively new nation-states can preserve diversity in religious, ethnic and cultural terms. Other Asian nations such as China, dominated culturally by its Han population, cannot be said to have the same character. Matters are made that much more complicated in India by the fact that in the late twentieth and early twenty-first centuries, fairly sweeping changes in the domestic and international economic environment may be expected, which will surely be accompanied by a social transition of some importance. Given the relatively non-authoritarian character of the political system in India (compared once more to, say, China), the articulation of this social transition will surely be reflected in political terms.

Unlike what has often been assumed, both in western writings, and by simple-minded apostles of liberalization in India, the Indian economic performance in the post-independence years has not been wholly dismal. Comparisons between India and China do not always reflect badly on the former, whether in respect of famine prevention, or other aspects of social policy. Where India has not fared well is in the persistence of mass poverty, as well as a poor level of some other key indicators, from literacy, to morbidity and infant mortality. Again, it is necessary to bear in mind that important regional differences exist within India; the case of Kerala has been cited by Amartya Sen and others to show that rapid economic growth is not a necessary prerequisite for a reasonable standard of living or well-being. In terms of certain common indicators of the standard of living, Kerala actually fared better than even the best districts of China.

Nevertheless, it is clear that the economic changes of the coming years, which are often summed up under the broad head of 'liberalization', will be significant and of consequence not only for the Indian economy, but will also create new social and political tensions the fallout of which is not entirely predictable. Sectarian conflict in India will find echoes outside; conflicts on the outside will increasingly find reflection in India. As trans-national funding of religious and political groups grows, the fate of local issues in India will be tied up as much to the finances mobilized by Sikhs in Vancouver, as with remittances from the Gulf, with German funding to Christian missionary activity in India, and with non-resident support for increasing Hindu militancy. Will this exacerbate the conflict of 'civilizations' that some Western political scientists insist is under way, in particular with the Islamic underbelly of Europe in mind? Or will it strengthen the hands of a 'westernized' and 'secular' middle class in India, as others insist ? Will increasing economic prosperity and competition drive away sectarian tensions, or will the market help create a disenfranchized underclass that will further complicate the formation of sectarian and communal identities, and further fuel tensions ?

The present book does not venture to predict outcomes. But it is put together in the belief that these are complex questions of a great immediacy, with possibly momentous consequences depending on how they are resolved. We believe that an essential step towards answering these questions and grappling with the problems is first to try and understand them; to examine the political, economic and social faces of sectarianism and sub-nationalism. Towards this end, we invited some of the leading economists, sociologists, psychologists and historians of India to help us examine and understand our present predicament. The book is a collection of essays by them.

It begins with an essay of considerable sweep by Amartya Sen which investigates the idea of secular India. 'Secularism' is an ambiguous concept, with many possible interpretations. In the context of India, Sen suggests that her secular ideal is essentially that of pluralism, not just in terms of religion but language groups, culture, and social practices. The principle of secularism does not require dissociation between the state and religions. What it requires is a *symmetry* of treatment of different religions and different religious communities. The idea of secularism was widely accepted at the time of India's independence. But now, as we approach this century's end, there is increasing dissent being voiced against the idea. Sen considers six standard arguments against secularism and as an 'unreformed secularist', defends the idea. In the process, he garners support from a range of lucidly constructed philosophical arguments and historical vignettes.

To understand our present situation and to 'construct' solutions requires us to look back at the past. But the past provides no black and white answers. Though communal political parties often drastically simplify the historical record to fit their ideology, history provides us with no representative citizen or ideal ruler. Aurangzeb's intolerance was by no means representative of the attitudes of his contemporaries, and Akbar's openness to religious and cultural experimentation cannot be divorced from a consideration of the political and cultural context within which it was affirmed. Similarly, the history of Hindu-Sikh relations of one century turns out to be no easy predictor of relations in another. The past decade has witnessed a number of significant political processes in India, some of which have undoubtedly left enduring and traumatic scars. The emergence of Khalistani militancy in the post-Emergency period, the anti-Sikh violence that followed the assassination of Indira Gandhi in October 1984, and the subsequent suppression of militancy in Punjab through the use of draconian measures, have not resolved the problems of Sikh identity either in India or abroad. In the 1990s, assertive Sikh groups in localities of Delhi have begun, like aggressive Hindu organizations, to lay claim to public land for religious purposes, and are supported both by Sikh groups abroad, and more recently even by the BJP government in India's capital. An analysis of the intricacies of such problems requires a detailed examination of the politics (and economic balance) of particular localities, as well as an awareness of the broader macro-context of assumptions within which religiously-constituted groups operate. As Veena Das points out in her essay on anti-Sikh violence in 1984, important variations may be observed from one micro-locality to another, as local dynamics render more complex what appears superficially from the outside to be a uniform phenomenon.

In the aftermath of the traumatic events of the mid-1980s, and especially in the 1990s, the major change in the nature of Indian politics has been the emergence into prominence of another politico-religious phenomenon, namely the *Hindutva* movement, organized around the parties and organisations of the *Sangh parivar*. Although their emergence is the result of a long period of gestation, ranging back to the late nineteenth century, there is clearly a shift in the political weight of such groups in the post-Janata government phase of national politics. In the 1990s, the politics of *Hindutva* have acted as a magnet, drawing former radicals (including even some contributors to the early volumes of *Subaltern Studies*), former communists (who have now discovered that a 'cultural faultline' had long existed between Hindus and Muslims), and, above all, erstwhile adherents of Congress-style socialism. G. Balachandran's essay attempts to contextualise the emergence of such a brand of Hindu communal politics, by placing it against the background of the latter part of the colonial period, and various other ethnic and regional movements of the post-independence era.

It is clear that the 'new Hindu identity' that the *Sangh parivar* wishes to foster is based on a series of binary oppositions between Hindus and others (usually Muslims), but also on the creation of a new, violent, and grandiose, political rhetoric, audible for example in the widely circulated cassettes of Sadhvi Rithambra. Sudhir Kakar in his essay examines these tendencies, and what he regards as their inherent narcissism, and concludes that they are largely triggered off by the global phenomenon of modernization, to which they represent a particular, perhaps pathological, response.

The definition of this new identity depends crucially in turn on the use of the past as a resource. In this the *Hindutva* movement is not alone; Soviet nationalism used such improbable figures as

6

Aleksandr Nevski and even Peter the Great; the French have been free with the myths of Vercingetorix, Clovis and Charlemagne; in the Maghreb, the Sultan Ahmad al-Mansur and others who 'heroically resisted' Portuguese imperialism in the late sixteenth century have been enshrined in the pantheon of heroes. It is surely no coincidence that the emergence of the BJP-RSS-VHP combine centred around a dispute over a historical monument, the Babri Masjid at Ayodhya, and that some of their sharpest attacks have been (and are) directed at what they view as 'pseudo-secular', leftist Indian historians who have distorted India's pre-colonial history. This view represents a shift from the traditional nationalist emphasis on the colonial state as responsible for all the social, economic and political evils to be found in India, and even curiously absolves colonialism of many faults. While the nationalist position is still held to a greater or lesser extent by left-radical historians, who either attribute sectarian tensions in India to British 'divide and rule' policies, or to the British construction of a communalist 'discourse' which then insidiously infiltrated Indian minds, amateur and professional historians attached to the *Sangh parivar* have scoured colonially patronized translations of pre-colonial sources in Persian and Arabic to find in them evidence of large-scale, and one-sided, violence. The brunt of this position, variously argued by such writers as Arun Shourie and Sita Ram Goel, is to argue that the historical grievances of 'Hindus', stemming above all from the destruction and desecration of temples, must now be redressed retrospectively.

In the face of this attack, the response of left and liberal historians has been altogether curious. They have either denied the empirical validity of the statement that large-scale sectarian violence took place in pre-colonial India, or they have argued that the violence that took place, while ostensibly sectarian or religious, was in fact motivated by purely materialistic intentions such as the accumulation of loot, the destruction of the power-base of rivals, and so on. If indeed it were true that sectarian and religious violence did not take place in pre-colonial India, the subcontinent would be a glaring exception to the rule that one observes practically everywhere in the medieval and early modern world. Where India is different, is that unlike Europe, where nation-states tended in their formative stages to destroy or expel minorities – the Reconquest of Iberia and the concomitant expulsion of Jews and Muslims, the religious wars between Catholics and Protestants in France, the Netherlands and Germany, anti-Catholic and anti-Puritan movements in England – in the South Asian subcontinent a relatively diverse population has survived into modern times, and has been constituted in at least two cases (Sri Lanka and India) into nation-states. The issues of this complex medieval legacy are discussed in Sanjay Subrahmanyam's contribution to the volume.

Indeed, it is not clear that western Europe holds out any example to India in this respect. Even in recent times, faced with the issue of immigration of Muslim minorities from the Maghreb, Turkey and the former Yugoslavia, the response of European governments has been curiously ambivalent. Anti-Islamic rhetoric has heated up, fuelled by the very real tensions that exist at an international level between some Islamic states in West Asia and North Africa, and the states of the EEC and the United States. It is also often stated in France, at a popular level, that North African communities constitute a threat, because of their relatively large family size (the somewhat impolite French expression *smala*, from the Arabic *zmala*). The spectre of a rapidly increasing minority which will soon turn itself into a majority is evoked.

This parallels similar statements that are often made in the Indian context, and which are investigated in the present volume by Alaka Malwade Basu. It is certainly true that the rate of growth of population of the Muslim minority in India since independence has been slightly higher than that of the population taken as a whole. But this difference does not appear all that significant once one takes into account the impact of socio-economic factors. It is often forgotten that despite the presence of a limited number of elite Muslims in positions of power and authority, a very large proportion of India's Muslim population comprises poor agriculturists and artisans, whose lot has not greatly improved in the decades since independence. Basu goes on to show how politicians routinely distort fertility and migration statistics in order to bolster their prejudices. She argues in effect against the politicization of demography.

8

The volume does not directly address another frequently voiced accusation: that the Indian state pampers certain minorities, whether defined through religion or caste. Taking a leaf out of the book of western social scientists, who have argued from the point of view of economic efficiency against affirmative action, some Indian analysts too have argued that the state has introduced serious distortions into the efficient functioning of the economy by such policies. This argument has three clear flaws in it. *First*, it often assumes that in the absence of such affirmative action by the government, resources would be allocated in a first-best fashion, as if other distortions did not exist. *Second*, it fails to take note of the fact that even if some efficiency loss is incurred in the short-term, the computation of dynamic losses and gains is not clear. And *third*, such a view neglects the weakness of focussing exclusively on efficiency, which is in fact compatible with what to common sense appears the most flagrant form of injustice, that of favouring the *status quo*.

Conceived of as part of a larger project on common security, this collection is by no means comprehensive in its coverage. Yet by paying attention to cultural, historical and economic aspects of the problems of community and nation in India, these essays do attempt to present a coherent, reasoned, and astringent alternative perspective to those produced in recent times. The debates, needless to say, will continue, both with others writing on South Asia, and with those who have formulated wide-ranging comparative arguments, such as Benedict Anderson, Ernest Gellner, and Eric Hobsbawm. Unlike these latter authors, the contributors to the present volume have for the most part laid limited emphasis on issues of language in relation to nationalism, which in itself may be a reflection on the difference between the core bases of Indian and western nationalisms. Whatever be the case, it seems worthwhile to emphasize once more that nationalism and the problems of the nation-state will continue to remain central both to inhabitants of, and researchers on, South Asia, for better or for worse, for a good many years to come. Whatever shape 'globalization' takes in the decades to come, immigration barriers that separate and distinguish national labour markets are likely to remain as high, if not higher, than before; it is information, commodities and capital that will flow internationally. The owl of Minerva may have begun to circle nationalism, as Eric Hobsbawm has recently written; but it is far too soon to conclude that we are hence at the twilight of this phenomenon.

Secularism and Its Discontents[1]

Amartya Sen

1. Introduction

WHEN India became independent nearly half a century ago, much emphasis was placed on its secularism, and there were few voices dissenting from that priority. In contrast, there are now persistent pronouncements deeply critical of 'Indian secularism, and attacks have come from quite different quarters. In this essay, I want to examine these discontents.

Before proceeding further, I should say a few words on the audience to which this analysis is addressed. Issues of national, social and communal identities, and their political correlates, have received, in recent years, extensive analyses from scholars with much expertise in the field. The subject, however, is also of interest to many others — within India and outside as well. It would be a pity if an insistence on extensive prior knowledge about details of Indian history or contemporary state were to shut out potential readers from joining in this discussion. This heterogeneity of readership calls, I believe, for a style of presentation that might well be irritating to the knowledgeable expert.[2] I must, therefore,

---

[1] For helpful discussion I am grateful to Sabyasachi Bhattacharya, Akeel Bilgrami Sugata Bose, Joshua Greene, Emma Rothschild, and the editors of this volume.
[2] In a somewhat comparable context, in presenting his essays on 'Africa in the philosophy of culture', Kwame Anthony Appiah notes that a work of this kind 'is bound to spend some of its time telling each of its readers something that he or she already knows', and he anticipates that some readers will ask why the author has 'explained what does not need explaining' (*In My Father's House*, New York: Oxford University Press, 1992, p. xi). This reader is grateful to Appiah for not assuming knowledge of things that any 'Africanist' would know very well. The present essay, similarly, is not for the 'Indianist' only.

ask for tolerance from the bored, but given the assertive nature of this essay, I am well aware that boredom is not the thing that would most irritate *some* readers.

Many of the barbed attacks on secularism in India tend to come from activists engaged in practical politics, often associated with the BJP (the Bharatiya Janata Party), which has been described as 'the principal political party representing the ideology of Hindu nationalism in the electoral arena'.[3] Sometimes the attacks have come from the Shiv Sena, the locally powerful militant Hindu party based in Maharashtra and its capital, Bombay. Persistent critiques of secularism are also associated with the R.S.S. (Rashtriya Swayamsevak Sangh), which does not participate in elections, but which has been the moving force behind a good deal of Hindu activist politics, including providing leadership and direction to the BJP and other parts of the so-called '*Sangh parivar*' (the 'family' of like-minded organizations oriented towards a Hinduism-based Indian politics).

However, intellectual scepticism about secularism is not confined to those actively engaged in politics. Indeed, eloquent expressions of this scepticism can be found also in the high theory of Indian culture and society.[4] Many of the attacks are quite removed from the BJP and other official organs of Hindu nationalism. In addressing the issue of Indian secularism it is important to take note of the range as well as the vigour of these critiques, and also the fact that they come from varying quarters and use quite distinct arguments. If today 'secularism, the ideological mainstay of multireligious India, looks pale and exhausted',[5] the nature of that predicament would be misidentified

[3] Ashotosh Varshney. 'Contested Meanings: Indian National Unity, Hindu Nationalism, and the Politics of Anxiety', *Daedalus*, 122 (1993), p. 231.

[4] See particularly T.N. Madan, 'Coping with Ethnic Diversity: A South Asian Perspective', in Stuart Plattner, ed., *Prospects for Plural Societies* (Washington. DC: American Ethnological Society, 1984), and 'Secularism in Its Place', *Journal of Asian Studies*, 46 (1987); and Ashis Nandy, 'An Anti-Secular Manifesto', *Seminar*, No. 314 (1985), and 'The Politics of Secularism and the Recovery of Religious Tolerance', *Alternatives*, 13 (1988).

[5] Varshney, 'Contested Meanings: Indian National Unity, Hindu Nationalism, and the Politics of Anxiety' (1993), p. 227.

— and somewhat minimized — if it were to be seen simply in terms of the politics of Hindu sectarianism. While the attacks on secularism have often come from exactly that quarter, there are other elements as well, and the subject calls for a wider analysis and response.

Despite this broad and forceful challenge, secularist intellectuals in India tend to be somewhat reluctant to debate on this rather unattractive subject. Reliance is placed instead, usually implicitly, on the well-established and unquestioning tradition of seeing secularism as a good and solid political virtue for a pluralist democracy. As an unreformed secularist myself, I understand, and to some extent share, this reluctance, but also believe that addressing these criticisms is important. This is so not only because the condemnations have implications for political and intellectual life in contemporary India, but also because it is useful for secularists to face these issues explicitly — to scrutinize and reexamine the habitually accepted priorities, as well as the reasoning behind them. There is much need for self-examination of beliefs — nowhere more so than in practical reason and political philosophy.[6] Hence this attempt at discussing some of the critical questions about secularism that have been forcefully raised.

2. Incompleteness of Secularism and the Need to Go Beyond

The nature of secularism as a *principle* calls for some clarification as well as scrutiny. Some of the choices considered under the heading of secularism lie, I would argue, beyond its immediate scope. Secularism in the political — as opposed to ecclesiastical — sense requires the separation of the state from any particular religious order. It goes against giving any religion a privileged position in the activities of the state. It is important to be clear as to what the denial of such a privileged position would or would not imply. The requirement is not that the state must stay clear of any association with any religious matter whatsoever. Rather, what is needed is to make sure that insofar as the state has to deal with

[6]In this context, see also Charles Taylor, *et al, Multiculturalism and 'The Politics of Recognition'* (Princeton: Princeton University Press, 1993).

13

different religions and members of different religious communities, there must be a basic symmetry of treatment.

Therefore, to be secular in the political sense, the state does not have to withdraw from dealing with religions and religious communities altogether. For example, it is no violation of secularism for a state to protect everyone's right to worship as he or she chooses, even though in doing this the state has to work *with* — and *for* — religious communities. In the absence of asymmetric solicitude (such as protecting the rights of worship for one religious community, but not others), the preservation of religious freedom does not breach the principle of secularism.

The important point to note here is that the requirement of symmetric treatment still leaves open the question as to what *form* that symmetry should take. To illustrate with an example, the state may decide that it must not offer financial — or other — support to any hospital with any religious connection whatever. Or, alternatively, it can provide support to *all* hospitals, without in any way discriminating between the respective religious connections (or lack of these). While the former may appear to be, superficially, 'more secular' (as it certainly is in the 'associative' sense, since it shuns religious connections altogether), the latter is also *politically* quite secular in the sense that the state, in this case, supports hospitals *irrespective* of whether or not there are any religious connections (and if so, what), and in this way, it keeps the state and the religions quite separate.

Since the two forms are both politically secular, a 'secularist' has to face the choice between them (and other options with secular symmetry). Secularism closes some alternatives, but still allows several distinct options. There is, thus, a need in dealing with religions and religious communities to take up questions that lie 'beyond' secularism. While this essay is concerned with scrutinizing attacks on secularism as a political requirement, the organizational issues that lie beyond secularism must also be characterized.[7] In analysing the role of secularism in India, note

[7]Some of the arguments presented here draw on an earlier paper (my Nehru Lecture at Trinity College, Cambridge, on 5 February 1993), published under the title 'Threats to Indian Secularism', in *The New York Review of Books*, April 8, 1993. See also the illuminating paper of Akeel Bilgrami, 'Two Concepts of Secularism', *Yale Journal of Criticism*, 7 (1994).

must be taken of its intrinsic 'incompleteness', including the problems that this incompleteness leads to, as well as the opportunities it offers.

3. Critical Arguments

Scepticism about Indian secularism takes many different forms. I shall consider, in particular, six distinct lines of argument. This may be enough for one paper, but I do not claim that all anti-secularist attacks are covered by the arguments considered here.

(1) The 'non-existence' critique

Perhaps the simplest version of scepticism about Indian secularism comes from those who see nothing much there, at least nothing of real significance. For example, Western journalists often regard Indian secularism as essentially non-existent, and their language tends to contrast 'Hindu India' (or 'mainly Hindu India') with 'Muslim Pakistan' (or 'mainly Muslim Pakistan'). Certainly, Indian secularism has never been a gripping thought in broad Western perceptions, and recent pictures of politically militant Hindus demolishing an old mosque in Ayodhya have not helped to change these perceptions. Indian protestations about secularism are often seen in the West as sanctimonious nonsense — hard to take seriously in weighty discourses on international affairs, and in the making of foreign policy by powerful and responsible Western states that dominate the world of contemporary international politics.

(2) The 'favouritism' critique

A second line of attack argues that in the guise of secularism, the Indian constitution and political and legal traditions really favour the minority community of Muslims, giving them a privileged status not enjoyed by the majority community of Hindus. This 'favouritism' critique is popular with many of the leaders and supporters of the Hindu activist parties. The rhetoric of this attack can vary from wanting to 'reject' secularism to arguing for what is called 'true secularism' ('shorn of favouring the Muslims').

(3) *The 'prior identity' critique*

A third line of critique is more intellectual than the first two. It sees the identity of being a Hindu, or a Muslim, or a Sikh, to be politically 'prior' to being an Indian. The Indian identity is 'built up' from the *constitutive* elements of separate identities. In one version of the identity argument, it is asserted that given the preponderance of Hindus in the country, any Indian national identity cannot but be a function of some form or other of a largely Hindu identity. Another version would go further and aim at a homogeneous identity as a necessary basis of nationhood (in line with the picturesque analogy that 'a salad bowl does not produce cohesion; a melting pot does'[8]), and move on from that proposition to the claim that only a shared cultural outlook, which in India can only be a largely Hindu view, can produce such a cohesion. Even the unity of India derives, it is argued, from the 'cementing force' of Hinduism.

(4) *The 'Muslim sectarianism' critique*

In another line of critique, the proposed dominance of Hindu identity in 'Indianness' turns not on the logic of numbers, but is 'forced on the Hindus', it is argued, by the 'failure' of the Muslims to see themselves as Indians first. This form of argument draws heavily- on what is seen as the historical failure of Muslim rulers in India to identify themselves with others in the country, always seeing Muslims as a separate and preferred group. It is also claimed that Muslim kings systematically destroyed Hindu temples and religious sites whenever they had the chance to do so.

Jinnah's 'two-nation theory', formulated before independence

---

[8]See Varshney's helpful characterizations of different claims associated with 'Hindu nationalism', in his 'Contested Meanings' (1993), pp. 230-1; see also Ashis Nandy, 'The Ramjanmabhumi Movement and the Fear of Self', mimeographed paper, presented at the Harvard Center for International Affairs, April 1992.

(and historically important in the partition of India), is seen as a continuation of the evident Muslim refusal to identify with other Indians. It is argued that while the partition of India has provided a 'homeland' for the Muslims of the subcontinent, the Muslims left in India are unintegrated and are basically not 'loyal' to India. The 'evidential' part of this line of critique is, thus, supposed to include suspicions of Muslim disloyalty in contemporary India as well as particular readings of Indian history.

(5) The 'anti-modernist' critique

Contemporary intellectual trends, primarily in the West but also (somewhat derivatively) in India, give much room for assailing what is called 'modernism'. The fifth line of critique joins force with this assault by attacking secularism as a part of the folly of 'modernism'. While post-modernist criticisms of secularism can take many different forms, the more effective assaults on 'secularism as modernism' in India, at this time, combine general anti-modernism with some specific yearning for India's past when things are supposed to have been less problematic in this respect (particularly, in terms of peaceful co-existence of different religions). Elements of such understanding tend to form integral parts of the intellectual critiques of some contemporary social analysts.

Ashis Nandy notes that 'as India gets modernized, religious violence is increasing', and he expresses admiration for 'traditional ways of life [which] have, over the centuries, developed internal principles of tolerance'.[9] The denunciation of secularism that follows from this line of reasoning is well captured in Nandy's sharp conclusion: 'To accept the ideology of secularism is to accept the ideologies of progress and modernity as the new justification of domination, and the use of violence to achieve and sustain ideologies as the new opiates of the masses' (p. 192).

---

[9] Nandy, 'The Politics of Secularism and the Recovery of Religious Tolerance' (1988), p. 188. See also Madan, 'Secularism in Its Place' (1987).

(6) *The 'cultural' critique*

The sixth — and the last — critique I shall consider takes the ambitiously 'foundational' view that India is, in essence, a 'Hindu country', and that as a result it would be culturally quite wrong to treat Hinduism as simply one of the various religions of India. It is Hinduism, in this view, that makes India what it is, and to require secularism, with its insistence on treating different religions symmetrically, must turn an epistemic error into a political blunder.

This line of criticism often draws on analogies with formally Christian states such as that of Britain, where the particular history of the country and the special role of its 'own religion' are 'fully acknowledged'. For example, the Archbishop of Canterbury conducts political ceremonies of the state at the highest level ('no nonsense about secularism there'). Similarly, the British laws of blasphemy are specifically protective of Christianity and of no other religion (just as in Pakistan the domain of blasphemy laws penalize 'insults' only to Islam). India, it is complained, denies its indigenous cultural commitment in not providing anything like a similarly privileged status to its 'own' tradition, to wit, the predominantly Hindu heritage.

I shall consider these half a dozen critiques in turn. As was stated before, other grounds for rejection of secularism have also been offered. Some of these critiques involve elaborate conceptual compositions and estimable intricacy of language, and are not breathtakingly easy to penetrate (even armed with a dictionary of neologisms on the one hand, and courage on the other). I shall confine myself only to the six lines of criticism of secularism identified earlier, without pretending to be dealing with all the arguments against secularism that have actually been proposed.

4. On the 'Non-existence' Critique

Is the 'non-existence' critique to be taken seriously? Many Indian intellectuals tend to view this kind of opinion with some contempt, and are rather reluctant to respond to what they see as obduracy (or worse) of Western observers. This is sometimes combined with a general theory that it does not really matter what 'others' think about India (at most, this is something for the Indian embassies to worry about). This studied non-response is not only insular (ignoring the importance of international understanding in the contemporary world), it also overlooks how crucial the outside perceptions have historically been to the identity of Indians themselves.[10] Even the composite conception of Hinduism as one religion includes the impact of the outsiders' view of the classificatory unity of the religious beliefs and practices in the country.

There is also the recent phenomenon of the support provided by opulent expatriates from the subcontinent to community-based political movements — of Sikhs, Muslims *and* Hindus — back at 'home'. And because of the relevance of what they read and react to, we can scarcely take foreign reporting on India as 'inconsequential' — even for immediate issues of internal politics in India.

The 'non-existence' critique certainly has to be addressed (even if the more informed reader would decide to switch off while that addressing takes place). Is India really the Hindu counterpart of Pakistan? When British India was partitioned, Pakistan chose to be an Islamic Republic, whereas India chose a secular constitution.[11] Is that distinction significant? It is true that in standard Western journalism, little significance is attached to the contrast, and those in India who would like the country to abandon its secularism often cite this 'forced parity' in Western vision as proof enough that there is something rather hopeless in India's attempt at secularism when the new masters of global politics cannot even tell what on earth is being attempted in India.

Yet the distinction between a secular republic and a religion-based state is really rather important from the legal point of view, and its political implications are also quite extensive. This applies

---

[10]I have touched on this question in my paper 'India and the West', *The New Republic*, June 7, 1993.

[11]The emergence of Pakistan as a 'Muslim state', under the leadership of Mohammad Ali Jinnah, has a complex — and circumstantially quite contingent — history, on which see particularly Ayesha Jalal, *The Sole Spokesman: Jinnah, the Muslim League and the Demand for Pakistan* (Cambridge: Cambridge University Press, 1985).

to different levels of social arrangements, including the operations of the courts, going all the way up to the headship of the state. For example, unlike Pakistan, whose constitution requires that the head of the state be a Muslim, India imposes no comparable requirement, and the country has had non-Hindus (including Muslims and Sikhs) as Presidents and as holders of other prominent and influential offices in government and in the judiciary (including the Supreme Court).

Similarly, to take another example, it is not possible, because of the secularist constitution of India, to have asymmetric laws of blasphemy, applied to one religion only, as it is in Pakistan. There is a difference between the legal status that Pakistan gives to Islam (as it must in an 'Islamic Republic') and the lack of a comparable legal status of Hinduism in India. Not surprisingly, the 'non-existence' critique is aired much more frequently abroad than at home, and often takes the form of an implicit presumption — colouring Western analyses of the subcontinent — rather than being aired as an explicit assertion. That hardened belief turns on overlooking extensive and important features of the Indian constitution and polity.

Two qualifications should, however, be introduced here. First, the 'non-existence' critique must not be confused with the claim — not infrequently made (often by staunch secularists) — that despite the elements of legal symmetry, Hindus still have a substantive advantage over Muslims in many spheres. This would be, typically, an argument for practising secularism 'more fully' in India, rather than for 'rubbishing' the secularism that is already there. Second, the rejection of the 'non-existence' critique does not identify the exact form of secularism that exists in India (nor of course assert anything like the 'superiority' of that specific form of secularism). Indeed, as was discussed earlier, the acceptance of secularism still leaves many questions unanswered about the attitude of the state to different religions. Even when the basic need for symmetry in the political and legal treatment of different religious communities is accepted, we still have to decide on the shape that this symmetry should take, and what the exact domain and reach of that symmetry might be.

To illustrate, symmetry regarding blasphemy laws can be

achieved with different formulae — varying from applying it to all religions, to applying it to none. While the latter option fits in immediately with a secularist withdrawal of the state from religious affairs, the former option pursues symmetry between religions in a way that favours no religion in particular. Just as a secular state can protect the liberty of all citizens to worship as they please (or not to worship), irrespective of their religious beliefs (and this could not be seen, as was analysed earlier, as a violation of secularism), secularism can, in principle, take the form of 'shielding' every religious community against whatever that community seriously deems as blasphemy. I am not, of course, recommending such 'universal anti-blasphemy laws' — indeed I would argue very firmly against anti-blasphemy laws in general. But my rejection of 'universal anti-blasphemy laws' is not based on seeing them as anti-secular, but on other grounds that go beyond secularism: in particular, the need to prevent religious intolerance and persecution, and the practical unfeasibility of making anti-blasphemy laws really 'universal', covering all religions in India (including those of the variety of tribal communities that constitute an underprivileged minority in India). The need to choose between different secular forms remains, but this is a very different contention from saying that the requirement of Indian secularism makes no difference — that it is 'immaterial'.

5. On the 'Favouritism' Critique

The 'favouritism' critique turns on interpreting and highlighting some legal differences between the various communities. They have been much discussed recently in the activist Hindu political literature. The differences in 'personal laws' have been particularly in focus.

It is pointed out, for example, that while a Hindu can be prosecuted for polygamy, a Muslim man can have up to four wives, in line with what is taken to be the Islamic legal position (although, in practice, this provision is extremely rarely invoked by Indian Muslims). Attention is drawn also to other differences, for example, between the provision for wives in the event of a divorce, where Muslim women (in line with a certain reading of Islamic law) have less generous guarantees than what other Indian women have — a subject that came to some prominence in the context of the Supreme Court's judgement on the famous 'Shah Bano case' (involving the right of support of a divorced Muslim woman from her estranged and more opulent husband). The existence of these differences has been cited again and again by Hindu political activists to claim that Hindus, as the majority community, are discriminated against in India, whereas Muslims are allowed to have their own 'personal laws' and 'special privileges'.

This line of reasoning has many problems. First, if these examples indicate any 'favouritism', in giving special 'privileges', in the treatment of the different communities, this can hardly be a favouritism for Muslims in general. Any unfairness that is there is surely one against *Muslim women*, rather than against *Hindu men*. A narrowly 'male' — indeed sexist — point of view is rather conspicuous in the form that these political complaints often take.

Second, it is not the case that the personal laws of the Hindus have been somehow overridden in post-independence India by some uniform civil code. The separate status of Hindu personal laws has *in general* survived. The issue of uniform civil codes has to be distinguished from the fact that the Hindu laws were reformed after independence, particularly during 1955 and 1956 (with little opposition — indeed they resulted from political movements *within* the Hindu communities). The possibility of polygamy was explicitly ruled out by the reforms of the Hindu laws. It did not follow from some 'uniform' civil codes being imposed on the Hindus but not the Muslims. Nor did it make the Hindu personal laws inoperative — quite the contrary. Several other provisions were introduced within the Hindu laws themselves, but the domain of Hindu personal laws continues to be quite substantial.

The makers of the Indian constitution did express some preference for 'uniformity of fundamental laws, civil and criminal', which was seen by Dr. Ambedkar (the leader of the team that framed the constitution of India) as important for maintaining the unity of the country.[12] In the event, however, such uniformity was

---

[12]On the history of this aspect of Indian laws, see John H. Mansfield, 'The Personal Laws or a Uniform Civil Code?', in Robert Baird, ed., *Religion and Law in Independent India* (Delhi: Manohar, 1993), which also provides a balanced

not incorporated in the constitution that emerged, and the preference for uniformity was only included as a 'Directive Principle of State Policy' — *without* enforceability. The principle that was adopted demanded that 'the State shall endeavour to secure for the citizens a uniform civil code throughout the territory of India'. Like all the 'Directive Principles' enunciated in the Indian constitution, this was seen as 'fundamental in the governance of the country' and it was specified that 'it shall be the duty of the State to apply' this principle, but at the same time this principle (like the other 'directive' ones) 'shall not be enforceable by any court'.[13]

It is, of course, up to the courts to see how far to go in line with this Directive Principle. In the much-debated case of the 'Shah Bano judgement', involving a Muslim woman's right to a better financial deal at the time of divorce, the Supreme Court did indeed make a move in the direction of uniformity.[14] The court also revealed some disappointment at the government's failure to move in the direction of a uniform civil code in line with the 'constitutional ideal' (and noted that this constitutional provision had 'remained a dead letter'). In fact, as one observer has noted, 'the intensity of Muslim reaction to the Supreme Court's judgment in that case was partly explained by the inclusion of this utterance and the suggestion that what the government had failed to do, the Court itself might undertake'.[15] The 'Muslim reaction' was not, however, by any means uniform, and there was support as well as

---

review of the pros and cons of the case for submerging different personal laws in India in a 'uniform civil code'. See also Tahir Mahmood, *Muslim Personal Law, Role of the State in the Indian Subcontinent* (Nagpur, second edition, 1983).

[13] *Constitution of India*, Article 37.

[14] This was done by the Supreme Court by giving priority — over the provisions of Islamic law for divorce settlements — to section 125 of the Code of Criminal Procedure, which requires a person of adequate means to protect from destitution and vagrancy one's relations (including one's spouse, minor children, handicapped adult children, and aged parents). For critical analyses of the rather complex considerations involved in the Shah Bano case, see Asghar Ali Engineer, *The Shah Bano Controversy* (Delhi: Ajanta Publishers, 1987), and Veena Das, *Critical Events* (Delhi: Oxford University Press, 1992, Chapter IV). Also see Mansfield, 'The Personal Laws or a Uniform Civil Code?' (1993).

[15] Mansfield, 'The Personal Laws or a Uniform Civil Code', p. 140.

criticism for the Supreme Court's judgement, from different sections of that community.[16] It was Rajiv Gandhi's Congress government that ultimately 'caved in', and made fresh legislation that further supported the 'separatist' view, rather than following the Supreme Court's push in the direction of more uniformity.

The general issue of asymmetric treatment is indeed an important one, and there would, of course, be nothing non-secular in pursuing the possibility of making the provisions of a set of uniform civil laws apply even-handedly to individuals of all the communities. On the other hand, as was argued earlier in this paper, the principles of secularism will also permit an arrangement by which separate personal laws continue well into the future (so long as the different religious communities are treated with symmetry). In arguing against the latter option, considerations of justice may well be raised which demand some symmetry not only in the way the different religious communities are treated, but also in the way fairness is applied across other classificatory distinctions (for example, between the different classes, between women and men, between the poor and the rich, between the 'elite' and the 'subalterns', and so on).

The choice between these two options — and intermediate ones — remains open, and certainly cannot be closed in one direction or the other by the requirements of secularism alone. To note this is not a concession of the failure of secularism, but rather an acknowledgement of its circumscribed domain, and the affirmation of the need to go beyond secularism — with other principles of fairness and justice — to identify specific legal and social forms. While there is not much substance in the charge of 'favouritism' benefiting Muslims, and certainly no general case against secularism can be constructed on that line of reasoning, it is useful to integrate the discussion on secularism with the principles — such as those of justice — that lie beyond it. We have to distinguish, in particular, between (1) the need for symmetry

---

[16]The Supreme Court had also taken this opportunity of commenting on the disadvantaged position of women in India (not just among the Muslims, but also among the Hindus), and had called for more justice in this field: The Shah Bano case did, in fact, get much attention from the women's political groups as well.

24

among different religious communities (a secularist consideration), and (2) the question of what form that symmetry should take (a concern that has to be consolidated with other principles of justice which take us well beyond secularism into, on the one hand, the importance that may be attached to group autonomy of religious communities, and on the other, the inescapable issue of equity for different groups of Indians, classified in non-religious categories: class, gender, etc.).

6. On the 'Prior Identity' Critique

The question of political and religious identities raises issues of a rather different kind. There can be little doubt that many Indians — indeed most Indians — have religious beliefs of one kind or another, and regard these beliefs to be important in their personal lives. The issue that is raised by the claimed priority of this identity in the political context is not the general importance of religious beliefs in *personal* or even *social* behaviour, but the specific relevance of that identity in *political* matters (with and without the involvement of the state).

It is useful in this context to recollect the contrast between the religiosity of political leaders in pre-independence India and their respective beliefs in a secular identity. Jinnah, the great advocate of the 'two-nation theory' and the founding father of the Islamic Republic of Pakistan, was scarcely a devout Muslim, whereas Maulana Abul Kalam Azad, the President of the Indian National Congress and a major leader of the Indian Union, was a deeply religious Muslim.[17] Similarly, Shyama Prasad

---

[17]In fact, Azad was among the 'traditionalist' Muslims, as opposed to the 'reformers' (for example from the Aligarh school). On the intricacies of Azad's religious and political attitudes, see Ayesha Jalal, 'Exploding Communalism: The Politics of Muslim Identity in South Asia', in Sugata Bose and Ayesha Jalal, eds., *Nationalism, Democracy and Development: Reappraising South Asian States and Politics*, forthcoming. Jalal also discusses the much broader question of a general misfit between (1) the reformism-traditionalism division among Muslims in pre-partition India, and (2) the division between Muslims who favoured an undivided India and those who wanted Pakistan. In particular, quite often the Muslim traditionalists opted for staying on in India (as Azad himself did), especially after the Khilafat movement.

Mukhopadhyay, the leader of Hindu Mahasabha, had very few Hindu practices, compared with, say, Mahatma Gandhi, who was both actively religious in personal life and in social practice (for example, he held regular prayer meetings which were open to the public), and also staunchly secularist in politics (insisting on symmetric political treatment of different religions and on an effective separation of the state and religions). When Mahatma Gandhi was murdered by an extremist Hindu politician, the complaint against him was not that he did not follow Hinduism in his personal life or in his social activities, but that he was, allegedly, very 'soft' on the Muslims in political matters, and did not give priority to Hindu interests in these.

The importance of religious identity has to be separated from the relevance of that identity in the political context. It is, thus, odd to require that an Indian must 'go through' her religious identity first, *before* asserting her Indianness, and even less plausible to insist that the Indian identity *must* be 'built up' on the constitutive basis of the different religious identities. That assertion of priority comes not only from religious sectarians (particularly, in recent years, the so-called 'Hindu nationalists'), but also from those who have been especially worried about the usurping role of the state (as opposed to community), and about the violences committed by the state. In this context, the issue of a national identity is often identified, misleadingly, I believe, with the philosophy of a 'nation state', thus giving an inescapably 'statist' orientation to the very conception of any political unity *across* religious communities and other social divisions. It is certainly true that in the emergence or consolidation of that unity, the nation state may well have an important instrumental role, but the state need not be central to the conceptual foundation of this unity, nor provide its constructive genesis. It is, for example, not a 'category mistake' to think of the Indian nation prior to 1947 as encompassing the residents of the so-called 'native states' (such as Travancore), and also of the non-British colonial territories (such as Goa), even though they did not 'belong to' the same *state* at all. It is a mistake to think that the idea of a nation requires the prior presence of a national state.

A second problem in this line of reasoning concerns the use

of this route to arrive at the proposed Hindu view of India. Even if the religious identities were somehow 'prior' to the political identity of being an Indian, one could scarcely derive the view of a Hindu India based on that argument alone. The non-Hindu communities — Muslims in particular but also Christians, Sikhs, Jains, Parsees and others — are scarcely 'marginal' even in numerical terms in the country.

India has well over a hundred million Muslims, not much less than Pakistan, and rather more than Bangladesh. Indeed, in terms of the number of Muslim citizens, India is the third largest Muslim country in the world. To see India just as a Hindu country is a fairly bizarre idea in the face of that fact alone, not to mention the intermingling of Hindus and Muslims in the social and cultural life of India (in literature, music, painting, and so on). Also, Indian religious plurality extends far beyond the Hindu-Muslim division. There is a large and prominent Sikh population, and a substantial number of Christians, whose settlements go back at least to the 4th century A.D. (considerably earlier than Britain had any Christians at all). There have also been Jewish settlements in India from just after the fall of Jerusalem. Parsees moved to India many hundreds of years ago, to escape less tolerant Iran. To this we have to add the millions of Jains, and practitioners of Buddhism, which had been, for a long period, the official religion of many of the Indian emperors (including the great Ashoka in the third century B.C., who had ruled over the largest empire in the history of the subcontinent).

Furthermore, large also is the number of Indians who are atheist or agnostic (as Jawaharlal Nehru himself was), and that tradition in India goes well back to the ancient times (to Carvaka and the Lokayata, among other agnostic schools). The classificatory conventions of the Indian social statistics tend to disestablish the recognition of such heterodox beliefs, since the categories used represent what in India has come to be called 'community', without recording actual religious beliefs (for example, an atheist born in a Hindu family is classified as Hindu, reflecting the so-called 'community background').

Those who framed the Indian constitution wanted to give appropriate recognition to the extensive religious pluralism of the

Indian people, and did not want to derive the notion of Indianness from any specific religious identity in particular. As Dr. Ambedkar, the leader of the Indian Constituent Assembly, put it, 'if the Muslims in India are a separate nation, then, of course, India is not a nation'.[18] Given the heterogeneity of India and of the Indians, there is no real political alternative to ensuring some basic symmetry and an effective separation of the state from each particular religion.[19]

The programme of deriving an Indian identity via a Hindu identity, thus, encounters problems from two different directions. First, it suffers from insufficient discrimination between (1) *personal* and *social* religious involvement, and (2) giving *political* priority to that involvement (against symmetric treatment of different religions). Second, it fails to recognize the implications of India's immense religious diversity.

In fact, the issue of religious plurality does not relate only to the relationship between Hindus and followers of other faiths (or none). It also concerns the divergences *within* Hinduism itself. The divisions do, of course, include those of caste, and the nature of contemporary Indian politics reflects this at different levels with inescapable force. But the diversities that characterize Hinduism are not just of caste. They also encompass divergent beliefs, distinct customs, and different schools of religious thought.

Even the ancient classification of 'six systems of philosophy' in India had acknowledged deeply diverse beliefs and reasoning. More recently, when the authoritative Hindu scholar Madhava Acarya of 14th century (head of the religious order in Sringeri in Mysore) wrote his famous Sanskrit treatise *Sarvadarsana Samgraha* ('collection of all philosophies'), he devoted sixteen chapters to as many different schools of Hindu religious thought (beginning, in

---

[18]In his insightful paper 'Hindu/Muslim/Indian' (*Public Culture*, vol. 5, no. 1, Fall 1992), Faisal Devji begins with this (and another) quotation from Ambedkar, and goes on to scrutinize critically the relation between different identities (raising issues that are much broader than those addressed in this paper).

[19]See also Nur Yalman, 'On Secularism and Its Critics: Notes on Turkey, India and Iran', *Contributions to Indian Sociology*, 25 (1991). See also Gary Jeffrey Jacobsohn, 'Three Models of the Secular Constitution', mimeographed, Williams College, 1995, and the literature cited there.

fact, with the atheism of the Carvaka school, which is the subject of the first chapter). He examined in some detail how each religious school differed from the others, and what their own arguments were in favour of their respective beliefs and what counterarguments could be raised against them (even though he did not flinch from coming out, ultimately, in support of his own Vaishnavite beliefs in the last chapter).

In fact, seeing Hinduism as a unified religion is a comparatively recent development. The term 'Hindu' was traditionally used mainly as a signifier of location and country, rather than of any homogeneous religious belief. The word derives from the river Indus or 'Sindhu' (the cradle of the Indus valley civilization which flourished from around 3,000 BC), and the name of that river is also the source of the word 'India' itself. The Persians and the Greeks saw India as the land around and beyond the Indus, and Hindus were the native people of that land. Muslims from India were at one stage called 'Hindavi' Muslims, in Persian as well as Arabic, and there are plenty of references in early British documents to 'Hindoo Muslims' and 'Hindoo Christians', to distinguish them respectively from Muslims and Christians from outside India.

A pervasive plurality of religious beliefs and traditions characterizes Hinduism as a religion. The point can be illustrated with the attitude to Rama (in modern Hindi, Ram), in whose name so much of the current Hindu political activism is being invoked (including demolishing the Babri mosque in Ayodhya, 'the birth place of Rama'). The identification of Rama with divinity is common in the north and west of India, but elsewhere (for example, in my native Bengal), he is largely the heroic king of the epic *Ramayana*, rather than God incarnate. *Ramayana* itself is, of course, widely popular, as an epic, everywhere in India, and has been so outside India as well — in Thailand and Indonesia, for example (even Ayutthaya, the historical capital of Thailand, is a cognate of Ayodhya). But the power and influence of the epic *Ramayana* — a wonderful literary achievement — has to be distinguished from the particular issue of Rama's divinity.

In fact, in *Ramayana* itself, the epic hero Rama is treated very much as a good and self-sacrificing king rather than as God, and there is even an interesting occasion on which he is lectured by a sceptical pundit called Javali: 'O Rama, be wise, there exists no world but this, that is certain! Enjoy that which is present and cast behind thee that is unpleasant.'[20] Even though the *Ramayana* records that Rama chose to spurn that fearless advice, he emerges mainly as a good and pious king, not as divinity incarnate.

Indeed, Rabindranath Tagore, in his *Vision of India's History*, showers Rama with special praise precisely because Rama, as Tagore put it, 'appeared as divine to the primitive tribes, some of whom had the totem of monkey, some that of bear.'[21] Tagore's remark, which might appear to be rather irreverent to a Rama-disciple, only serves to illustrate the extent to which the attitude to Rama varies across the country. Another great Bengali poet, Madhusudhan Dutt, chooses Rama's adversary, Meghnad, as the hero of his dramatic poetry, and Rama and his brothers do not emerge as particularly admirable in that classic — and highly popular — book.

The same can be said about the claims to pre-eminent divinity of the other putatively divine characters in one part of India or another. If we must use the analogy of the 'melting pot' and the 'salad bowl' to which a reference was made earlier, the Hindu traditions do not constitute a melting pot in any sense whatever. This need not, of course, prevent Hindus from living together in great harmony and mutual tolerance, but then the same goes for a community of Hindus, Muslims, Christians, Sikhs, Jains, Buddhists, Parsees, Jews, and people without any religion. Not only is there, in general, no necessity to build up an Indian identity from any 'prior' assertion of individual religious identities, it is hard to get to a unified Indian identity from the rich diversity of Hindu traditions across the country.

7. On the 'Muslim Sectarianism' Critique

I turn now to the issue of the alleged Muslim disloyalty to India.

---

[20]English translation from H.P. Shastri, *The Ramayana of Valmiki* (London, 1952), p. 389.

[21]Rabindranath Tagore, *A Vision of India's History* (Calcutta: Visva-Bharati, 1951, reprinted 1962), p. 32.

Spirited anecdotes abound on this subject, varying from the alleged frequency of Indian Muslims spying for Pakistan to their tendency, we are told, of cheering the Pakistan cricket team in Test matches (whether or not Indian Muslims do this in any significant number — I don't know of any evidence in that direction — I ought to confess that this non-Muslim author often does just that, when the Pakistan team plays as well as it frequently does).

There is, in fact, no serious evidence for the hypothesis of the political disloyalty of the Indian Muslims. A great many Muslims stayed on in post-partition India (instead of going to Pakistan) as a deliberate decision to remain where they felt they belonged. In the Indian armed forces, diplomatic services and administration, Muslims have no different a record on loyalty to India than Hindus and other Indians have. (Even on the momentous subject of cricket, India has been led for many years by its Muslim captain, Mohammad Azharuddin.) There is no significant empirical evidence to substantiate the critique, and the unfairness of this specious line of reasoning is quite hard to beat.[22]

Allegations of Muslim 'sectarianism' are sometimes linked up with a certain reading of Indian history (though 'reading' may well be the wrong word to use here). Muslim kings were, it is claimed, consistently alienated from their Hindu subjects. They destroyed, allegedly, as many Hindu temples as they could, and asserted their alienation in other noticeable ways.

Was that, in fact, the case? Muslim invaders in north India did indeed destroy many Hindu temples, and certainly between the 11th and the 13th century, the early Muslim invaders and raiders had demolished or mutilated remarkably many temples, along with causing general devastation. For example, Sultan Mahmud, coming

---

[22]The case of Kashmir is, of course, different in several respects, including its separate history and the peculiar politics of its accession to India and its aftermath. The evident disaffection of a substantial part of the Kashmiri Muslim population relates to the very special political circumstances obtaining there and the treatment they have received respectively from both India and Pakistan. The Kashmir issue certainly demands political attention on its own (I am not taking up that thorny question here), but the special circumstances influencing the viewpoints of 3 million Kashmiri Muslims can scarcely be used to question the strong record of national loyalty and solidarity of the 110 million Muslims in general in India.

from Ghazni (in what is now Afghanistan), repeatedly invaded north and west India in the eleventh century, and devastated cities as well as temples, including famous ones in Mathura, Kanauj, and what is now Kathiawar (where the Somnath temple had been widely renowned for its treasures). The destructive record gradually receded with the Indianization of Islamic rulers, but it would still be foolish to claim that no demolition of Hindu sites ever occurred under the Indian Muslim kings, no matter how infrequent such demolitions might have become. The real question is what to conclude from these facts.

In the context of defending the importance of secularism in contemporary India, it is not in any way essential to make any claim whatsoever about how Muslim emperors of the past had behaved — whether they were sectarian or assimilative, oppressive or tolerant. There is no intrinsic reason why a defence of India's secularism must take a position on what, say, the Mughals did or did not do. The 'guilt' of Muslim kings, if any, need not be 'transferred' to the 110 million Muslims who live in India today. Also, we can scarcely form a view of the political commitments of Muslims in contemporary India, or of their political loyalties, by checking what Muslim kings might or might not have done many centuries ago.

However, in the political discussions that accompanied the activist incursions of Hindu communal politics (for example, the demolition of the Babri mosque), a certain characterization of the Mughal rule — not just of Aurangzeb but more sweepingly of Mughals in general — was constantly invoked. No view of Muslims in contemporary India can really be formed on the basis of the conduct of Muslim kings in the past (this general point must be firmly asserted first). Nevertheless, we cannot escape addressing this contingent historical issue, since the two questions are strongly linked in the minds of many political activists, and a non-response would appear to them, and to those influenced by that line of reasoning, to be unsatisfactory — or worse.[23]

---

[23]This relates to a methodological point I have tried to discuss elsewhere that the historical arguments in which we have to engage given their *supposed* political importance may not be the ones we ourselves would accept as particularly significant. To leave unaddressed the charge of a generally 'anti-Hindu attitude'

It is, in fact, not possible to find any kind of uniformity in the attitude of Muslim kings to the Hindu population. They varied greatly in terms of sympathy for their subjects, as had the Hindu and Buddhist kings before them. Some were friendly to their subjects, others were not. Some were keen on converting the Hindus, others were not. It is hard to construct a picture of persistent persecution of Hindus by Muslim kings — tempting though that hypothesis clearly is to some Hindu politicians.[24]

The anti-Hindu bias of Emperor Aurangzeb is often cited and made much of. He clearly did have considerable intolerance of Hinduism, and there is indeed evidence of his destroying some temples, imposing special taxes on the Hindus, and so on. But to see Aurangzeb as the representative Muslim monarch of India — or for that matter as the typical Mughal emperor — would be serious falsification of history.

None of the other Mughals, in fact, showed anything like the intolerance of Aurangzeb, and some had made great efforts to treat the different religious communities in an even-handed way. The great emperor Akbar, who reigned between 1556 to 1605, was deeply interested in Hindu philosophy and culture, and had attempted to establish something of a synthetic religion (the Din Ilahi) drawing on the different faiths in India. His court was filled

---

of the Mughal kings would be politically unconvincing to those with whom we argue, even though we may not ourselves think that the behaviour of the Mughals would matter one way or the other in assessing the claims of Muslims in contemporary India. On this see my 'Interpreting India's Past', mimeographed.
[24]The present political attempt to portray the Muslim rulers in general, and the Mughals in particular, as intolerant of Hindus contrasts sharply from the assessments of earlier Hindu religious leaders. For example, Sri Aurobindo, who established the famous ashram in Pondicherry, had seen the history of Muslim rule in India in a very different light (*The Spirit and Form of Indian Polity*, Calcutta: Arya Publishing House, 1947, pp. 86-9.):

[T]he Mussulman domination ceased very rapidly to be a foreign rule. ...The Mogul empire was a great and magnificent construction and an immense amount of political genius and talent was employed in its creation and maintenance. It was as splendid, powerful and beneficent and, it may be added, in spite of Aurangzeb's fanatical zeal, infinitely more liberal and tolerant in religion than any medieval or contemporary European kingdom or empire.

with Hindu as well as Muslim intellectuals, artists and musicians, and he tried in every way to be non-sectarian and symmetric in the treatment of his subjects. But Akbar was not by any means unique among the Mughal emperors in seeing Hindus differently from the way Aurangzeb preferred to view them.

It is actually interesting to consider Aurangzeb in his familial setting (in the context of others with whom he was associated) — not in isolation. None of his immediate family seem to have shared Aurangzeb's intense sectarianism. His elder brother, Dara Shikoh, was greatly interested in Hindu philosophy and had himself, with the help of some scholars, prepared a Persian translation of some of the Upanishads. Dara Shikoh had somewhat stronger claims to the Mughal throne than Aurangzeb had, since he was the eldest and the favourite son of his father, Emperor Shah Jahan. Aurangzeb grabbed the throne after fighting and defeating Dara, who was tortured and beheaded by Aurangzeb, who also imprisoned their father Shah Jahan for the rest of his life (leaving him, the builder of the Taj Mahal, to gaze at his creation, in captivity, from some distance). Aurangzeb's anti-Hindu position contrasted sharply — and may even have been dialectically influenced by — the eclectic and somewhat Hinduized brother whom he hated so much.

But Dara was not the only relation Aurangzeb had to encounter; he was, in fact, surrounded by people who differed from him in their attitude towards Hindus. Even his own son, also called Akbar, who had rebelled against his father in 1681, joined the Hindu Rajput kings to fight his father. After the Rajputs were pushed back by Aurangzeb's army, Akbar continued his battle by joining Raja Sambhaji, the son of Shivaji who fought the Mughals and who is much revered by contemporary Hindu activists. Even the name of the Hindu activist party 'Shiv Sena', referred to earlier, invokes Shivaji who has become such a cult figure among militant Hindus.[25] Also, among the proposals that

---

[25]Shivaji himself was, it appears, quite respectful of other religions. Some historians (such as Sir Jadunath Sarkar, the author of *Shivaji and His Times*, published in 1919) attribute to him a forceful letter sent to Aurangzeb on religious tolerance. The letter contrasts Aurangzeb's intolerance with the policies of earlier Mughals (Akbar, Jahangir, Shah Jahan), and then says this:

If Your Majesty places any faith in those books by distinction called divine,

the Shiv Sena made immediately after its victory in the state elections in Maharashtra was the motion to rename the city of Aurangabad after Raja Sambhaji himself. Akbar also had fairly acrimonious correspondence with his father, defending the excellence of his Hindu allies against his father's vilification of such people. Aurangzeb had to encounter his son's theorizing, in addition to his elder brother's philosophy, on the subject of respect for the Hindus.

No general picture of consistent hostility of the Muslim kings to their Hindu subject emerges from Indian history. No matter what the relevance of this line of inquiry is in judging Muslim integration today (as already stated, I believe that relevance to be rather little), this line of reasoning breaks down even in terms of the basic facts on which the thesis is meant to draw. The overwhelming fact that remains is the loyalty of the large Muslim population in India, and the clear recognition that their record is not in any way different from those of the other religious communities, including Hindus.

8. On the 'Anti-modernist' Critique

Turning now to the 'anti-modernist' critique of secularism, is it the really the case that 'as India gets modernized, religious violence

---

you will there be instructed that God is the God of all mankind, not the God of Muslims alone. The Pagan and the Muslim are equally in His presence....In fine, the tribute you demand from the Hindus is repugnant to justice (Vincent Smith, *The Oxford History of India*, 4th edition, edited by Percival Spear, London: Oxford University Press, 1974, pp. 417-8).

This letter may or may not have been actually authored by Shivaji (an alternative hypothesis attributes the authorship to Rana Raj Singh of Mewar/ Udaipur), but it would be consistent with his attitude to the religions of others. In fact, the Mughal historian Khafi Khan, who was no admirer of Shivaji in other respects, nevertheless had the following to say about his treatment of Muslims:

[Shivaji] made it a rule that wherever his followers were plundering, they should do no harm to the mosques, the book of God, or the women of any one. Whenever a copy of the sacred Quran came into his hands, he treated it with respect, and gave it to some of his Mussalman followers (Vincent Smith, *The Oxford History of India*, p. 412).

is increasing' (as Ashis Nandy says)? There are certainly periods in history in which this is exactly what has happened. For example, the communal riots immediately preceding the partition of the country in 1947 almost certainly took many more lives than any violence between the different communities earlier on in Indian history. But as the country has moved on from there (presumably not decreasing in 'modernity'), the general level of violence has fallen from its peak in the 1940s — indeed the number of incidents have been quite tiny *in comparison* with what happened half a century ago.

We must not, however, interpret Ashis Nandy's statement too literally. The thesis presented deals with a presumed shift in the long run, away from a pre-modern situation in which 'traditional ways of life' had 'over the centuries, developed internal principles of tolerance'. There is undoubtedly some plausibility in such a diagnosis — there is some evidence that the level of communal violence did indeed increase with colonial rule. On the other hand, even in the pre-colonial past of India, there have been periods (for example, between the 11th and the 13th century, as discussed earlier) in which violence, especially by sectarian armed forces, had escalated sharply, and then ebbed. But Nandy is right to assert that, in general, 'principles of tolerance' have tended to develop eventually, as people of different backgrounds have settled down to live next to each other. It is not, I believe, central for Nandy's thesis to check whether the time trend of communal violence has been consistently upwards, nor particularly interesting to compare the numbers killed in recent years *vis-a-vis* those in the past (the massive increase in the absolute size of the population would bias those numbers anyway). The point rather is the thesis that principles of tolerance do develop in multi-community societies, unless they are disrupted by contrary moves, and Nandy sees the development of 'modernism' as just such a move.

But what exactly *is* 'modernism' that could so disrupt the process of tolerance? The concept of modernity is not an easy one to identify, even though many post-modernists seem to share the modernists' comfortable belief in the easily characterized nature of modernism. We might resist being sent off on an errand of finding the 'true meaning of modernism', and concentrate instead on the specific depiction of 'secularism as modernism', which is central to Nandy's concern. The point of departure would then be the argument forcefully presented by Nandy (as was quoted earlier): 'to accept the ideology of secularism is to accept the ideologies of progress and modernity as the new justification of domination, and the use of violence to achieve and sustain ideologies as the new opiates of the masses.' This is quite a grand vision, but would seem to be, nevertheless, based on an odd characterization of secularism. The principle of secularism basically demands (as was discussed earlier) symmetric treatment of different religious communities in politics and in the affairs of the state. It is not obvious why such symmetric treatment must somehow involve 'the use of violence to achieve and sustain ideologies as the new opiates of the masses'.

I am aware that the nation-state is under great suspicion these days as a constant perpetrator of violence, and indeed the state does manage to do many violent things. What is not clear is why taking a symmetric attitude to different communities would encourage, or add to, such state violence. To invoke some concepts much favoured in contemporary theory, it is not, of course, difficult to conceive that a state might 'homogenize' to 'hegemonize', but it seems, at best, intensely abstract to see this happening whenever the state stops favouring one religious community over another (as secularism requires). If the experience of British colonial rule is meant to be taken as a guide on how secularism can be used to accentuate communal violence, surely we ought to see more clearly how 'divide and rule' is used for this purpose, rather than a programme of 'unite and homogenize'. Indeed, a non-sectarian and symmetric approach to governance and statecraft may do a lot to reduce tension and violence. Also, since the concept of secularism applies to politics in general (not just to state policy), it is also worth asserting that secular politics may well reduce, rather than add to, the violence that many societies standardly have (when political attitudes are non-symmetric, sectarian and suspicious across the boundaries of the respective communities).

It is, thus, hard to escape the suspicion that something has gone oddly wrong in the cited diagnostics. Nor is it obvious why secular symmetry should be a characteristic only of 'modernity'. Indeed, even ancient states run by, say, an Ashoka or an Akbar did some things to achieve just such symmetric treatments, and there is no evidence that these historical attempts at secular symmetry *increased*, rather than lessening, communal violence.

I would argue that it is not really helpful to see secularism and modernism in these oddly formulaic terms. Indeed, 'the principles of tolerance', on which Nandy relies, are not really that remote from taking a symmetric view of other communities, and it is less than fair to political secularism to be depicted in the way it is in these indictments. The development of secular attitudes and politics can surely be a *part* of that mechanism of tolerance, rather than running against it, unless we choose to define secularism in some very special way.

The idea of 'modernity' is deeply problematic — in general and also in the postulated relation with secularism. Was Ashoka or Akbar more or less 'modern' than Aurangzeb? Perhaps the question being raised here can be illustrated with another historical example, involving differences between contemporaries. Consider the contrast between the sectarian destruction caused by Sultan Mahmud of Ghazni in the 11th century (to which reference was made earlier), and the reactions of Alberuni, the Arab-Iranian traveller (and distinguished mathematician), who accompanied Mahmud to India and felt revolted by the violence he saw:

> Mahmud utterly ruined the prosperity of the country, and performed there wonderful exploits, by which Hindus became like atoms of dust scattered in all directions.[26]

He went on to suggest — perhaps overgeneralizing a little — that the Hindus, as a result, 'cherish, of course, the most inveterate aversion towards all Muslims'. That 'aversion' was, happily, not enough to prevent Alberuni from having a large number of Hindu friends and collaborators, with whose help he mastered Sanskrit

---

[26]*Alberuni's India*, translated by Edward C. Sachau, edited by Ainslie T. Embree (New York: Norton, 1971), Chapter I, p. 22.

and studied the contemporary Indian treatises on mathematics, astronomy, sculpture, philosophy, and religion.[27]

However, Alberuni did not stop there, but proceeded to provide an analysis of why people of one background tend to be suspicious of those from other backgrounds, and identified the need for a balanced understanding of these problems — a good starting point for the symmetry that is essential for secularism.

> ...in all manners and usages, [the Hindus] differ from us to such a degree as to frighten their children with us, with our dress, and our ways and customs, and as to declare us to be devil's breed, and our doings as the very opposite of all that is good and proper. By the bye, we must confess, in order to be just, that a similar depreciation of foreigners not only prevails among us and the Hindus, but is common to all nations towards each other.[28]

Those who like 'modernism' would probably prefer to see Alberuni as a 'modern' intellectual of some kind (albeit from the 11th century), but that would be a rather far-fetched reaction.

In fact, modernism is not really the issue at all. The substantive view of Alberuni, with its emphasis on unbiased understanding and symmetric tolerance of different communities, is a positive force in the direction of reducing violence and mindless destruction, and that approach cannot be torn away from the pursuit of secularism, no matter whether we call it 'modern', 'pre-modern', or 'post-modern'. I conclude this section by noting that the characterization of secularism as modernism is not particularly cogent, nor does it provide an especially persuasive basis for rejecting secularism. (There is also the 'bigger' issue, not unrelated to the preceding discussion, as to whether the 'anti-modernists' are not too respectful of 'modernism', seeing the idea of modernity as cogent and coherent — but that subject I have to postpone for a later occasion.)

---

[27]In fact, Alberuni's work and his translations of Indian mathematical and astronomical treatises had great influence in continuing the Arabic studies (well established by the 8th century) of Indian science and mathematics, which reached Europe through the Arabs.

[28]*Alberuni's India*, Part I, Chapter I, p. 20.

9. On the 'Cultural' Critique

I turn, finally, to the 'cultural' critique, and to the suggestion that India should really be seen as a 'Hindu country' in cultural terms. This, it is argued, militates against secularism in India, since secularism denies that basic recognition.

There are two questions to be raised here. First, even if it were right to see Indian culture as basically Hindu culture, it would be very odd to alienate on that ground the right to equal political and legal treatment of minorities (including the political standing and rights of the 110 million Indian Muslims). Why should the cultural dominance of one tradition, even if true, reduce the political entitlements and rights of those from other traditions? What have they done to lose their rights, as citizens, to fair and equal treatment?

Incidentally, the analogy — often invoked — with religious asymmetry in Britain is quite misleading in this context, despite all the role that the Archbishop of Canterbury plays in state functions. True, the domain of symmetric treatment can be fruitfully extended in Britain, for example, through more even-handed financing of different community-oriented schools (not favouring only Christian schools), or, for that matter, through removing the disparity in blasphemy laws (perhaps by removing these laws altogether). Nevertheless, in most matters of legal or political rights, or of protective and supportive state action, the treatment of citizens from different religious communities in Britain is fairly symmetric already, and the limits of asymmetry are well-defined and stationary.[29] The stationarity is quite important, since a self-conscious rejection of secularism in India today would almost certainly usher in fresh and serious asymmetry of treatment.

The second problem with the thesis under examination is that its reading of Indian culture is extremely narrow. The cultural inheritance of contemporary India from its past combines Islamic influences with Hindu and other traditions, and the results of their interaction can be seen plentifully in literature, music, painting,

---

[29]The treatment of immigrants, or of suspected immigrants, in Britain is, however, a different matter altogether — not a subject of much glory for Britain. The remark in the text refers to citizens.

architecture, and many other fields. The point is not only that so many of the major contributions in these various fields of Indian culture have come from Islamic writers, musicians, painters, and so on, but also that their works are thoroughly integrated with those of others.

Indeed, even the nature of Hindu religious beliefs and practices has been substantially influenced by contact with Islamic ideas and values.[30] The impact of Islamic Sufi thought is readily recognizable in parts of contemporary Hindu literature. Further, religious poets like Kabir or Dadu were born Muslim but transcended sectional boundaries (one of Kabir's verses declares: 'Kabir is the child of Allah and of Ram: He is my Guru, He is my Pir'[31]). They were strongly affected by Hindu devotional poetry, and in turn, profoundly influenced it. There is, in fact, no communal line to be drawn through Indian literature and arts, setting Hindus and Muslims on separate sides.[32]

Another serious problem with the narrow reading of 'Indian culture as Hindu culture' is the entailed neglect of many major achievements of Indian civilization that have nothing much to do with religious thinking at all. The focus on the distinctly Hindu religious tradition effectively leaves out of the accounting the rationalist traditions of India. This would be a serious neglect for a country in which some of the decisive steps in algebra, geometry and astronomy were taken, where the decimal system emerged, where classical philosophy dealt extensively with epistemology and logic along with secular ethics, where people invented games like

---

[30]On this see Kshiti Mohan Sen, *Hinduism* (Harmondsworth: Penguin Books, 1960). He discusses the interrelations in greater detail in his Bengali book *Bharaté Hindu-Mushalmaner jukto sadhana* (Calcutta: Visva-Bharati, 1949).

[31]See *One Hundred Poems of Kabir*, translated by Rabindranath Tagore (London: Macmillan, 1915), Verse LXIX. See also Kshiti Mohan Sen, *Hinduism*, Chapters 18 and 19, and his collection of Kabir's poems and his Bengali commentary in *Kabir* (Calcutta: Visva-Bharati, 1910, 1911), reissued with an Introduction by Sabyasachi Bhattacharya (Calcutta: Ananda Publishers, 1995).

[32]The tradition of integrated work has continued straight through to modern art forms, such as the cinema, where Muslims and Hindus thoroughly intermingle. Even the films on Hindu themes frequently rely on Muslim writers or actors (for example, Rahi Masoom Reza wrote the script for the hugely successful television version of the Hindu epic *Mahabharata*).

chess, pioneered sex education, and initiated systematic political economy and formal linguistics. It would be absurd to overlook, in characterizing the culture of India, the works of mathematicians such as Aryabhata or Brahmagupta, or poets and dramatists such as Kalidasa or Sudraka, or logicians such as Nagarjuna, or linguists such as Panini, or sex educationists such as Vatsayana, or political economists such as Kautilya.

To be sure, in his famous *History of British India*, published in 1817, James Mill did elaborate just such a view of India, an India that is intellectually bankrupt but full of religious ideas (not to mention Mill's pointer to barbarous social customs). Mill's 'history', written without visiting India or learning any Indian language, may have, in some ways, served well the purpose of training young British officers getting ready to cross the seas and rule a subject nation, but it would scarcely suffice as a basis of understanding the nature of Indian culture. The identification of Indian culture specifically with Hinduism not only demotes the role of Muslim and other non-Hindu contributors, but also the major creations outside the fields of religious thought in general. The cultural bigotry that ignores the contributions of Muslims also demolishes much else.

The 'cultural' critique of secularism, based on identifying India in distinctly Hindu terms, thus suffers from both (1) a spurious cultural diagnosis, and (2) a political *non sequitur* on making rights conditional on historical cultural contribution.

10. A Concluding Remark

The discontent with secularism in India has produced many distinct and interesting lines of argument, which are certainly worth scrutinizing, but — as has been argued here — they do not do much to undermine the basic case for secularism in this country. It is hard to escape the need to see India as an integrally pluralist society, and to accept the necessity of symmetric treatment and secular politics as crucial parts of that recognition.

Secularism is basically a demand for symmetric political treatment of different religious communities, and its acceptance still leaves open many other questions, particularly dealing with the choice between the forms that symmetry can legitimately take. Balanced political treatment can be achieved, as I have discussed, in rather disparate ways, and it does make a difference as to which of the ways is chosen. These issues must remain central to the political debates and arguments that India must have.

It is not being claimed here that the secular approach is trouble-free. Among the many forms that secularism can take, there are some that are clearly less just or fair than others. The communal lines are not the only contrasts that divide the country — there is class, and gender, and language, and location, and many other lines of separation. There are also difficult issues of balancing group autonomy and individual freedom.

There is, furthermore, a real difference between getting symmetry through the sum-total of the collective intolerances of the different communities, rather than through the union of their respective tolerances. Anything that causes the wrath of any of the major communities in India is presently taken to be a potential candidate for proscription. We have to ask whether that is the form that symmetric treatment should take.

There remain many uncomfortable questions of this kind. But the case for re-examining these issues does not contradict the overarching argument for secularism and the overwhelming need for symmetric treatment of different communities and religions in India. There are good reasons to resist the contrary enticements that have been so plentifully offered recently. The winter of our discontent might not be giving way, right now, to a 'glorious summer', but the abandonment of secularism would make things far more wintry than they currently are. There is work to be done, but not through moving in the constricted and constraining direction that is being so forcefully proposed at this time. There is more force in the proposal than reason.

Before the Leviathan:
Sectarian Violence and the State in
Pre-Colonial India

Sanjay Subrahmanyam

> "The Muslim fears the flame,
> and the Hindu the tomb,
> Both die in this fear,
> such is the hatred between them".
>
> - Bullhe Shah (1680-1758)[1]

In recent years, the perception of India's pre-colonial past has come to play an ever more important role in the rhetoric and conduct of contemporary politics. The results have often been distressing. The past is thus now cast in the role of a crucial (though not particularly scarce) resource, over which contending groups engage in a tussle, which is as much methodological as empirical.[2] The revival of methodological subjectivism in the social sciences, the claim that there may really be nothing 'out there' anyway, has permitted an attitude of anything goes, empirically speaking. Religious fundamentalists, allied with a particular shade of indigenist post-modernists, have taken to arguing that 'history' is only one of several ways in which the past can be read, and further that it is a particularly tainted procedure, since History

---

[1] Text cited in Denis Matringe, 'Kṛṣṇāite and Nāth elements in the poetry of the eighteenth century Panjabi Sufi Bullhe Sah', in R.S. McGregor, ed., *Devotional Literature in South Asia: Current Research, 1985-1988*, Cambridge, 1992, p. 196. The translation has been slightly modified in keeping with the text.

[2] For two different overviews of recent literature, see the contributions by Amartya Sen and G. Balachandran to this volume.

was invented in the West anyway.[3] It is suggested therefore that in order to return to their own real 'roots', Indians should seek other, more indigenous forms of approaching the past, a statement that usually serves as a preamble for some largely arbitrary procedure, deriving more often than not from an opportunistic use precisely of *Western* social science, and reflecting no more than the authors' fancies and prejudices of the moment. Along with the bathwater of History, both the babies of rigour and logic are summarily thrown out, and we are left with essays that deliberately resemble pulp films from Bombay not just in their populism and pyrotechnics, but in their celebration of a lack of coherence. Not only this: epistemological hats are changed in the midst of an essay with the same facility with which Bombay film heroes and heroines change their wardrobe in the midst of a scene.

Now, as can be demonstrated without a great deal of difficulty, the argument against History is a version of the 'Errington thesis', developed a decade and a half ago by a linguistically naive American anthropologist of Southeast Asia, and based on a considerable ignorance concerning the wide variety of modes and forms of history-writing in pre-colonial India (as well as the rest of the non-Western world), which were not simply the product of the European Renaissance, or of the European Enlightenment.[4] The idea that in pre-colonial and early colonial India, the past was approached solely through the *purāṇa* genre, popularized by

---

[3] The academic end of this position is well represented by the recent writings of Ashis Nandy; but also see Dipesh Chakrabarty, 'Postcoloniality and the Artifice of History: Who Speaks for "Indian" Pasts?', *Representations*, No. 37, 1992. A recent essay by Gyanendra Pandey, attacking 'historians' history', comes perilously close to this position; cf. Pandey, 'The Prose of Otherness', in David Arnold and David Hardiman, eds., *Subaltern Studies VIII: Essays in Honour of Ranajit Guha*, Delhi, 1994. One is entitled to wonder what sort of history Pandey imagines he himself writes, if not 'historians' history'.

[4] Cf. Shelly Errington, 'Some comments on Style in the Meanings of the Past', *Journal of Asian Studies*, Vol. 38, No. 2, 1979, pp. 231-44, which argues among other things that history is purely a 'post-Renaissance Western genre'; contrast V. Narayana Rao and David Shulman, 'History, Biography and Poetry at the Tanjavur Nayaka Court', *Social Analysis*, No. 25, 1989, pp. 115-30, and the more elaborate discussion in V. Narayana Rao, David Shulman and Sanjay Subrahmanyam, *Symbols of Substance: Court and State in Nayaka-period Tamil Nadu*, Delhi, 1992.

some recent writers, is as grotesque a distortion of the record as any produced by European Orientalists.[5]

The present essay will not address these methodological and epistemological questions further, saving that task for another occasion. Instead, the approach here will remain premised on the legitimacy and desirability of history as a form of approaching the past; we shall be concerned in that context to deal with the empirical issue of the place of violence in pre-colonial India, and its interface with the state in that context. Our principal theses will oppose those of Golden Age theorists of various stripes, whether those 'secular' nationalists, who wish to argue that colonial rule should be held responsible for all the ills of Indian society, or those Hindu nationalists, who wish to use the pre-colonial past to create an image of a ceaselessly violent Islam, acting on hapless, innately tolerant, 'Hindu' populations. This last view, we should note, is no longer confined to right-wing Hindu groups alone; some western academics, whether studying Indian society from a 'Hindu point of view', or making sweeping generalizations between the iconoclasm of the Peoples of the Book as contrasted to the comportment of Hindus, Buddhists and Jainas, are equally responsible for and complicit in the spread of such distortions.[6]

An anecdote may help bring out the flavour of the problem at hand; this is an exchange in the Indian newspapers concerning the demolition of the mosque at Ayodhya on December 6, 1992, which serves as a convenient and appropriate entry-point into the subject of the essay. On October 10, 1993, D. Mandal, professor of archaeology at Allahabad University, and author of a pamphlet in the series 'Tracts for the Times', entitled 'Ayodhya: Archaeology after demolition', wrote a guest column in the *Times of India*. There he argued that contrary to the claims of the right-wing

---

[5]This is the implicit assumption of Partha Chatterjee, 'Claims on the Past: The Genealogy of Modern Historiography in Bengal', in Arnold and Hardiman, eds., *Subaltern Studies VIII*, pp. 1-49.

[6]This is equally true of some erstwhile Indian Marxists; for a particularly extreme instance, see Shashi Joshi and Bhagwan Josh, *Struggle for Hegemony in India 1920-47: Culture, Community and Power*, New Delhi, 1994, of which Chs. 2 to 6 comprise a virulent and scarcely comprehensible diatribe on the 'cultural faultline' in medieval India between Hindus and Muslims.

Vishva Hindu Parishad (VHP) and the Historians' Forum supported by it, there was no archaeological evidence for a temple of either stone or brick during the three centuries (1200-1500 A.D.) preceding the building in Ayodhya of the Babri Masjid by Mir Baqi.[7] He implied that the VHP had manufactured evidence after December 6, in order to support its claim, and this has also been the view of many historians engaged in the debate on the Ayodhya site, notably those of the Centre for Historical Studies, Jawaharlal Nehru University.

A letter appeared in response a week later by a certain D. Singh from New Delhi. The brunt of this letter was to argue that before Professor Mandal's conclusions regarding Ayodhya were to be deemed 'correct', he needed to establish his credentials by investigating another case: that of the Gyan Vapi mosque in Benares, which it was claimed was built on the site of a demolished temple by the Mughal ruler Aurangzeb (or 'Alamgir: reign 1658-1707). The implication of the letter was as follows: if it could be shown that a temple had been demolished to build a mosque in Benares, it must have been the case at Ayodhya as well: since the argument 'of eminent Muslim scholars that according to Islam a masjid cannot be built on disputed land and that even Allah does not accept the prayers offered in a disputed masjid' would have been shown to be false.[8]

The letter contains its share of *non sequiturs*. But there is a cunning that underlies its choice of example: the evidence regarding Benares is indeed quite explicit. Saqi Must'ad Khan's official Mughal chronicle, *Ma'asir-i 'Ālamgīrī*, makes it clear that a Visvanath temple was destroyed there on the Mughal ruler's orders in mid-1669. Its account runs somewhat flatly as follows:

'It was reported [in September 1669] that, according to the

---

[7] D. Mandal, 'The myth of archaeological evidence', *The Sunday Times of India*, October 10, 1993, p. 16.

[8] 'Myths and evidence' (Sunday Forum), *The Sunday Times of India*, October 17, 1993, p. 16. For the complex nature of evidence from another, albeit far more obscure, site, see Sunil Kumar, 'Making Sacred History or Everyone his own Historian', *The India Magazine*, September 1993, pp. 46-55.

Emperor's command, his officers had demolished the temple of Viswanath at Kashi'.[9]

Architectural historians seem to agree that a wall of this temple was used to provide the *qibla* wall of the Gyan Vapi mosque. Scholarly dispute continues however on the motives behind the razing of the temple, whether these were solely political (as an act of vengeance against the family of Jai Singh, which had built the temple), or at least partly religious.[10] Such niceties scarcely interest the single-minded activists of the VHP and Bajrang Dal, who gather periodically in fairly large numbers (for example, on the occasion of Mahashivaratri) to demand the demolition of the mosque and its substitution by a temple.[11]

In any event, the seventeenth-century episode mentioned above is not an isolated instance. From the reign of 'Alamgir, the Mughal chronicles provide numerous others. Thus, for January 1670, we have the following, somewhat more detailed account from the same official chronicle:

'During this month of Ramzan abounding in miracles, the Emperor as the promoter of justice and overthrower of mischief, as a knower of truth and destroyer of oppression, as the zephyr of the garden of victory and the reviver of the faith of the Prophet, issued orders for the demolition of the temple situated in Mathura, famous as the Dehra of Kesho Rai. In a short time, by the great exertions of his officers, the destruction of this strong foundation of infidelity was accomplished, and on its site a lofty mosque was built at the expenditure of a large sum. This temple of folly was built by that gross idiot Bir Singh Deo Bundela. Before his accession to the throne, the Emperor Jahangir was displeased with Shaikh Abul Fazl. This infidel [Bir Singh Deo] became a royal favourite by slaying him, and after Jahangir's accession

---

[9] Saqi Must'ad Khan, *Ma'asir-i 'Alamgiri: A History of the Emperor Aurangzib-'Alamgir (Reign 1658-1707 AD)*, tr. Jadunath Sarkar, Calcutta, 1947, p. 55.
[10] Catherine B. Asher, *Architecture of Mughal India* (The New Cambridge History of India, I.4), Cambridge, 1992, pp. 277-79.
[11] 'Security geared up at Kashi temple', *The Pioneer* (New Delhi), February 27, 1995, p. 1.

was rewarded for this service with the permission to build the temple, which he did at an expense of thirty-three lakhs of rupees'.

Thus, the construction of the temple was, in the first place, done under Mughal rule, and in the second place by a *mansabdār* and tributary raja of the Mughals, in the early seventeenth century. The chronicle's author, Saqi Must'ad Khan, implies that permission was granted to do this as a political favour, rather than through any spirit of tolerance on Jahangir's part. He then goes on:

'Praised be the august God of the faith of Islam, that in the auspicious reign of this destroyer of infidelity and turbulence [Aurangzeb], such a wonderful and seemingly impossible work was successfully accomplished. On seeing this instance of the strength of the Emperor's faith and the grandeur of his devotion to God, the proud Rajas were stifled, and in amazement they stood like images facing the wall. The idols, large and small, set with costly jewels, which had been set up in the temple, were brought to Agra, and buried under the steps of the mosque of Begam Sahib, in order to be continually trodden upon. The name of Mathura was changed to Islamabad.'[12]

Here then, what is stressed by the chronicler is precisely the political impact of such a destruction, in cowing down the rajas (rather than the Vaishnava population in general) and asserting the Emperor's grandeur, rather than its purely religious dimensions.

On the other hand, during the wars of the eighteenth century, the destruction and desecration of Muslim religious sites (and even royal tombs) was not unknown; the case of Akbar's tomb at Sikandra, desecrated by the Jats of Bharatpur, is one of them. Equally, Hindu temples were at times attacked by other Hindu warriors and chieftains, as we gather from the following account of a dispute between the Maratha rajas of Tanjavur, and Murarirao Ghorpade of Gutti, also a Maratha chieftain (albeit a minor one), in the early 1750s. Pratapasimha, the Maratha raja, wrote on this occasion from Tanjavur:

---

[12]Saqi Must'ad Khan, *Ma'asir-i 'Alamgiri*, p. 60.

'Murari was enraged that the Nawab was suffered to pass through my country and sent some horsemen [or] robbers who entered the Cholamandalam alias my country and have plundered and ruined it entirely. They have killed about 100 or 200 Brahmins and ravished a great many women. The Sudras (alias the Malabars etc.) murdered by them were so numerous that it was impossible for one to count them. The chariots of our Gods were burnt and they defiled our pagodas [temples] by committing hostilities in various manner. No one has hitherto committed the like insults in my country. They have been so barbarous as to set the paddy heaps and the houses on fire. I dare say that Chanda [Chanda Sahib, Husain Dost Khan] never did the like injury though he acted against me. My loss was computed at ten lakhs ...' [13]

Destruction could at times be followed by construction, desecration by conversion. It is likely that in South Asia, as in most other parts of the world, some proportion of the major religious monuments of today are built on the sites of earlier structures, not least of all because of persistent geomantic beliefs concerning the properties of particular sites. This happens most conspicuously with the conversion of communities who are attached to a particular site, but is not at all uncommon even otherwise. We may take the case of the northern Indian town of Sambhal, visited by the eighteenth-century Khatri merchant and courtier from Delhi, Anand Ram Mukhlis, in the early 1740s, and described in some detail in his well-known *Safar Nāma*.[14] A large part of the town, considered to be one of the older ones of the region, was at that time in ruins, but the people of the town were as cultured as those of

---

[13]Letter from Pratapasimha, King of Tanjavur, received the 17 May 1753, in Records of Fort St. George, *Country Correspondence, Military Department, 1753*, Madras, 1911, Letter No. 98, pp. 57-58. Spellings have been modernized. It is an instructive irony that Murarirao Ghorpade is nevertheless a minor hero in the pantheon of Maratha nationalist historiography.

[14] *Safar Nāma-i Mukhlis* (The Diary of the Travel of Anand Ram Mukhlis, d. 1164 A.H.), ed. with notes by Sayyid Azhar 'Ali, Rampur, 1946. An English translation of the first part of the journey, from Delhi to Garh Mukteshwar, by William Irvine, may be found in the rather obscure *Indian Magazine and Review* (1903), pp. 66-71, 102-106, 116-121, 151-56 and 169-72.

Delhi, in Anand Ram's view; Amin al-daula, a well-known notable (of 7,000 *mansab* rank) from the time of Bahadur Shah had originally been from there, and had had his own *haveli* constructed at Sambhal, besides having patronized a number of gardens and market-places. But Mukhlis also noticed on the town's other side a high dome, that he states was at one time a temple called Har Mandal. Of this it used to be said (in the vernacular): *Bhâg baḍe sambhal ke/ ke Harjî har maṇḍal âveṅge* ('Great is the fortune of Sambhal/ where Harji (Siva) will come to the Harmandal'), reflecting a belief in the imminent return of the god incarnate. When Babur took Hindustan, writes Mukhlis, he gave Sambhal as a *jâgîr* to his son Humayun Mirza, and the latter converted this ancient building into a mosque, so that it was now the *jama' masjid* of the town. 'Earlier too it was a place of worship (*'ibâdat kadah*), and even now it is a place of worship', concludes Anand Ram calmly, apparently finding this a perfectly normal procedure. He even cites the chronogram inscribed on one of its arches, noting that it was constructed on Babur's orders by a certain Hindu Beg. Further, Anand Ram notes the existence of a tank, now in poor condition, but thought to be holy, where people still came and bathed in some numbers in the 1740s. Brahmans and flower-sellers too still came there in numbers to sell flowers and recite *shlokas*.[15]

The point should be clear. Historians who are willing to concede that the central political issue is of whether a particular religious structure was indeed destroyed to make way for another in the sixteenth century are thus unwittingly giving hostages to fortune. The empiricist in each one of us knows that there is a rather significant probability that further evidence may turn up, in the form of a chronicle, a set of letters, or a travelogue, that could transform the certainties of today concerning a sixteenth-century event into an indefensible position. Would 'progressive historians' be willing to concede, were such evidence to turn up concerning the existence of a temple at Ayodhya before 1526, that the demolition of December 6, 1992, was justified ? If this is indeed

---

[15] For an earlier brief mention of the Har Mandal, see Abu'l Fazl, *The A-in-i Akbari*, tr. H.S. Jarrett, revised Jadunath Sarkar, reprint, Delhi, 1989, Vol. II, p. 285. For details of the mosque, also see Asher, *Architecture* of *Mughal India*, pp. 28-29. Asher follows Jarrett in reading 'Hara' (Shiva) as 'Hari' (Vishnu).

the case, then the VHP's tripartite programme is well on its way: *Yah to keval jhānki hai; Mathurā, Kāshi bāki hai* ('This is only a preview; Mathura and Kashi still remain'), as their slogan ran in the aftermath of December 1992. This, to my mind, had been these historians' blunder with respect not only to the particular issue of Ayodhya, but to the entire medieval Indian record of sectarian violence. Rather than analyse it in order to transcend it, there has been strategic selectivity and misuse on the one hand, and strategic obfuscation on the other.

Two vignettes from Gujarat

Let us further our analysis by considering two accounts regarding Gujarat, separated by nearly five hundred years. The first is in the text *Jawāmi' al-Hikāyāt fi Lawāmi' al-Riwāyāt* of Sadid al-Din Muhammad 'Awfi from Bukhara, and derives from the early 1220s, when 'Awfi was at the Gujarat port of Khambayat (Cambay), then under the rule of a Hindu raja. At Khambayat, 'Awfi found a significant population of Muslim merchants from Iran, Central Asia and the Arab lands, whose relations with the non-Muslims were, he reports, generally amicable. However, incidents of violence were not unknown, and he cites one from the earlier reign of a certain Raja Jai Singh. In this period, a *jama'* (congregational) mosque with a minaret was built at Khambayat to serve the Muslims, and became the target of an attack by some 'Hindus ... instigated by the Zoroastrians', also resident in the port. The mosque was set on fire, the minaret demolished, and eighty Muslims were killed. The Muslim preacher (or *khatīb*) called 'Ali, presented a complaint in the court at Nahrawala, but to no avail since some powerful courtiers were unsympathetic. The text now takes a surprising turn, and 'Awfi reports that matters ended well; for the *khatīb* managed to catch the ruler's attention while he was out on a hunting expedition, and presented another petition directly to him. The ruler then is said to have himself come incognito to Khambayat, looked into matters, and being convinced that the *khatīb* was right, ordered the punishment of those responsible, the payment of damages to the Muslims, and the restoration of the mosque and minaret (besides bestowing signal honours on the *khatīb*). The restored mosque was later demolished once more by the invading Paramara rulers of Malwa, but then again re-built by a merchant from Bam in Iran. 'Awfi's conclusions are thus ambiguous: on the one hand, he praises the even-handed justice of the Hindu raja, but on the other concludes his discussion by implying that Muslims in Gujarat still require the protection of the Sword of Islam — that is of the Sultan of Delhi, Shams al-Din Iltutmish ![16]

The second account comes from the Mughal chronicle *Muntakhab ul-Lubāb* of Muhammad Hashim Khafi Khan, completed almost exactly five hundred years after 'Awfi's account, in the early 1730s. It concerns affairs in the provincial capital of Ahmadabad in Gujarat, in the year 1713 (1125 A.H.), during the reign of the Mughal sovereign Farrukhsiyar, when the governor was a noble of Afghan origin called Da'ud Khan Panni. Da'ud Khan, from a family that had long been in the Deccan and in the service of the Sultans of Bijapur, had earlier held posts of some importance for the Mughals in southern India, in the area around Arcot; he appears to have belonged to the Mahdawi sect, a millenialist group which also flourished in some limited pockets in the Deccan and western India. The occasion described by Khafi Khan in Ahmadabad was the bacchanalian spring festival of Holi, when on the eve of the main festivities a bonfire was (and still is) often burnt symbolizing the destruction of the demoness Holika. A certain Hindu, writes Khafi Khan, whose house shared a common courtyard with that of a Muslim, decided to burn the Holi, but his neighbour objected. The matter was taken before Da'ud Khan, who decided in favour of the former. However, since the governor himself was married to a Hindu woman, he was accused at this time (as on other occasions) of partiality.

The next day, the chronicle reports, the Muslim neighbour decided for his part to honour the Prophet with a feast in which a cow was slaughtered. He argued that if his neighbour could burn the Holi, since 'he had a right to do as he liked in his own house', so too did he have the right to slaughter a cow. The Hindus of the

---

[16] Iqtidar H. Siddiqui, *Perso-Arabic Sources of Information on the Life and Conditions in the Sultanate of Delhi*, Delhi, 1992, pp. 24-26; for the text, see *Jawāmi' al-Hikāyāt fī Lawāmi' al-Riwāyāt*, ed. Muhammad Nizam-ud-din, Vol. I, Part II, Hyderabad, 1966, pp. 255-58.

quarter are reported to have gathered around the house in protest, forcing the Muslims present there to conceal themselves. The crowd then escalated the level of violence, seized a cow-butcher's son aged fourteen or fifteen, and slaughtered him. This brought a violent response in turn. A great number of Muslims, including several thousand Afghans in Da'ud Khan's service, are reported to have assembled from the town and even from outlying quarters. They appealed to the *qāzi* for justice, but he shut his doors to them. This crowd now set fire to the door of the *qāzi's* house, and went on to burn a number of houses of Hindus. Several shops too were burnt, and an attack was planned on a jeweller called Kapur Chand, reputedly a friend of Da'ud Khan. He, however, prepared to defend his house with armed force, and even closed off the gates to the quarter where he lived. (Quarters in Ahmadabad apparently were well equipped for such occasions !) The violence went on, bringing business to a standstill for three or four days. Kapur Chand now sent a petition to the Mughal court at Delhi, countersigned by Da'ud Khan, but others at the court presented petitions for their part against Da'ud Khan. Violence and contention seems to have spread even to Delhi as a consequence.[17]

Khafi Khan's sympathies in the matter are plain: he believed that Da'ud Khan Panni was culpable, because he was partial to the 'infidels', and even had close relations with some of them like Kapur Chand. The fact that he was a deviant and heterodox Muslim (a Mahdawi, as noted above) may have had a role to play as well in this disapprobation. At issue too is a curious question of the domain of the public and the private, which we are often told by historians of India did not ever arise in pre-colonial India. Could one in the privacy of one's own house light a large bonfire and organize noisy celebrations around it, or slaughter a cow ? Further, the state is clearly implicated in the violence, and becomes a sphere where contests on the issue are played out. The chronicle is also sweeping in its categories: 'the Hindus', 'the Muslims', with a

---

[17] Muhammad Hashim Khafi Khan, *Muntakhab ul-Lubāb*, Vol. II, ed. K.D. Ahmad and Wolseley Haig, Calcutta, 1869, pp. 755-56; translation in H.M. Elliot and J. Dowson, ed. and compil. *The History of India as told by its own historians: The Muhammadan period*, 8 vols., London, 1867-77, Vol. VII, pp. 454-56.

concession being made at one point to the slightly more nuanced category 'the Afghans'.

Such examples of urban sectarian violence and its portrayal in contemporary materials in pre-colonial South Asia can be multiplied, especially from the first half of the eighteenth century. Yet they are seldom admitted into academic discussions of the question of sectarian or communal violence, which in recent years have reached industrial proportions.[18] Why? It appears that the debate on 'communal' violence in India has in recent years thrown up at least three distinct positions. The *first* of these, associated with nationalist-Marxist writers, and thus logically more recently to an extent with their heirs, the secular historians of the *Subaltern Studies* school, pinpoints the colonial period as not merely crucial but wholly determining for an understanding of current sectarian violence. Whereas nationalist-Marxist writers located causation squarely in British 'divide and rule' policies, writers such as Gyanendra Pandey (in his acclaimed *The Construction of Communalism in Colonial North India*)[19] argue that the British 'discourse' on communal identities served as a midwife in the creation of precisely such identities. In this view, which has assumed the dimensions of a new orthodoxy, of which most writers in a special section on India of the journal *Annales ESC* (July-October 1992) also seem to partake in a more or less nuanced fashion, the actual history of communal (or sectarian) relations in *pre-colonial* India is largely irrelevant, for it is assumed that such relations were either largely harmonious or at least *random* in their generation of conflict, and thus not amenable to systematic analysis.[20] Besides, if the crystallization of what are today

---

[18] A rather typical instance of woolliness on the part of a medievalist scholar is M. Athar Ali, 'Encounter and Effloresence: Genesis of the Medieval Civilization', *Presidential Address to the Indian History Congress, Golden Jubilee Session*, Gorakhpur 1989.

[19] Gyanendra Pandey, *The Construction of Communalism in Colonial North India*, Delhi, 1990; earlier Romila Thapar, Harbans Mukhia and Bipan Chandra, *Communalism and the Writing of Indian History*, New Delhi, 1977. Finally, the recent analyses in Gyanendra Pandey, ed., *Hindus and Others: The question of identity in India today*, New Delhi, 1993.

[20] Cf. in particular Jackie Assayag, 'La Déesse et le Saint: Acculturation et "communalisme" hindou-musulman dans un lieu de culte du sud de l'Inde (Karnataka)', *Annales ESC*, Vol. XLVII, (4 5), 1992, pp. 789 814, especially p. 806.

recognizable communities and community identities is itself a recent phenomenon, what could be the purpose of shifting the focus of analysis to the earlier period ? Far better to accept the position, simplistic though many would admit it to be, of a recent Aligarh historian, writing on the eighteenth century !

'The very rarity of the references to communal conflict among the ordinary populace in the eighteenth century is of singular importance. In spite of political decay, the century marks the apex of the process of attainment of a composite culture which had been generated in medieval times. An admiration for Perso-Muslim culture on the part of the Hindus and an attachment to their Indian heritage on the part of the Muslims marked the "higher culture" of the time. At folk levels the two communities had long learned to live together, and this mutual tolerance was easily reflected in their mode of life, customs and festivals.'[21]

Yet, despite this resolute disavowal of its significance to any discussion, the medieval past is very much a resource, whether directly or indirectly, in political writings of a communalist inspiration in South Asia today. The major target of the writers summarized above (of the first group), is of course the writings of this second group, namely the ideologues of sectarian groups and parties themselves, be they historians like I.H. Qureshi arguing that the roots of Pakistan may already be found in the Mughal period, or others like Koenraad Elst (attached more or less explicitly to the RSS, VHP, BJP and so on) who argue that the 'Muslim ruling class' in the seven centuries before colonial rule systematically affronted the 'Hindus' and their institutions.[22] Since the medieval record serves so clearly as a justification for current politics, it might have seemed worthy of more than the cursory mention it has so far received. Further, rather than survey the

---

[21] Mohammad Umar, *Islam in Northern India during the Eighteenth Century*, New Delhi, 1993, pp. 394-95.

[22] I.H. Qureshi, I.H. *The Muslim Community of the Indian Subcontinent*, The Hague, 1962; for a general perspective, also see Mubarak Ali, 'Akbar in Pakistani Textbooks', paper presented to a seminar on *Akbar and His Age*, I.C.H.R., New Delhi, 15-17 October 1992.

modern historiography on the pre-colonial period, in order to show how this or that twentieth-century historian is either 'secular' or 'communalist', we might turn more resolutely to analysing the record of the pre-colonial period itself.

Indeed, a third point of view also exists, even if it is as yet imperfectly articulated. Chosen as his particular 'straw man' by Gyanendra Pandey at the outset of his book cited above, this is the view of C.A. Bayly that there might indeed have been a 'pre-history' of religion-based strife, before colonial rule in north India.[23] Pandey notes, astutely enough, that in its present rather elementary form, Bayly's argument can be boiled down to a statement of Indian changelessness. He seems to assert no more than that, periodically, clashes of material interests and the hunger for land have led to tensions and violence between communities, which might thus seem much the same whether in the eighteenth or in the twentieth century (or for that matter in the tenth or the thirteenth century).

While this polemically disposes of Bayly's argument with a suspicious deftness, it does not do all that much damage to the substantive question that underlies it. The thorny question does remain: What was the nature of sectarian relations and sectarian strife in pre-colonial India, and how was it articulated ? When sectarian violence did occur, on what lines was it, and what part did the state have to play? It is only once we have delineated some elements of this problem, that we can move on to asking how the logic of violence changed with colonialism, to say nothing of its scale and impact. This is precisely what this essay sets out to do, albeit in a preliminary way. The term 'sectarian' is deliberately used in place of 'communal', for 'communal' violence is a concept largely peculiar to the South Asian historiography of the colonial and post-colonial periods, and is thus likely to be incomprehensible to a historian of Africa, China, or Indonesia, on the face of it.

The particular line of analysis that will be followed is premised on my conviction, which has grown from many years of working on the sources of pre-colonial history (and with which many

---

[23] C.A. Bayly, 'The pre-history of "communalism"?: Religious conflict in India, 1700-1860', *Modern Asian Studies*, Vol. XIX, (2), 1985.

colleagues privately at least agree), that medieval and late pre-colonial Indian society was violent, and that the texts and ideological statements produced in the epoch are often suffused with this violence, which was seen as legitimating for a number of purposes. A certain violence, even in the choice of metaphors and in the portrayal of social relations, underlies the statements of some of the most touted apostles of 'harmony' of the period, from the fifteenth-century mystic Kabir, to the Mughal ruler Akbar, proponent of the ideology of *sulh-i kull* ('universal peace'). Yet, this was no war of all against all. Violence was still somewhat fragmentary and local; but even so, certain common logics and patterns can be discerned. Nevertheless, there was relatively little harnessing of devices of collective memory or the recollection of 'historical grievances' to orchestrate mass violence. Such notions remained, with a few exceptions, in the domain of private rather than sectarian violence, of the feud rather than the pogrom.

The concluding section of this essay will raise larger comparative issues, once more something that historians of colonial and post-colonial India have almost without exception shied away from doing. It will be argued that sectarian violence in late pre-colonial India conforms to a larger pattern, and that certain demographic and other peculiarities have obscured this pattern. No doubt the South Asian case is unique and peculiar in some respects. But were it not so, history would not be – as it is partly at least – an empirical discipline !

Religious violence and violent religiosity

States in their expansionary campaigns have always used violence, and violence is thus bound up most intimately with the political sphere. The Mauryan ruler Ashoka, cited by official Indian ideologues as an ideal of proto-secularism, was mythologized as publicly renouncing violence after embracing Buddhism, but only after a series of bloody campaigns culminating in Kalinga. Non-violence could however never be a meaningful tenet of state policy: at best non-aggression could be aimed for. States in South Asia even after Ashoka continued to have instruments of internal coercion and external expansion at their disposal, and we are not aware that the political logic of Buddhist kingdoms differed systematically from those of others which adhered less explicitly to ideals of *ahimsa*. The very concept of *ahimsa* has suffered some distortion in modern times; it has been shown recently that in classical Brahmanical literature at least, it did not have the connotations given to it by Gandhi in modern times.[24] Indeed, there is nothing surprising in the fact of states, or of warrior-groups, using violent means to expand, or to crush internal dissent. Far more interesting is to consider the interface between the state's violence and sectarian strife within society.

Even apologists of Hindu nationalism have, to the present writer's knowledge, never claimed in the Indian context that South Asian society before the arrival of the first Islamic elements was not characterized by violence of any sort. Indeed, the very epic texts around which their writings are so often located (and which they seek naively to historicize) are impregnated with violence, and certainly date to much before the Hijra. These texts, notably the *Rāmāyaṇa* and *Mahābhārata*, are, among other things, elaborate statements of warrior values, and of legitimating and even cleansing (thus also, crucially, heroic and legitimate) violence in the context of internecine and even intra-clan conflict. Like the Greek epics (and in particular the *Iliad*), the dramatic logic of these texts centres around battlefield violence; however, this violence is not immediately assimilable to the notion of sectarian violence, save if one identifies the epic's categories with ethnic divisions, as indeed some naive Marxists and modern-day Dravidian nationalists have tended to do.

These texts formed a part of the literary and cultural resources and reference points for writers of the medieval period, when sectarian violence became more explicit. At the risk of some simplification, it appears that the latter centuries of the first millenium witnessed a resurgence in certain forms of Hindu sectarianism, centering around a series of figures such as Sankara (ca. 788-820 A.D.), then later Ramanuja, Yamuna and Madhavacharya, who appear in their own hagiographies either in

---

[24] Madeleine Biardeau, 'Le Brahmanisme ancien, ou la non-violence impossible', in D. Vidal, G. Tarabout and E. Meyer, eds., *Violences et Non-Violence en Inde* (Collection Puruṣārtha 16), Paris, 1994, pp. 125-39.

conflict with Buddhists and their religious complexes, or in conflict with rival forms of sectarian Hinduism. It is to these conflicts of the late years of the first millenium and the early years of the present millenium that we must turn for an explanation of the origins of certain militant forms of sectarian Hinduism, as well as the explicit use of texts like the *Rāmāyaṇa* as political devices. In a recent essay, the American Sanskritist Sheldon I. Pollock claims to demonstrate that the association of the figure of Rama with specific dynastic myths and royal figures was a post-twelfth century, specifically northern Indian response to rampant Islam (in reaction to the expeditions of Mahmud of Ghazni, the Ghaznavids, and the Ghurids).[25] This idea appears not merely simplistic (Islamic challenge leading to Hindu response), but empirically unsound: the early inscriptions of the Cholas of Tanjavur (predating the twelfth century) associate the eponymous founding-figure of the dynasty explicitly with Rama, and the Cholas also provide the political context for the writing of Kampan's *Irāmāvatāram*, a retelling with explicit local cultural and political overtones, in Tamil, of the *Rāmāyaṇa*.[26] Although Kampan probably wrote in the twelfth century, we can hardly attribute his vision or version to a supposed Hindu reaction to Mahmud's raids on north India ! Still another Chola text, the *Kaliṅkattuppāraṇi* of Jayankontar, describes the campaigns of Kulottunga I in Orissa, and explicitly compares him to divine incarnations in the epics as follows:[27]

> That one who, long ago,
> fought against Lanka
> and destroyed it

[25] Sheldon Pollock, 'Ramayana and Political Imagination in India', *The Journal of Asian Studies*, Vol. LII, (2), 1993, pp. 261-97; this is an ambitious extension of a far more limited argument presented by Hans Bakker, for which see by way of example Bakker, 'Vormen van religieus geweld in India: De zaak Ayodhya', in Martin Gosman and Hans Bakker, eds., *Heilige Oorlogen: Een onderzoek naar historische en hedendaagsche vormen van collectief religieus geweld*, Kampen, 1991, pp. 155-175.

[26] For a discussion, see David D. Shulman, *The King and the Clown in South Indian Myth and Poetry*, Princeton, 1985.

[27] In the translation of David Shulman, 'Poets and patrons in Tamil literature and literary legend', in Barbara Stoler Miller, ed., *The Powers of Art: Patronage in Indian Culture*, Delhi, 1992, p. 103.

and who later brought the war of the Bharatas
to an end
appeared again as Vijayadhara (= Kulottunga)
whose command brings victory !

This, then, was the political-cum-sectarian vocabulary already in vogue in the medieval period, thus chronologically *before* Islam could make its impact felt on this Indian region. On the other hand, any reconsideration of medieval Hindu sectarian movements, and especially those associated with *bhakti*, has to combat the myth that these were essentially pacific and syncretistic not merely in their actions (which are relatively difficult to verify), but even at the level of self-representation. Such a view, of which all scholars studying these movements have not necessarily partaken, nevertheless has a hold over a larger collective imagination, not least of all on account of post-independence state propaganda from India, notably the pamphlets and books produced by the Government of India's Directorate of Audio-Visual Publicity. Reality was, of course, far more complex. We may consider in this context the case of Parakala, one of the Alvars or 'saints' of south Indian Vaishnavism, who historians believe flourished some time between the sixth and the ninth century A.D.; hagiographical and literary works associate his career with the reign of the Chola dynasty in the Kaveri delta, or less frequently with the earlier Pallavas. Parakala is a warrior in many versions, who took it upon himself to feed thousands of Vishnu-*bhaktas* daily after a dramatic initiation into the Vaishnava faith, that had him branding a conch and discus on his own shoulders. This continuous expenditure led him to embezzle money belonging to the Chola ruler, and then to resist the latter's demands that he return the money. One of the hagiographies, the twelfth-century Sanskrit text *Divyasūrīcaritam*, even introduces a gory battlefield scene, in the epic style, to depict his resistance — all in a good sectarian cause. Thrown into prison, Parakala was miraculously released, but given his considerable financial needs (stemming from his devotion to his sect) he now turned to banditry.[28]

---

[28] My discussion here derives from Friedhelm Hardy, 'The Srivaiṣṇava Hagiography of Parakala', in Christopher Shackle and Rupert Snell, eds., *The Indian Narrative: Perspectives and Patterns*, Wiesbaden, 1992, pp. 81-116.

Indeed, further enlightening details follow on his career, one of which is of some significance, namely a raid on the major Buddhist shrine at Nagapattinam, with the intention of stealing a golden statue of the Buddha there in order to finance the building of a Vaishnava temple. In one version, Parakala's gang found an entry into the shrine large enough to lower one man through; the one chosen was Parakala's brother-in-law. He managed to hand up the Buddha but was unable to climb back; to prevent him from being identified, Parakala cut off his head (which he obligingly stuck out of the hole) and left the headless trunk inside. Some texts elaborate at length on this episode, which involved concealing the statue in a rice-field, pursuit by Buddhist agents, and their tricking by Parakala. The corpus of texts is clearly organized around themes of ruthless, single-minded, and often violent actions to meet a sectarian ideal. The well-being of those outside the sect is totally subordinate to the sect's own needs: there is no universalistic ambition on display here.

And yet, the analysis of the materials on Parakala contains some further surprises. As has been argued convincingly by Friedhelm Hardy, the Parakala corpus — though a Vaishnava corpus with a good deal of emphasis on rivalry with both Buddhists and Saivas — in fact borrows a great deal from Saiva hagiographical materials, with their insistent emphasis on a 'strong element of violence ... coupled with a ruthless, single-minded pursuit of a very limited, specific ideal'. Thus, sectarian conflict went together with unacknowledged borrowings across sectarian divisions, and the corpus provides what to a modern sensibility may be an unlikely religious hero or 'saint'.

The state too is implicated in Parakala's story, albeit in an oblique way. The later Chola rulers are often used in Vaishnava sectarian texts as villainous figures, and are portrayed by them as partisan of an ascendant Saivism. The hagiographies of Ramanuja, who is thought to have lived in the eleventh or early twelfth century, insist, for example, that he was forced to flee the Tamil country from fear of a Chola king; two other Vaishnava ācāryas are said to have been blinded by the same ruler. The implication is thus clearly of a sectarian strife in which rival factions make appeals to, and try even to 'capture', the state. In the particular instance of Parakala, the conflict arises in the fiscal domain, but the underlying logic could not have been occult to the Vaishnava devotee.

Writers on the medieval Saiva tradition, for their part, have rarely concealed the violent religiosity that inheres therein. To the south Indian *nāyanmār*, the Saiva equivalent of the *ālvār*, their god was a violent and jealous one, with whom they cajoled, pleaded, and even threatened, often using the device of violence on themselves or on their family.[29] This is as evident in the Tamil corpus, addressed at some length over the years by scholars like David Shulman, as in some extremely important Telugu works like Palkuriki Somanatha's *Basavapurāṇa* (significantly translated recently as *Siva's Warriors*), or in the poems addressed by the sixteenth-century poet Dhurjati to the god of the southern Andhra temple of Kalahasti.[30] We are at some distance here from the rarefied philosophizing of certain texts of antiquity: religion has assumed more palpable, sensate dimensions, which are expressed through outpourings of anguished and indeed violent emotion.

Once more, it should be clear that representations in sectarian religious materials are not the same as historical events. The violence of these texts, it could be argued with a certain simple logic, might represent not the direct counterpart of social violence in the epoch, but a sublimation and 'taming' of the violence by closing it off within the bounds of text and even ritual. Besides, the violence in these texts is not always sectarian: it is often located within the sphere of the family or the kin-group. Yet even when one has taken all these caveats into account, the logic and nature of the violence that is portrayed remains striking. An illustration of this relationship between textual representation and social violence may help. Many of the major foundation myths of both princely clans and fortified centres in southern Andhra and northern

---

[29] An excellent recent introduction to these themes is David Shulman, *The Hungry God: Hindu Tales of Filicide and Devotion*, Chicago, 1993, especially chapters 2 and 3. I have unfortunately been unable to consult a paper by Shulman of obvious relevance for my argument, namely 'Die Dynamik der Sektenbildung im mittelalterlichen Sudindien', in S. Eisenstadt, ed., Kulturen der Achsenzeit, Vol. II, Frankfurt, 1992.

[30] Velcheru Narayana Rao (with Gene H. Roghair), trans., *Siva's Warriors: The Basava Purana of Palkuriki Somanatha*, Princeton, 1990.

Tamil Nadu go back to the medieval centuries and contain familiar elements: there is a hunt in which the animals behave strangely, the hunter falls asleep and dreams, and on waking he discovers a fortune. But, often, there is a sacrifice that has to be made either to propitiate the ghosts that defend the site (this is the case of the foundation-myth of the fortress at Chandragiri, for example), or to gain access to the treasure.[31] Now, almost inevitably, there is an untouchable servant (or servants) who comes forward to be sacrificed, and who is/are thereafter associated with the foundation by means of associating the place-name or clan-name with their names. There is thus the permitting violence of sacrifice that holds the key to the foundation-myth: and this violence reproduces the direction of the social violence exercised — whether overtly or implicitly — by landed castes on untouchables.

Indeed, some illuminating historical examples do exist that confirm that the sectarian violence (*not* involving Islam) of which we have spoken was neither solely interior nor imagined. One of these concerns Chidambaram in Tamil Nadu, where there was a long tussle in Vijayanagara times over the Govindaraja shrine, earlier located within the complex of the Saiva temple, but which had been done away with at the behest of Kulottunga Chola II. Restored by Aliya Rama Raya in the mid-sixteenth century, Saiva lore (in the form of the text *Jangama kālajñāna*) claims that this act led in turn to Rama Raya's defeat in 1565; the shrine was thus dismantled after his death. Then, in 1597, the Nayaka ruler of Senji in northern Tamil Nadu, Muttu Krishnappa, who was a devout Vaishnava, ordered it replaced and made extensive additions to the Govindaraja shrine. The Saiva temple priests refused to countenance the 'innovation' and threatened to throw themselves down from a gopuram if the Nayaka went ahead with his plans. He did so, leading to several suicides, with other priests allegedly being killed by his harquebusiers.[32]

A somewhat later set of incidents appears in the context of Wodeyar Mysore in the early eighteenth century, wherein the

---

[31] India Office Library and Records, London, Mackenzie Collection, General, Vol. 25, pp. 45–47, 'Historical Account of Chendragerry'.

[32] H. Heras, *The Aravidu Dynasty of Vijayanagara*, Madras, 1927, pp. 544, 553–54.

protagonists once more are in one case Saiva *jangamas*, who enter into conflict with Chikkadevaraja Wodeyar, leading to a massacre of them, in another the (probably Vaishnava) Brahmins of the *agrahāras* of western Mysore, who were particularly brutally treated in the raids on the region by the Kodava forces of Dodda Virappa.[33] It is possible in the case of the *jangamas* to attempt a purely 'materialistic' interpretation of the violence perpetrated on them in view of the privileged position of the Lingayat community in the region; the careful violence visited on the western Mysore Brahmins is however rather hard to interpret in any light other than that of a sectarian-cum-ethnic conflict.

Finally, it is instructive to review the considerable literature from the seventeenth and eighteenth centuries on 'caste conflict' in urban centres in India, which historians and sociologists have by a definitional sleight-of-hand sealed away into a separate category from religious or sectarian violence. Yet, the elements are very often similar: the disputes over urban space in respect of processions, the mobilization across classes and occupations, and the occasions for such violence (typically religious observances). A well-known example is the violent dispute between the shoe-sellers of Delhi and the adherents of a certain Subh Karan, a jeweller, in the eighteenth century. Subh Karan's men killed a certain Haji Hafiz, prompting a large section of the shoe-sellers to attack his house and that of jewellers in general; he then took refuge with a Muslim notable, Raushan ud-daula, who protected him. It is clear in this instance that mobilization was not solely across a Hindu-Muslim chasm; whether the fact that Raushan ud-daula was a Sunni who had converted to Shi'ism may have had a role to play, is a matter of speculation.[34] Equally, looking further south, a very large literature exists, for example, on right- versus left-hand caste (*idangai-valangai*) disputes in urban centres such as Madras, and it is curious indeed that fanciful anthropological

---

[33] For details, see Sanjay Subrahmanyam, 'Warfare and state finance in Wodeyar Mysore, 1724-25: A missionary perspective', *The Indian Economic and Social History Review*, Vol. XXVI, (2), 1989, pp. 203-233.

[34] Umar, *Islam in Northern India*, p. 394.

models have been built around these without noting that they belong to a far larger domain of very similar conflict.[35]

To sum up this section, therefore, the logic of early medieval sectarian violence, stemming from the desire of certain resurgent Vaishnava and Saiva sects initially to compete with Buddhist and Jaina orders and their state patrons, and later from the internecine conflicts between these sects and others, provided a groundswell of violent sectarian activity that preceded, and then ran concurrent to the major impact of Islam on South Asia. It is a gross oversimplification to argue that the collective organization of all such non-Islamic sectarian groups was a mere reaction to Islam; a good deal of suggestive contrary evidence exists (and we have not even touched on the large, and alas, rather violent late Jaina and Buddhist corpus of materials, analysed amongst others by Phyllis Granoff).[36]

This fact of fragmenting conflict and violence also imposed certain demands on the state, which had emerged clearly by the sixteenth century as an arbiter of such conflicts at a number of levels. A famous incident at Thaneswar in 1567, involving the Mughal ruler Akbar, is a minor case in point, and has the advantage not merely of being described in the official chronicle, the *Akbar Nāma*, but providing the subject of a splendidly gory contemporary painting by Basawan. It is reported in the chronicle that Akbar made his way in 1567 to Thaneswar, near which there was a tank, associated with the revered site of Kurukshetra. A long-standing dispute existed at the site of this tank between two rival groups, probably of Saivite Dasnami *saṁnyāsis* (termed 'Kurs', perhaps for 'Giri'; and 'Puris'), over rights to alms-collections, and the leader of the latter, Kesava, hence came on this occasion and petitioned Akbar to intervene. Before the matter could be

---

[35] For an elaborate but less-than-convincing theoretical formulation, see Arjun Appadurai, 'Right and left hand castes in south India', *The Indian Economic and Social History Review*, Vol. XI, (2-3), 1974, pp. 216-59; in contrast, useful materials may be found in Joseph J. Brennig, 'Chief merchants and the European enclaves of seventeenth-century Coromandel', *Modern Asian Studies*, Vol. XI, (3), 1977, pp. 321-40.

[36] This seems to be the argument in David Lorenzen, 'Warrior ascetics in Indian history', *Journal of the American Oriental Society*, Vol. XCVIII, 1978, pp. 61-75; also see Pollock, 'Ramayana and Political Imagination', cited above.

pursued much further, violence broke out between the two groups (who in Basawan's painting are shown as armed with swords, staves, tridents, and other metal implements). Akbar was inclined to favour the 'Puris', who had appealed to him in the first place; he hence encouraged some of his camp-followers to aid them, leading to the defeat of the other group and the killing of their leader 'Ananda Kur'.[37] This figure, with the upper part of his trunk partly severed, is an important part of Basawan's composition; also carefully set out are the sectarian marks of the two groups, making it evident that the 'Kurs' are Saivas, and the 'Puris' Vaishnavas.[38]

Conquest and martyrdom

The first incursions of Sultan Mahmud of Ghazna (967-1030 A.D.) into northern India, and the gradual establishment of first Ghaznavid and then Ghurid control over north-western India has of course been much discussed by historians of India. Treated as the quintessential Islamic marauder and despoiler of temples in a certain set of late nineteenth and early twentieth century writings, attempts were then made to reinterpret Mahmud's actions in largely materialistic terms by historians such as Muhammad Habib.[39] The interpretation is one that is hard to sustain in order to explain the actions of any medieval actor, and is no less so for this Sultan. Certainly, many medieval chroniclers did not wish to see him in this light at all; the sixteenth-century *Tārīkh-i Alfī* reports that when offered a large amount of money in order not to destroy the stone image at Somnath, he replied that on Judgement Day he

---

[37] Abu'l Fazl, *The Akbar Nama*, tr. H. Beveridge, reprint, New Delhi, 1989, Vol. II, pp. 422-24; for another contemporary account, see 'Abd al-Qadir al-Badayuni, *Muntakhab ut-Tawarikh*, Vol. II, tr. W.H. Lowe, reprint, New Delhi, 1990, pp. 94-95. For a discussion, see Véronique Bouiller, 'La violence des non-violents, ou les ascètes au combat', in D. Vidal, et al., *Violence et Non-Violence*, pp. 218-20.

[38] Geeti Sen, *Paintings from the Akbar Nama: A visual chronicle of Mughal India*, New Delhi, 1984, pp. 104-109. The visual evidence is, however, at odds with the identification of both the groups as Dasnamis.

[39] Muhammad Habib, *Sultan Mahmud of Ghaznin*, Aligarh, 1951.

would have something to answer for if he sold the 'greatest of the idols to the infidels for gold' instead of destroying it.[40]

One of the long-term legacies of Sultan Mahmud's numerous expeditions to northern and western India is a particularly curious one: here I refer to the elaborate shrine and myth surrounding a certain Salar Mas'ud, or Ghazi Miyan, located in the northern town of Bahraich. Testified to by the late thirteenth century, this tomb of a *ghāzī* – thus almost by definition, a warrior of Islam – embodies some of the most crucial paradoxes that flow from the sectarian violence of medieval times.[41] Revered through a very large stretch of territory, from the Punjab to the eastern reaches of Bengal, and even into Nepal, Ghazi Miyan's devotees cut across many religious, sectarian and class divides.[42] Yet a large part of the hagiography of the saint, defined already in the early seventeenth century by a Sufi text of 'Abd al-Rahman Chishti, the *Mirāt-i Mas'udī*, makes it clear that the Ghazi – reputedly a nephew of Sultan Mahmud himself – died at the age of nineteen fighting the infidels, the Rajput rulers of the territory, and this version persists in later texts too.

Historians today largely reject any connection between Salar Mas'ud and Sultan Mahmud, arguing that at the date given for his death in the hagiographies (1033 A.D.) Muslim warriors simply could not have penetrated as far as the Bahraich region. Such arguments from silence must be treated with a little caution, since stray expeditions over even several hundred kilometres are not totally out of the realm of possibility. It has even been suggested that the tomb is in fact of a soldier of the thirteenth century from the Sultanate of Delhi; whatever be the case, it is certainly true

---

[40] Translation in Elliot and Dowson, *The History of India*, Vol. II, p. 472.

[41] See Tahir Mahmood, 'The Dargah of Sayyid Salar Mas'ud Ghazi in Bahraich: Legend, tradition and reality', in Christian W. Troll, ed., *Muslim Shrines in India*, Delhi, 1989, pp. 24-43. The cult of Ghazi Miyan will be discussed at length in a forthcoming monograph by Professor Shahid Amin of the University of Delhi.

[42] Useful references to the literature, and a discussion of ethnographic materials for Banaras may be found in Sunthar Visuvalingam and Elizabeth Chalier-Visuvalingam, 'Between Mecca and Banaras: Towards an acculturation model of Hindu-Muslim relations', *Islam and the Modern Age*, Vol. 24, No. 1, 1993, pp. 20-69.

that it was only in the fourteenth century that Bahraich became a major centre of pilgrimage.[43]

Since medieval times, and even today, the shrine has certain healing properties associated with it, for sufferers from leprosy, as also for forms of possession, persistent sickness, and – significantly – is equally thought to confer fertility. Ghazi Miyan himself is, importantly, a virgin warrior in most legends, who is thus also known as *bāle mīyān* (thus stressing his childlike and innocent qualities, and also perhaps the parallels with Krishnaite devotion), which in turn is linked with his power over the domain of childbearing and fertility. It is this aspect that draws the devotees in their largest numbers, despite periodic attempts by Islamic reformers, both in the medieval period and in more recent times, to decry the attribution of miraculous powers to Salar Mas'ud as un-Islamic superstition.

Even though the distribution of devotees by religious denomination has never been subjected to rigorous analysis, it is generally agreed that over an annual ritual cycle (which encompasses several occasions, including the *'urs* festival marking the anniversary of his death), both Hindus and Muslims in large numbers are linked to the main shrine and its subsidiaries (whether shrines of other members of his family and entourage associated with the legend, or symbolic tombs built elsewhere). This despite the fact that Ghazi Miyan represents not some saccharine myth of religious syncretism, but a quintessential moment of confrontation between expanding Islam and pre-Islamic polities of 'infidels'.

This was already clear to 'Abd al-Rahman Chishti when he wrote his *Mirāt-i Mas'udī* over three centuries ago, during the reign of Jahangir, in an attempt to rehabilitate and historicize the legend of Salar Mas'ud before a critical Islamic audience.[44] He hence claimed to base his work on an earlier text which is lost to

---

[43] Iqtidar Husain Siddiqui, 'A note on the Dargah of Salar Mas'ud in Bahraich in the light of the standard historical sources', in Troll, ed., *Muslim Shrines*, pp. 44-47; S.A.A. Rizvi, *A History of Sufism in India*, Vol. I, New Delhi, 1978, pp. 311-14.

[44] This text has never been published to date; for extensive translated excerpts by R.B. Chapman see, Elliot and Dowson, *The History of India*, Vol. II, pp. 513-49. For a larger, but still incomplete, manuscript translation from which these excerpts are taken, see British Museum, Manuscript Room, London,

us, the *Tawārīkh-i Mahmūdī*, written by a contemporary of Salar Mas'ud and Sultan Mahmud, called Mulla Muhammad Ghaznawi. Refuting the claims of those who placed Salar Mas'ud as a contemporary of Mu'izz al-Din Ghuri and Khwaja Mu'in al-Din Chishti of Ajmer (ca. 1142-1236 A.D.), 'Abd al-Rahman sought to insist that he had belonged to an even earlier wave of Islamic conquest – one that had, significantly, failed in the face of infidel resistance. The enemies of Salar Mas'ud are shown as both external (the rajas of the region around Bahraich and Kanauj, as well as earlier Delhi and Meerut), and internal to the Ghaznavid court. The most important amongst the latter is shown to be a certain Khwaja Hasan Maimandi, who is portrayed in turn as allied by marriage to a Hindu *zamīndār* family. It is on account of Khwaja Hasan's machinations that Mas'ud leaves the court of Sultan Mahmud for his long north Indian *jihād*. Once in north India, his victories over the infidels are shown to be many and sanguinary: 'Abd al-Rahman makes no attempt to soften his portrayal of the conflictual nature of relations. For example, in discussing Sultan Mahmud's actions in respect of the image from Somnath, it is made plain that even when the Sultan hesitated, his nephew Mas'ud showed no signs of compromise, going so far as to grind pieces of the image and feed it unbeknownst to Hindu supplicants together with lime and betel.

The action in and around Bahraich is also depicted in clearly confrontational terms. A central place in the portrayal is the so-called Suraj Kund at Bahraich, which the *Mirāt-i Mas'udī* insists was a place of sun-worship of considerable importance with a tank attached to it. Salar Mas'ud is shown as entering into a rage each time he saw the idol worship practised on the spot. It is later into this very Suraj Kund that Mas'ud, on the eve of his final battle, has the dead bodies of many of his soldiers thrown in, 'in the hope that through the odour of their martyrdom the darkness of unbelief might be dispelled from that spot'.[45] Thereafter, attacked

---

Additional Manuscript, 30,776. For a manuscript, see Asiatic Society of Bengal, Calcutta, Curzon Collection, I, 136 (IvC 103), ff. 50. Another Persian text, to my knowledge still unexploited, is also in the Asiatic Society of Bengal, D 47 (IvASB 322), and is entitled *Qissa-i Mas'ud Sālār Ghāzī*.

[45] Elliot and Dowson, *The History of India*, Vol. II, p. 546.

by the forces of the Raja Sahar Deo and Har Deo, Salar Mas'ud attains martyrdom, on the 14th of Rajab 424 A.H. (14th June 1033), at the hour of the evening prayer.

There is little doubt that the *Mirāt-i Mas'udī* was written in the seventeenth century for a particular political purpose. Together with it, 'Abd al-Rahman also authored the *Mirāt-i Asrār* and the *Mirāt-i Madārī*, the first a biographical dictionary of Sufi saints and a general reflection on Sufism in an Indian context, and the latter a biography of Shah Madar, another saint of some importance in northern and eastern India, to whom magical properties are attributed. Born in about 1315 to a Jewish family from Aleppo, Shah Madar is supposed to have converted to Islam, and on arriving in India been heavily influenced by a pilgrimage he made to Mu'in al-Din Chishti's tomb in Ajmer. Thus, these works, like some other commentaries and exegeses also attributed to 'Abd al-Rahman, suggested that he was constantly concerned to project a particular view of Islamic expansion in India which would give a central roie to the Chishti order: it is no coincidence that at the close of the *Mirāt-i Mas'udī*, a triumphal note is struck with the establishment at Ajmer of Mu'in al-Din Chishti, which augurs the dawn of the permanent establishment of Islam in northern India. Further, his main concern in the instance seems to have been to protect the Bahraich cult from criticism for its heterodoxy by showing its impeccable Islamic credentials, as indeed the impeccable familial pedigree of its hero. The reading of this text is a salutary correction for those who believe that the explicit, politically-flavoured reinterpretation of history and legend is a modern-day phenomenon !

Nor should the elevation to the status of pan-sectarian hero of a figure whose historical logic is always portrayed as pre-eminently sectarian, be entirely surprising. Violence and violent heroism, valorised through widely accepted notions of pride, obduracy, and even hubris, when combined to produce a tragic hero, can transcend sectarian logic. The same hero, with a core myth surrounding a historical kernel, can thus appear in a wide variety of hagiographical contexts, with very different connotations.[46] Besides, sites and legends like that of Ghazi Miyan are so direct in their portrayal of a form of historically recognizable (even if not historically true') violence that they may cauterize much rather than wound. Indeed, the first four centuries of the present millenium provide us with a number of similar examples, including those of the *ghāzī sūfīs*, whose careers Richard Eaton has examined in the context of the Deccan.[47] Eaton, basing himself on the Sufi hagiographical accounts for the Bijapur region in the western Deccan, has identified a number of figures such as Sufi Sarmast, Pir Ma'bari Khandayat, Shaikh 'Ali Pahalvan, and Shaikh Shahid (a disciple of Sarmast), all of whom were active in the late thirteenth and early fourteenth centuries in pushing along the Islamic frontier in the region. The tale of Sarmast, involving in large measure his conflicts with a local Hindu raja called Kumaram, has certain parallels with that of Salar Mas'ud. As with the Ghazi Miyan of Bahraich, there is some difficulty in reconciling the chronology attributed to his actions with that of other historical sources; if indeed Sarmast died in 1281 A.D., as suggested by the *Tazkira-i Auliya*, he preceded any other form of Islamic presence in the region by a good three decades. Rather, it seems best to see Sarmast as a sort of archetypal figure, representing the notional conflict between an expanding Islam, enmeshed with state power, and autochthonous resistance.

Eaton has noted a certain resistance among historians to his formulation of the 'warrior Sufi': he attributes this to 'the image of pious quietism commonly (and mistakenly) associated with Sufis in general, which conflicts with the militancy of the Sufis considered [by him]'.[48] Comparisons with North Africa, the

---

[46] This is the case of Desinguraja of Senji, of whose legend at least half a dozen versions exist, including at least one with an explicit Saivite flavour, and a number of others with a Vaishnava colouring. Desinguraja was, we may note, the same as the Bundela Rajput chieftain Tej Singh, who died in battle in 1714 near Senji; I am preparing a monograph on this subject with V. Narayana Rao and David Shulman. For a brief, recent, discussion see Alf Hiltebeitel, *The Cult of Draupadi 1: Mythologies: From Gingee to Kurukṣetra*, Chicago, 1988, pp. 99-100.

[47] Richard M. Eaton, *Sufis of Bijapur, 1300-1700: Social Roles of Sufis in Medieval India*, Princeton, 1978, pp. 19-44.

[48] Eaton, *Sufis*, p. 19. It is believed that the editors of at least one Indian journal refused to publish this chapter as an article for this very reason.

Ottoman Empire, and especially Iran under the Safavids enable him to demonstrate that this vision of the Sufi orders is simplistic, to put it mildly.[49]

This leads us to the last of the warrior-martyr cults that we wish to consider, namely that of the last Sultan of Ma'bar at Madurai in the late fourteenth century, Sikandar Shah (also known as Qurbat Hasan Kangu). Sikandar Shah's reputation amongst contemporary chroniclers cannot be said to be altogether positive. The Sanskrit poem *Madhuravijayam* of Gangadevi is devoted in good measure to his defeat and death at the hands of the Vijayanagara prince Kumara Kampana; prior to this campaign, its justification is set out in terms of the unholy and sanguinary acts of the sultans of this principality, who ostensibly oppressed peasants, and desecrated monuments. Nor does he fare much better at the hands of Shams-i Siraj 'Afif, the contemporary chronicler who wrote the *Tārīkh-i Fīrozshāhī* for Sultan Firoz Shah Tughluq of Delhi.[50] To Shams-i Siraj, Sikandar Shah was devoid of most praiseworthy qualities, being a pederast and inclined to appear in public 'decked out hand and foot in female ornaments'. Besides, he is portrayed as a rebel, who sought to deny the authority of Delhi over himself, and thus got his come-uppance, albeit at the hands of the infidels from Vijayanagara.

Yet, from these unpromising materials there emerges the stuff of a legend, associated with the hill-top site of Tirupparankunram, six and a half kilometres south-west of Madurai. Here, at a site known as Sikandarmalai, the figure of Sikandar Shah has become simultaneously assimilated into two other traditions: that of Skanda or Subrahmanya, a formidable martial figure from the Hindu tradition, and on the other hand with Iskandar Zulqarnain, the mythical and potent figure of Alexander the World-Conqueror celebrated in certain Islamic traditions. Both of these identifications

---

[49] More recently, in the context of a debate with Carl Ernst, Eaton's position has shifted somewhat, and he has expressed doubt on the *historical* accuracy of some of the hagiographical materials used in his earlier work.

[50] For a full discussion, see Mehrdad Shokoohy, 'Architecture of the Sultanate of Ma'bar in Madura, and other Muslim Monuments in South India', *Journal of the Royal Asiatic Society of Great Britain and Ireland*, 3rd Series, Vol. I, (1), 1991, pp. 31-92.

involve a play on words, the latter a facile use of a coincidence of names, and the former a more creative manipulation of similarities. Similarly, the terracotta images kept in various niches and crags at the hilltop of Sultan Sikandar Shah's warrior followers, who supposedly perished after a heroic last stand against the Vijayanagara forces, are sometimes assimilated into similar figures from the Tamil tradition of the god Aiyanar.[51]

It has been argued by Susan Bayly that in the eighteenth and early nineteenth centuries, the cult of the Madurai Sikandar witnessed an effloresence of some magnitude, first among the Deccani and other migrant warrior communities of the area, and then gradually gaining acceptance even among the relatively fastidious *maraikkāyars*, the Tamil Muslims of the port-towns. The shrine found a propagandist in Kunankuti Mastan Sahib (1800-1847), a *maraikkāyar* himself, who claimed to have undergone spiritual rapture and enlightenment while meditating at Tirupparankunram. In this process, the historical Sikandar Shah has received rather short shrift, and the fact that identifiable tombs exist at the hilltop site has been ignored until rather recently.[52]

In this context, a recent report concerning a children's textbook produced by the extremist Hindu Rashtriya Swayamsevak Sangh (RSS), entitled *Bāl-bodh kathāyen* (1991), assumes a particular and rather peculiar significance. As reported in the *Times of India*, the collection of stories contains one called 'The Kutty story', the plot of which runs as follows:

'Malik Kafur's rampaging Muslim hordes have destroyed many temples in Madurai. Everyone in the village of Tirupparkundram is at their wits' end as to how they should protect the Kartikeya [= Murukan] temple. Then, Kutty, a young 10-year-old boy, goes up to a village elder and asks: "What are the Muslims afraid of ?" The village elder replies despairingly, "The Muslims are only afraid of ghosts – and

---

[51] Susan Bayly, *Saints, Goddesses and Kings: Muslims and Christians in South Indian Society, 1700-1900*, Cambridge, 1989, pp. 109-110, 191-93. For the site as a Murukan/Skanda temple, see F.W. Clothey, 'Pilgrimage centres in the Tamil cults of Murukan', *Journal of the American Academy of Religion*, Vol. XL, (1), 1972, pp. 79-95.

[52] Shokoohy, 'Architecture of the Sultanate of Ma'bar in Madura'.

> it is only those who commit suicide who become ghosts".
> Kutty then decides to become a ghost to take on the Muslim
> warriors. He climbs on the topmost gopuram and jumps
> down, thus sacrificing his life for the temple'.[53]

Thus here, the Sikandar myth in its many variations (in both the Tamil and the southern Urdu literature) is set aside; in its place, Tirupparankunram is represented quite simply as the site of a conflict centering not around the existent warrior-martyr, but another. And yet, the story's very construction is more than a little ambiguous, not in purpose but in the message conveyed to the reader. It concedes that Malik Kafur's forces were fearless, and hence could only be defeated by supernatural means. It utilizes, moreover, the very themes of feminine resistance to Islam (and untouchable resistance to high-caste pressures) to be found in such stories as that of Padmini and 'Ala al-Din Khalji: suicide, here, becomes the highest form of heroism. Can this be reconciled with the aggressively masculine image that the ideologues of the RSS, VHP and other organizations wish to present not merely of the modern-day Hindu but his medieval forbear?

Comparisons and conclusions

The pre-modern past sits heavy, and not on India alone. Iran's ideologues still struggle to come to terms with the meaning of the Arab conquest of that land more than a thousand years ago: on the one hand, it brought Islam and thus appears necessarily defensible, but on the other the very roots of modern Iranian identity seem to lie in the reclamation of the pre-Islamic past (whether in the form of Firdausi's *Shāhnāmeh*, or in the Pahlawi fantasies that have now been discarded), and in the simultaneous rejection of Iran's Arab neighbours. Elsewhere, in Central Asia, and Afghanistan, new regimes that inherit the legacy of the defunct Soviet Union are bound to rewrite the history textbooks, not merely

---

[53] Lalit Vachani, 'RSS Indoctrination of Young Minds', *The Times of India*, 20 October 1993, p. 10.

to delete recent names, but to radically re-interpret the medieval past. Names such as Timur, Mirza Shahrukh, Shaibani Khan, and 'Abdullah Khan Uzbek will acquire a political urgency, belying the fact that they refer to individuals who lived from four to six hundred years ago. In the ex-Ottoman domains, whether the Arab lands, Cyprus, or the Balkans, issues of ethnic violence are constantly linked by modern-day participants with the 'historical injustices' of the distant past. No statute of limitations appears to hold, as 'primordial identities' are asserted and held to have existed over millennia, in constant opposition to other such identities.

In none of these cases has a panacea been found. Where certain sweeping solutions have been implemented, they appear dubious indeed. In the context of the five hundredth anniversary celebrations of 1492, a number of such issues were dredged up, and could not be satisfactorily dealt with. Was Columbus a 'villain' or a 'hero'? Did 1492 not lead to the decimation of indigenous populations in the New World, and if so was it really to be celebrated ? Were not the Discoveries the first step that led to the Atlantic slave trade, with its enormous human cost ? Radical activists with a collective 'bad conscience' set out these issues, but it was a luxury they could afford for the most part. At stake was not the political or societal future of Brazil or the United States, since no one suggested that the descendants of the victim popula-tions be recompensed by a countervailing pogrom, or by even giving political power to American Indian or black populations.

One gesture stands out in this context. On 31 March 1992, the Spanish king Juan Carlos went to the great synagogue of Madrid to ask pardon from the Chief Rabbi in the name of his ancestors for the decree by which the Most Catholic Monarchs, Ferdinand and Isabel had expelled the Jews from their domains on this day in 1492. He also revoked the edict of expulsion, which anachronistically had been left standing for five hundred years. Commemorations of the beginning of the Sephardic diaspora were held in many centres, notably in Toledo, where a large gathering of Jews from all over the world with the name 'Toledano' were collectively presented the keys of the city.

The Spanish state thus sought to resolve the issue of a part of its violent medieval past. But the gesture was not merely hollow but ethically largely meaningless and perhaps even dangerous.[54] How could Juan Carlos accept responsibility for and ask pardon for a series of acts committed five hundred years ago? In what sense was he, or any Spaniard living today, *responsible* for these acts? Does this apology mean that the historically constituted heirs of a collectivity that was wronged in the distant past can meaningfully ask for recompense from another group, even when there are no survivors left of either the victims or the perpetrators of violence? Should the ex-colonial powers of the nineteenth and twentieth centuries be asked then to apologize, and to make recompense to the colonized ? Should a large number of countries and politically active ethnic populations across a wide swathe of Eurasia demand apologies from Ulan Bator, the capital of a state that proudly claims the heritage of the conqueror Chinggis Khan? Cannot the Indonesians and the Sri Lankans claim injury for the expeditions of the Cholas against them in the eleventh and twelfth centuries? Should the French state apologize to the Huguenots for St. Bartholomew Day's Massacre, and reallocate the property they lost in Paris on that occasion to other Huguenots? And so on ....

The point is that Juan Carlos's gesture is politically and socially nearly costless, and thus easily made. It is also based on the dubious logic of monarchy, wherein the public and the private domains are insufficiently separated: as the heir to the throne of Spain, it is as if he is heir to the deeds of his distant ancestors Ferdinand and Isabella (like a party in a property dispute!). To make the leap from stating that the expulsion and suppression of the Jews in the fifteenth century is morally and ethically indefensible (not merely today, but even in the context of the values in vigour in the late fifteenth century) to apportioning responsibility for it in the modern world is a long distance indeed.

The legacy of the medieval past of India, much of West Asia, and Southeast Asia is in many crucial ways far more complex than that of Spain, Western Europe, or the Americas. This is not

---

[54] In a similar vein, the British Queen Elizabeth II has recently offered an apology (in July 1995) on behalf of the Crown to the indigenous populations of New Zealand, for unequal treaties signed in the early 19th century. But whether any redistribution of property follows remains open to doubt.

least of all because the 'ethnic cleansing' in these areas did not go as far as in those other parts of the world, where a series of state-sponsored projects in the medieval and early modern period disposed very largely of religious minorities and 'deviants', creating what were religiously rather homogeneous populations. The much touted 'separation of church and state' that accompanied the emergence of secularism in the West should be seen in context; it presumes that the state has to deal with only *one* religious authority. Whatever the ostensible legalistic or constitutional position, France, Spain, Britain and Germany implicitly remain Christian countries in which other religious minorities (usually of recent origin) reside; this is also the case with even Australia, Brazil or the United States of America, which are settler nations. In other parts of Eurasia, however, nation-states exist with fairly evenly balanced and heterogeneous populations, though long recorded histories of conflict exist in them. These could be between religious groups or 'caste' groups, linguistically defined groups or 'ethnically' defined ones. In India, Telugu warriors have a history of incursions into the Tamil country. The Marathas in the eighteenth century drew tribute, with its attendant violence, from areas as distant as Orissa, Bengal, and Rajasthan. The folk-tales of Bengal even today are thus equally replete with the Maratha menace and the Magh (Arakanese) slave-raids, even as Tipu Sultan of Mysore was long held as a bogeyman for children in the Tamil district of Tanjavur. Let us make no mistake, the medieval and early modern record of violence in India too is not a prepossessing one, making nonsense of claims of generalized non-violence or tolerance. In this, India is no different from her neighbours at a very broad qualitative level; the particular logic and level of sectarian and religious violence in each geographical area naturally carries distinctive features. India's distinctive contribution is its peculiar demography: majoritarianism is a far more difficult proposition here than in almost any society in its neighbourhood.

We may in this context briefly consider the case of Indonesia, a society with a majority Muslim population and rather small populations of other religions. Here, from the fifteenth century, several waves of Chinese immigration are recorded, for trade and commerce, as well as manual labour (coolies on plantations and

78

mines in the nineteenth century), leading to the consolidation of relatively small but nevertheless conspicuous minority Chinese populations, particularly in the port towns and urban centres. The same is true to an extent of some parts of mainland Southeast Asia and the Philippines. Associated in the first phases with trade, and to a lesser extent with the exercise of state power through revenue-farming and other means, those Chinese who were from the southeastern provinces of Fujian and Guangdong were first the victims of large-scale pogroms in the mid-eighteenth century in Java (they had already been under similar attack in Manila in the seventeenth century, in 1603 and 1639, for example).[55] Sporadic violence against them has since continued, and has even taken a rather serious turn at such moments as the political transition of the mid-1960s. The Chinese were set apart by stereotypes concerning their culture as well as their religion, and continue to be regarded with suspicion. A recent study sums up the state of affairs:

'After 1965-1966, assimilation is once more the order of the day, the spontaneous assimilation of thousands of Chinese who have converted to Christianity, but also an assimilation stimulated by the government, which has taken a whole series of measures to suppress Chinese "identity". the suppression of Chinese schools, the ban on the (polite) usage of the term Tionghoa and the requirement that the term Cina (which has wound up acquiring a strong pejorative connotation) be used in its place, a very strict limitation over all sorts of cultural manifestations (and a particular ban on all manner of processions and religious festivities outside the bounds of the temples), and finally the requirement that an "Indonesian" name be chosen, so as no longer to draw attention to the trisyllablic xing-ming. Even the old Chinese architecture is threatened to the extent that there is an attempt to make those facades that are stylistically too "typical" disappear by camouflaging them behind a cement front... After the pogrom

[55] Leonard Blussé, 'Batavia, 1619-1740: The Rise and Fall of a Chinese Colonial Town', *Journal of Southeast Asian Studies*, Vol. XII, 1981, pp. 159-78; Peter Carey, 'Changing Javanese Perceptions of the Chinese Communities in Central Java, 1755-1825', *Indonesia*, no. 37, 1984, pp. 1-47.

of Solo, one deputy even went so far as to propose that all Chinese be obliged to marry outside their ethnic group. All those who refused would be ostracised and at the end of thirty years, one would have the final solution to the "Chinese problem".[56]

This solution was, happily, not adopted, even at the risk of lowering the flame under the state-sponsored 'melting pot'. But enough has been said to suggest that this ethnic and religious problem has not been resolved, and that actions against the Chinese are often justified in terms of their alleged dominance of the mercantile sector in the colonial and late pre-colonial periods.

India's neighbours and even the West, with its claims to having come to terms with its past, offer her no obvious solutions on the issue of the historical legacy of sectarian violence. In a modern context, it actually remains to be seen how the significant minority populations in countries such as the Netherlands, France and Germany will be accommodated there in terms of a genuine 'secularism'; the recent record of race-related violence in even Portugal suggests that none of the EEC states has truly found a solution to *all* the stereotypes and prejudices that emerged in the 'Age of the Discoveries'. One can certainly assert with confidence that the solutions do not lie in claiming a medieval past without organized and systematic mass violence, a Golden Age to which we may return at will. The enigmatic words of poets like Bullhe Shah already give the lie to this myth. The Indian state since 1947 has essayed such a route half-heartedly in the name of a particular version of secularism: we have gone far enough to know today that it is a cul-de-sac, even if secularism itself, in its broader sense, is not.

---

[56] Denys Lombard, *Le Carrefour Javanais: Essai d'Histoire Globale*, 3 Vols., Paris, 1990, Vol. II (Les réseaux asiatiques), p. 308.

Religion and Nationalism in Modern India

G. Balachandran

IN MAY 1995, two judges of the Supreme Court directed the Government of India to bring forward legislation for a uniform civil code or family law. The case on which they were pronouncing judgement related to a man who converted to Islam in order to take a second wife. Although not unheard of, such cases are relatively uncommon. More the reason why the court's directive to the government on a contentious political and sectarian religious issue is deserving of notice. Maintaining that Hindu family law had been reformed in the 1950s, the judges argued that those who elected to remain in India after 1947 knew that 'there would be one nation', and as such 'no community could claim separate identity in the name of religion'.[1]

Sectarian religious mobilization is relatively muted now in comparison with the early nineties. But the latest judgement of India's apex court, and the reactions to it, serve once again to emphasize that more than a century after the idea of an Indian nation quickened the pulse of its early protagonists and offered the possibility of a platform to resist, and eventually end, colonial rule, the content and meaning of the concept are once again live issues. Even allowing for the burden of history, the contemporary salience of these issues does not, as it might seem on the surface or from the propaganda of Hindu chauvinists, arise from within

---

[1] As quoted in the *Times of India,* 13 May 1995, p. 4.

the narrow context of relations between the majority Hindu community and the Muslim minority, or between the latter and the state. The Shah Bano affair, and the then Prime Minister Rajiv Gandhi's action in reversing a Supreme Court judgement directing a Muslim man to pay maintenance to the wife he had divorced, is often cited as a major influence on the trajectory of sectarian religious mobilization in India. This it may have been. At the same time, it would be wrong to overlook the role of the Mandal controversy (1989) — which was in some sense a historical legacy of the caste system — in fuelling the agitation to replace the Ayodhya mosque with a temple dedicated to Lord Ram. This, and the nearly seamless telescoping of the Shah Bano, the Mandal, and the Ayodhya controversies suggests that whatever the perceived challenges to it, increasingly the unity of the Indian nation is now sought to be defined, constructed, and directed explicitly *against* a significant segment of her society, viz. the Muslims who constitute nearly an eighth of India's population.

Notwithstanding recent events, the idea of a secular (in the sense of non-sectarian in which it is used throughout this paper) and democratic Indian society continues to hold an appeal and generate a resonance not matched by any other. Even the most die-hard proponents of a sectarian Hindu order often claim to stand for 'genuine' secularism. Still central to the self-definition of a substantial segment of the country's middle classes, the idea of a secular and democratic India is commonly invested with a historicity deriving from the philosophy and practice of the national movement which freed the country from colonial rule in 1947. In this case, as in others, the 'advantages of "myth"' are not all on one side, and there is much to commend in it. For example, activists who campaign to promote the idea of a secular state and society promised by the Indian constitution regularly come face to face with its everyday denial, but they still find the idea of great value in combating this denial. There is also considerable strength in the more general argument that this particular method of attributing historicity to secular and democratic values in contemporary India presents her secular democrats with a key weapon in the attritional battle in which they are engaged. Therefore, to question the intrinsically secular character of India's modern national tradition is to give up an important *contemporary* instrument of realizing it.

At the same time, myths have a way of running away with their proponents. Belief in the essential secular character of the modern Indian state and society can often be little more than an exercise in self-congratulation which overlooks or rationalizes the sectarian religious outlook pervading large areas of contemporary social and political practice. Equally, the sense of the historical inevitability, and infallibility, of a secular and democratic outcome in India can, at times, be so overwhelming that the failure to realize it may often be attributed, even by individuals who are otherwise not disposed to thinking in religious sectarian terms, to the social and cultural 'exclusivity' of minority communities. Few would deny the mileage that religious clerics derive from preserving and nurturing the social and cultural exclusivity (as opposed to distinctiveness) of their communities. But to focus on such manifestations, to the exclusion of others, in a society characterized in recent times by deep social and religious divisions is, at best, to conflate the constitutional discourse of rights with that of every-day conflict where neither the constitution nor the rights it offers are seriously protected. At worst, it is to endorse the majoritarian agenda which can hide behind the liberal discourse of the constitution and point to the minority communities as its principal violators. More dangerous, an uncritical faith in the 'naturalness', as it were, of secular and democratic values in India relegates the role of human agency in realizing these values in everyday life and activity and weakens their already tenuous hold in contemporary India.

In what follows, therefore, I have taken a deliberately linear, some might say provocative, view of Indian history of the last century, mainly in an effort to highlight the sectarian origins of the national idea in modern India, and the central role played by sectarian issues, bodies, and individuals in the evolution of the platform of Indian nationalism. As the references show, these historical features of Indian nationalism are, by now, well recognized by historians. However, the latter are notably wary, with good reason, of pursuing their line of inquiry into the more recent period. To some extent, this silence arises from the apprehension

83

that the goal of a secular and democratic India might become more difficult to realize if social and political practices were allowed to be burdened by the full weight of a divisive and contentious past. But such silence can easily become collusive in a context where a particular construction of modern history, or the history of the national movement, is invoked to justify the practice of majoritarian nationalism in a liberal garb. Finally, to implicitly assume that change unambiguously dominated continuity in the trajectory of political and social developments in post-1947 India is not very helpful when one seeks to understand the relative 'calm' of the first two decades after partition against the background of the decades of 'friction' which preceded and followed them. Hence I carry my linear tale through virtually to the present. In this tale may lie a few pointers not only to how we handle issues affecting the two great religious communities in India, but also to the wider questions of social and economic mobility associated with the development of the Indian economy and the deepening of its social processes under the stimulus of representative democracy.

II

It is almost a truism to say that the concept of the Indian nation, in which the ideology of Indian nationalism is rooted, is mainly an outcome of the complex encounter between indigenous society and colonial rule. This encounter operated at various levels and led to the construction or hardening of several identities, each often superimposed upon, and nestling uneasily with another.

Most versions of modern Indian nationalism seem to take India's seemingly ageless and inherent cultural and civilizational unity, going back three millennia or more, for granted. It is clear however that thanks to British rule, India managed to achieve a degree of political unity which, as much as geographical boundaries, helped redefine the mental and emotional horizons of her indigenous elite. And yet, there was nothing inevitable, even given this overarching political unity, about the emergence of an Indian identity, whether alongside other identities, or by supplanting them. Thanks, for instance, to the spread of both English and 'vernacular' education, the later decades of the nineteenth century witnessed a 'renaissance' in some regional languages, notably Bengali, Marathi, and Tamil. As publishing activity in these languages expanded, new publications helped standardize and spread these languages and identities based upon them; at the same time, they became vehicles for regional histories, literature, social reform tracts, and some of the most bitter contemporary criticism of the British rulers. Thanks to the growth of a middle class and the spread of 'print capitalism', identities which may now be regarded as 'regional' began to take strong root with, for example, the sense of a somewhat mystical collectivity suffused with Hindu religious symbolism called the *Bangali jati* emerging ahead of a sense of any wider collectivity in Bengal.[2] A similar movement was underway in the Bombay Presidency as well.[3] At the same time, since these languages began to flourish and new identities based, loosely speaking, upon them were forming among a section of the middle classes in administrative provinces which brought together a number of language communities, other linguistic identities (Telugu in Madras, Assamese and Oriya in Bengal, Hindi in the Bombay Presidency, etc.) also came into contention.[4]

Despite the late-nineteenth century setting, the process of identity formation was not confined to the formation of 'national'

[2] On 'print capitalism', see Benedict Anderson, *Imagined Communities: Reflections on the Origins and Spread of Nationalism*, London, 1982, pp. 32-49; in the Bengal context, see Robert I. Crane, 'The Development of Nationalism in India in the Late Nineteenth Century: The Bengal Press and Associations in the Diffusion of Nationalism', in Paul Wallace, ed., *Region and Nation in India*, New Delhi, 1985, pp. 85-110; on the *Bangali jati*, see Sudipta Kaviraj, 'The Imaginary Institution of India', *Subaltern Studies VII*, Delhi, 1992, p. 15.

[3] Jayant Lele, 'Caste, Class and Dominance: Political Mobilization in Maharashtra', in Francine R. Frankel and M.S.A. Rao, eds., *Dominance and State Power in Modern India: Decline of a Social Order*, Delhi, 1990, vol. 2, pp. 149-52.

[4] Anil Seal, *The Emergence of Indian Nationalism: Competition and Collaboration in the later Nineteenth Century*, Cambridge, 1968, pp. 31-2; for the growth of Oriya nationalism, see J. Boulton, 'Nationalism and Tradition in Orissa, with special reference to the Works of Phakirmohan Senapati', in R.J. Moore, ed., *Tradition and Politics in South Asia*, pp. 239-49; and B. Mohapatra, The Politics of Oriya Nationalism, 1903-36, unpublished D.Phil. thesis, University of Oxford, 1990; for Hindi nationalism, see Paul Brass, *Language, Religion, and Politics in North India*, Delhi, 1974.

or 'regional' identities. In late-nineteenth and early-twentieth century Africa, for instance, colonial intervention enhanced social and economic mobility, and the emergence of an indigenous elite deriving its self-perceptions from the perceptions of colonial officials and missionaries led to kinship, lineage, or clan-based identities being replaced by those based on newer European constructions like tribes.[5] A similar process, though involving 'non-tribal' communities, colonial authorities, as well as missionaries, has been outlined for some regions of India as well.[6]

Other identities were similarly 'constructed', or existing definitions made more rigid and exclusive in the changing administrative, social, and economic environments of nineteenth century India. One of the more important of the processes at work pertained to the way the 'other' was perceived, and the 'self' and its world defined in relation to it.[7] An important unconscious contribution here of the later colonial authorities in areas where their influence was most visible, was perhaps to replace the earlier sense of different, diffused 'others' which prevailed, by the new dominant, and socially exclusive 'other', represented by the British official, soldier, trader, missionary, etc.. Equally, as well as European perceptions of themselves influencing indigenous evaluations of the 'superior' race, European/British perceptions of Indian society helped also to construct several aspects of the indigenous perception of the self and its environment.

Thus one important reason why Bengal saw the first efforts to perceive and define a wider India may, for instance, have owed to the fact that the Europeans identified Bengal with India; in seeing Bengal, they believed, they were seeing India.[8] Further, the British

---

[5] Terence O. Ranger, 'Race and Tribe in Southern Africa: European Ideas and African Acceptance', in R. Ross, ed., *Colonialism and Racism*, Leiden, 1982; also see Basil Davidson, *The Black Man's Burden*, London, 1990.

[6] S.M. Dubey, 'Inter-ethnic Alliance, Tribal Movements and Integration in North-east India', in K. Suresh Singh, ed., *Tribal Movements in North-east India*, Delhi, 1982, vol. 1, pp. 4-6; Susanne B.C. Devalle, *Discourses in Ethnicity: Culture and Protest in the Jharkhand*, New Delhi, 1992, pp. 49-76.

[7] Tapan Raychaudhuri, 'Europe in India's Xenology: The Nineteenth Century Record', *Past and Present*, 1992, pp. 156-82.

[8] Ainslee T. Embree, *Imagining India: Essays on Indian History*, Delhi, 1989, p. 101.

drew heavily on the tradition of European Orientalism to understand 'Hindu society', using selected Brahminical texts as their point of entry into, what consequently became, an unchanging, and so timeless, social order dominated by a rigid *varna* system. The world-view of the Brahmins thus found its most potent publicists. Their beliefs and their rituals also became definitive representations of these aspects of the 'religion' which, since the Arabs, India was associated with.[9] Their perspective also became the implicit basis of those parts of the Anglo-Indian legal order dealing with Hindu family or personal law, which all but reified the *varna* order 'as the ideal type of social structure across regions'.[10] This nineteenth century construct of Hinduism was, as it were, internalized, propounded, criticized, or defended, and through each of these means reproduced by an indigenous elite exposed to Western or 'vernacular' education.[11] The resulting 'objectification' of religious beliefs enabled individual elements within it to be taken out and reformulated for conscious, often overtly political, ends.[12] The centralization into a religion of disparate but loosely connected beliefs, rituals, practices, myths, and histories had begun; and this religion, as numerous cow-protection and Hindi language (anti-Urdu) agitations, and even the 'Swadeshi' movement of 1905

---

[9]T.N. Madan, 'The Quest for Hinduism', *International Social Science Journal*, 1977, pp. 261-78.

[10]David A. Washbrook, 'Law, State and Agrarian Society in Colonial India', *Modern Asian Studies*, 1981, pp. 652-8, 673-4; Francine R. Frankel, 'Conclusion: Decline of a Social Order', in Frankel and Rao, eds., *Dominance and State Power*, vol. 2, p. 483.

[11]Milton Israel, 'Ramananda Chatterjee and the *Modern Review*: The Image of Nationality in the National Press', in Milton Israel, ed., *National Unity: The South Asian Experience*, New Delhi, 1983; Raychaudhuri, 'Europe in India's Xenology', pp. 162-7; David Kopf, *The Brahmo Samaj and the Shaping of the Modern Indian Mind*, Princeton, 1979, pp. 179-86; for an interesting account of the impact of English education upon the world-view of an upper-caste Hindu from Bihar, see Surendra Gopal, 'An Elite Group in the Second Half of the Nineteenth Century in Bihar', in Sachidananda and A.K. Lal, eds., *Elites and Development*, New Delhi, 1980, pp. 171-86.

[12]Bernard S. Cohn, 'The Census, Social Structure, and Objectification in South Asia', in Bernard S. Cohn, *Anthropologist among the Historians and Other Essays*, Delhi, 1988, p. 229.

or the activities of 'terrorist' groups in Bengal and Maharashtra showed, also swiftly became a vehicle for militant political activity.[13]

Early nationalist discourse in India emerged out of this coalescence of the local, regional, religious, and supra-regional identities which European intervention, whether in the form of the Orientalists, or more directly in the form of colonial rule, assisted. The Indian identity was preceded by, or overlapped with, the new Hindu identity; and almost overwhelmingly, it was 'Hinduism' in the sense of a 'great tradition', and a perception of its history as constructed in the nineteenth century which mediated the distance between locality or region-based identities which were also emerging at this time, and a wider, all-India identity.[14] As Sudipta Kaviraj points out, whilst discussing the changing self-perceptions of middle-class Bengali intellectuals in the late-nineteenth century, the latter

> found ways of believing, against formidable evidence, their indisputable descent from the Aryan ancestors of the Vedas. ... they convinced themselves that their complexions had only somewhat darkened, their structure somewhat shortened, their noses had lost some of their aquilinity due to the ravages of the tropical weather. Otherwise their racial purity was self-evident. .... But even if their image of the past – of what the Aryans did – was correct, what was doubtful was the claim that it was their past, something that was taken for granted. Actually, what was happening inside the discourse was very complex. In the business of stitching together Bengalis with

[13] Embree, *Imagining India*, pp. 158-64; M.J. Harvey, 'The Secular as Sacred? The Religio-Political Rationalization of B.G. Tilak', *Modern Asian Studies*, 1986, pp. 321-31; McLane, *Indian Nationalism*, pp. 332-57.

[14] Seal, *Emergence of Indian Nationalism*, pp. 249-52; Embree, *Imagining India*, pp. 16-25; Kopf, *Brahmo Samaj*, pp. 193-214, 319-33; John R. McLane, 'The Early Congress, Hindu Populism, and the Wider Society', in Richard Sisson and Stanley Wolpert, eds., *Congress and India Nationalism: The Pre-Independence Phase*, Delhi, 1988, pp. 57-8; on early nationalist historiography of 'ancient India' and its roots in Orientalist constructions, see Romila Thapar, 'Interpretations of Ancient Indian History', *History and Theory*, 1968, pp. 318-35.

a certain past, they were also ... stitching Bengalis with others in the present.[15]

Similar perceptions spread rapidly in the fertile environment of late-nineteenth century India which saw the accelerated rise of the 'literal' and 'commercial classes' over large parts of the country. The vertical and lateral mobility which northern India witnessed during these decades also helped transform fairly passive and leisurely exercises to 'define' Hinduism into active efforts by a class of 'new-Hindus' to realize it through 'revival'. Such 'revivalist' activities were often conducted around single issues like the defence of the cow, the promotion of Sanskrit, Hindi, etc., and in the form of organizations like the Arya Samaj, the Sanatan Dharm Sabha, Bharat Dharm Mahamandal, the Hindu Sabha, etc.

Some of these agitations, particularly those to protect the cow, had distinct anti-British overtones. Others, such as the campaign for Hindi, were sometimes initiated by those who were not overtly sectarian in their attitude towards other religious communities. Yet, even their initiatives reflected an unself-conscious majoritarian conviction that there was no contradiction between 'Hindu' and 'Indian' identities. Thus, as Sudhir Chandra notes about the late-nineteenth century slogan of 'Hindi, Hindu, Hindustan', those who advanced it failed to realize that

> many of the 'children of Bharat' might feel attracted to the cause of the country without feeling enthusiastic about the other two causes; indeed, that (this) insistence on the latter might adversely affect their concern for the former.

Hence, even when they were not so intended, initiatives of this type had the effect of sharpening and reinforcing religious divisions.[16]

---

[15] S. Kaviraj, 'Imaginary History: Narrativizing the Nation in Bankimchandra Chattopadhyaya', in P.C. Chatterji, ed. *Self-Images, Identity and Nationality*, Simla, 1989, p. 231; also see Kaviraj, 'The Imaginary Institution', and Israel, 'Ramananda Chatterjee'; on Bankim Chandra and Bengali-Hindu nationalism, also see J. Boulton, 'Nationalism and Tradition in Orissa', pp. 236-8.

[16] The quotation is from Sudhir Chandra, 'Communal Elements in Late Nineteenth Century Hindi Literature', *Occasional Papers in Society and History*, no. 15, Nehru Memorial Museum and Library, 1984, p. 26; also see Chris A. Bayly, *Rulers, Townsmen and Bazaars: North Indian Society in the Age of British*

Moreover, the most decisive efforts to consolidate and reinforce a Hindu identity during these decades were decidedly sectarian in character. The Arya Samaj was the most prominent of the Hindu organizations founded in late-nineteenth century India. Deriving its perception of Hinduism from the West and drawing its inspiration, even its language, from Christianity, the Arya Samaj marshalled 'shastric authority ... for a new tradition' which strove to exclude rituals, idolatry, and the notion of 'pollution'. It defined Hindus in explicitly homogeneous terms, and seeking to create a Hindu religious order, launched mass 'reconversion' (or *shuddhi*) movements to salvage lapsed or converted 'Hindus', the depressed classes, and the 'untouchables' for the order.[17] Although born in Bengal, the Arya Samaj's influence was first felt in a big way in Punjab, where it helped a palpable religious identity mature among a section of the middle classes emerging from the growth of trade and the expansion of employment in the government sector. The Arya Samaj's efforts to 'convert' adherents of Sikhism (or Sikhs) to Hinduism forced the former to assert their separate religious identity, which since the British conquest of the Punjab had been on the wane. Apart from its proselytizing activities, the Arya Samaj's strident campaigns against cow slaughter and its virulent propaganda against Islam and Muslims in general, also helped widen the gulf between the two communities in urban Punjab.[18]

Expansion, Cambridge, 1983, pp. 450-7; Richard G. Fox, 'Urban Class and Communal Consciousness in Colonial Punjab: The Genesis of India's Intermediate Regime', *Modern Asian Studies*, 1984, pp. 459-89; Peter Robb, 'The Challenge of *Gau Mata*: British Policy and Religious Change in India, 1880-1916', *Modern Asian Studies*, 1986, pp. 285-319; Francis Robinson, *Separatism among the Indian Muslims: The Politics of the United Provinces' Muslims, 1860-1923*, Delhi, 1975, pp. 57-69.

[17] G. Pandey, 'In Defence of the Fragment: Writing about Hindu-Muslim Riots in India Today', *Economic and Political Weekly*, 1991, pp. 566-7.

[18] Indu Banga, 'The Emergence of Hindu Consciousness in Colonial Punjab'; J.S. Grewal, 'The Making of the Sikh Self-image before Independence', both in P.C. Chatterji, ed., *Self-Images*, pp. 201-17, and pp. 187-200 respectively; J.K. Dhillon, 'Emergence and Growth of Sikh Alienation', in *Journal of Sikh Studies*, 1988, pp. i-ii; also Fox, 'Urban Class and Communal Consciousness'; McLane, *Indian Nationalism*, pp. 280-8, 296-304; Kenneth W. Jones, *Arya Dharm: Hindu Consciousness in Nineteenth Century Punjab*, Delhi, 1976, pp. 149-52, 195-7, 202-15; Robinson, *Separatism among the Indian Muslims*, pp. 68-9, 77-8; Dhanpati Pandey, *The Arya Samaj and Indian Nationalism*, Delhi, 1972, pp. 75-80.

In the more caste-divided societies to the east of Punjab, in Bihar and the United Provinces, the Arya Samaj's influence was slow to spread. In these regions, it sought to make inroads through organizing the cultivator castes of Kurmis and Ahirs (or Yadavs) into separate caste associations, sanskritizing their rituals, encouraging them to challenge the priestly monopoly of the Brahmins, and establishing educational institutions for the children of these communities.[19] Confronted now with a rigid definition of their orthodoxy and the pressure to conform to and defend it, the upper castes responded to these reformist initiatives through bodies like the Sanatan Dharm Sabhas and the Dharma Mahamandal. Although overtly in competition and conflict, yet the growth of these and other outfits provided the organizational basis for competitive mobilization aimed at drawing wider areas into agitations of a religious nature on issues like cow slaughter, etc..[20]

It is important to note that campaigns on sectional and religious issues were the first organized agitational initiatives targeted at a middle class growing in numbers, affluence, and self-confidence. These agitations gave this middle class, as they did Lala Lajpat Rai, Punjab's foremost Hindu politician and an Arya Samaji, the 'first lesson in Hindu nationalism'.[21] Although the cow was an important aspect of popular religion, and not uncommonly a source of friction between those who consumed it for the spirit and others who consumed it for the flesh, by the latter part of the nineteenth century the animal had become an issue separating communities which were coming into new forms of being in the process of

[19] F.R. Frankel, 'Caste, Land, and Dominance in Bihar: Breakdown of the Brahmanical Order', in Frankel and Rao, eds. *Dominance and State Power*, pp. 63-5; R.K. Hebsur, 'Uttar Pradesh: Belated and Imperfect Mobilization of the Backwards', in R.K. Hebsur, 'Reactions to the Reservations of Other Backward Classes, a Comparative Study of Four States: A Report submitted to the Backward Classes Commission', Government of India, Ministry of Home Affairs, *Report of the Backward Classes Commission*, Delhi, 1980, part 2, vol. iv, pp. 159-61; one effect of the Arya Samaj influence on the peasant castes of this region may have been that the latter subordinated secular to ritual mobility for far longer than, say, their southern counterparts did.

[20] Chris A. Bayly, *Local Roots of Indian Politics: Allahabad, 1880-1920*, Oxford, 1975, pp. 105-17.

[21] Lala Lajpat Rai, quoted in Indu Banga, 'Emergence of Hindu Consciousness', pp. 215-6.

fighting over it, and forging new internal bonds of solidarity. Contemporary 'Hindu' leaders were not unaware of the import of these developments, Lala Lajpat Rai, for instance, welcoming religious riots because they helped consolidate the Hindu identity.[22] In this sense, the *gaurakshini* (cow protection) movement had already become a 'species of sub-nationalism', and although the campaign largely petered out after 1893, the new communal organizations founded in its wake continued to articulate religious identities more sharply.[23] Moreover, the cow's popular religious aspect meant that it would help spread community definitions widely, and even to the villages of northern India.[24]

The social perceptions of the colonial rulers also inevitably guided their administrative initiatives, some of which, such as the decennial census, also helped realize these perceptions. For example, the British rulers saw caste and religion as keys to the organization of Indian society, and these categories soon became critical inputs into their 'technology of governing'.[25] Apart from gathering information on aggregate numbers, censuses in British India were used to develop these inputs through gathering detailed information about the caste and religious affiliations of the population. However, while 'beginning as a set of categories in the minds of its creators, the census went on to define those categories....'[26] Introducing caste and religion into the census enumeration procedure meant that Indians were being encouraged to ask these particular questions about themselves, and about their

---

[22]McLane, *Indian Nationalism*, p. 335.

[23]McLane, *Indian Nationalism*, p. 275, pp. 328-9.

[24]Anand A. Yang, 'Sacred Symbol and Sacred Space in Rural India: Community Mobilization in the "Anti-Cow Killing" Riots of 1893', *Comparative Studies in Society and History*, 1980, pp. 576-96; Sandria B. Freitag, 'Sacred Symbol as Mobilizing Ideology: The North Indian Search for a "Hindu" Community', *Comparative Studies in Society and History*, 1980, pp. 597-625; McLane, *Indian Nationalism*, pp. 296-331; Bayly, *Local Roots of Indian Politics*, pp. 111-2; also see in a wider context, Mushirul Hasan, *Nationalism and Communal Politics in India, 1885-1930*, Delhi, 1991, pp. 225-41.

[25]Richard Saumarez Smith, 'Rule-by-records and Rule-by-reports: Complementary Aspects of the British Imperial Rule of Law', in Veena Das, ed., *The Word and the World: Fantasy, Symbol, and Record*, 1986, pp. 172-3.

[26]Kenneth W. Jones, 'Religious Identity and the Indian Census', in N.G. Barrier, ed., *The Census in British India: New Perspectives*, Delhi, 1981, p. 100.

cultural and social systems. Apart from involving the whole population, colonial perceptions of Indian society were most directly transmitted to the over half a million enumerators, all literate and educated Indians who were potentially capable of occupying key positions of leadership in indigenous society.[27]

Besides, census reports also

> provided a new conceptualization of religion as a community, an aggregate of individuals united by a formal definition and given characteristics based on qualified data;[28]

and as well as receiving these definitions, the groups involved grew self-conscious enough to take steps to alter them in their own favour. For instance, the 1881 census included the adherents of all residual and unspecified religious categories among the Hindus, and classified as a Hindu any 'native who was unable to define his creed, or who described it by any other name than that of some recognized religion or of a sect of some such religion'.[29] But as the distribution of government jobs and political power came to depend on census returns, this definition was challenged by a Punjabi Muslim deputation which noted that

> if a reduction be made for the uncivilized portions of the (Hindu) community enumerated under the heads of Animists, and other minor religions, as well as for those classes who are ordinarily classed as Hindus but properly speaking, are not Hindus at all, the proportion of Muhammadans to the Hindu majority becomes much larger.[30]

E.A. Gait, the Commissioner of Census at the time of the 1911 operations, seemed in agreement, and suggested creating a category of 'debatable Hindus'. The classification of the Sikhs in a separate religious category had already diminished the number of census Hindus. Members of 'untouchable' communities accounted for some

---

[27] Cohn, 'The Census', pp. 230-48.

[28] Jones, 'Religious Identity', p. 84.

[29] Government of Punjab, *Census Report*, 1881, p. 101, quoted in Jones, 'Religious Identity', p. 92.

[30] The *Punjabee*, 6 Oct. 1906, p. 2, quoted in Jones, 'Religious Identity', p. 89.

42% of the census Hindu population of Punjab, and the thought of losing them caused great alarm among the province's Hindu leaders.[31] As their attentions turned towards the 'reform of Hinduism', the Arya Samaj organization and its campaigns received a boost from an unexpected quarter.[32] As Lala Lajpat Rai noted, the

> Gait circular had a quite unexpected effect and galvanized the dying body of orthodox Hinduism into sympathy with *its* untouchable population, because that was necessary to avert its own downfall. The possibility of losing the untouchables has shaken the intelligent section of the Hindu community to its very depths....[33]

Preventing the secession of the 'untouchables' from the Hindu order has since been an important pre-occupation of many politicians and legislators in India.

By listing and describing castes and collecting returns on this basis, the census operations also helped 'liven up the caste-spirit'.[34] Caste ceased predominantly to be the local phenomenon it had been earlier; moreover by trying to rank castes in terms of social precedence based on the *varna* system, the British authorities all but froze the caste system and increased its significance. For, contrary to the contemporary British view, Indian society presented several opportunities for vertical mobility within the caste-*varna* order, particularly for the affluent, arms-bearing peasantry. So long caste identities could be re-negotiated, the former were relatively muted, and the building of vertical caste affiliations remained uncommon. But the government's efforts to rank castes seem to have reduced the possibility of upward mobility, since occupational

---

[31]The 42% figure is from the report of the Simon Commission (1928-30), quoted in Marc Galanter, *Competing Equalities: Law and Backward Classes in India*, Delhi, 1984, p. 124.

[32]Cohn, 'The Census', pp. 245-7; for the effects of these campaigns on relations between the two communities, see Jones, 'Religious Identity', pp. 91-5.

[33]Lala Lajpat Rai, *The Arya Samaj*, London, 1915, p. 2, quoted in Jones, 'Religious Identity', p. 93.

[34]G.S. Ghurye, *Caste and Race in India*, New York, 1932, quoted in Cohn, 'The Census'.

categories, caste, the latter's position in the *varna* order, etc. were all closely, and seemingly finally, matched in the census descriptions, especially after the 1891 and 1901 censuses. To the extent that upward mobility was possible at all within this order, it could be achieved only through the formation of caste associations to petition the authorities, usually on the basis of evidence drawn from historical, mythological, and literary sources.[35]

III

Competition for jobs in the public services helped elite mobilization along religious and caste lines, as well as along linguistic and regional lines. Although regional differences should not be overlooked, in general throughout India, upper-caste Hindus took more readily to Western education, and were therefore better equipped to fill jobs in the government. While the growth of linguistic movements was partly an outcome of this process of mobility, the latter acquired sectarian religious overtones in northern India as the Hindu literate classes began to press for the replacement of Urdu, written in the Persian script, by Hindi, written in the Nagari script, some (but not all) influential participants in the campaign seeing it as an opportunity to deprive '*mussalmans*' of their 'monopoly' of '*peshkarships, sarishtadarships, muharrir-ships*, etc.'[36]

In a few cases, the growth of religious and caste identities also helped fracture regional elite affiliations, and widen caste and religious alliances. For example, initially the Kayasth elites of the North-Western Provinces (later United Provinces) joined the region's Muslim elites in opposing recruitment through examination

[35] For a brief discussion of Risley's attempts to create an ordering of caste by rank at the time of the 1891 census, see Cohn, 'The Census', pp. 245-7; also see Frankel, 'Caste, Land and Dominance in Bihar', p. 64.

[36] Robinson, *Separatism among the Indian Muslims*, pp. 69-77; the quotation (pp. 76-7) is from Babu (Bharatendu) Harish Chandra's statement to the North-Western Provinces and Oudh Education Commission; also see Krishna Kumar, 'Hindu Revivalism and Education in North-Central India', in K.N. Panikkar, ed., *Communalism in India: History, Politics and Culture*, Delhi, 1991, pp. 173-95.

to the civil services out of fear that it would favour educated
migrants from Bengal. But once the region's Kayasths themselves
gained an educational edge over their Muslim allies, their objection
to merit-based recruitment weakened. Further they strove to
distinguish themselves from their erstwhile allies, and to use the
Congress Party to affiliate themselves with the higher status
Kayasths of Bengal.[37] Similarly, Bengali speaking settlers in Bihar
took the lead in the agitation to replace Urdu as the language of
the administration with Hindi since they found it easier to master
a new language in the Nagari script familiar to them.[38] Faced
with the challenge that a new and assertive upper-caste Hindu
elite might pose to their positions which derived their legitimacy
largely from pre-British social and administrative structures, the
campaign of the Muslim elites within the community in favour of
Western education, and outside it on the principle of communal
job representation, gained in strength.[39]

The widening of the political arena from early this century
also helped sharpen elite conflict, while the institution of separate
communal electorates and representation helped reinforce competing
identities. Initiated at the time of the Minto-Morley reforms of
1909, communal electorates were legitimized through the Lucknow
pact concluded in 1916 between the Congress Party and the Muslim
League, and the Montagu-Chelmsford reforms of 1919. Whatever
its perceived merits, in practice, constitutional separatism narrowed
the focus of political debate within and between increasingly self-
conscious religious communities, made it more rewarding for them
to stress their separate religious identities, and helped transform
'socio-cultural identity into political identity'.[40] Designed also to
give the British rulers control over the evolving political framework,
separate electorates meant that leaders of one community did not
have to contend with voters belonging to the other communities.

---

[37] Seal, *Emergence of Indian Nationalism*, pp. 320-9; John R. McLane, 'The
Early Congress', pp. 51-2; Jones, *Arya Dharm*, pp. 241-52.

[38] Seal, *Emergence of Indian Nationalism*, (pp. 326, f.n.) quoting A.K. Majumdar,
Advent of Independence, Bombay, 1963, pp. 41-2, 57.

[39] Robinson, *Separatism among the Indian Muslims*, ch. 3.

[40] J.S. Grewal, 'The Making of the Sikh Self-image before Independence', in
P.C. Chatterji, ed., *Self-Images*, p. 197.

Communal bastions could thus be established more easily, and this might partly explain why, during the mid-1920s, the Congress, though professing a non-sectarian ideology, could seem to speak in the voice of the Hindu Mahasabha in northern India.[41]

As well as a widening of the franchise, the 1920s saw an increase in the political and agitational activities of the Congress party organization, particularly below the provincial level. Although more overtly political than the Hindu revivalist or separatist movements of the late nineteenth and early twentieth centuries, the support bases of these movements and the Congress movements overlapped to a great extent. The Congress Party at the local level was 'sometimes indistinguishable from the movement for the protection of cattle or for the propagation of Hindi', and there was a 'sharp contradiction between the secular, and non-communal, catch-cries used in the Congress publicity or official pronouncements, and the idioms adopted by its orators'.[42] The religious and mythical associations which the idea of India evoked in the middle-class consciousness also helped strengthen the tradition of articulating the goals of the national movement in religious terms, and of using religious (or caste) slogans, symbols, and sanctions to effect popular mobilization. The involvement of the United Province Congress Party's volunteer organization in arranging and conducting Hindu fairs and festivals, for example, kept Muslims away from it even at the height of the Khilafat movement. The widening of the Congress Party's support base during the 1920s, when it attracted growing numbers of the provincial middle and lower middle classes, increased the use of Hindu instruments and idioms in terms of which the party's goals were represented or interpreted, and mobilization effected. These features helped reinforce the Hindu image which the party seemed to present to all except its most uncritical admirers.[43] Gandhi himself was

[41]David Page, *Prelude to Partition: The Indian Muslims and the Imperial System of Control*, Delhi, 1982, ch. 4.

[42]Bayly, *Local Roots of Indian Politics*, p. 132, 142; McLane, *Indian Nationalism*, pp. 322-51.

[43]Ambree, *Imagining India*, p. 158-64; Sandria Freitag, *Collective Action and Community: Public Arenas and the Emergence of Communalism in North India*, Delhi, 1990, pp. 288-90; Ranajit Guha, 'Discipline and Mobilize', *Subaltern Studies VII*, pp. 79-90; Ghanshyam Shah, 'Caste Sentiments, Class Formation

sometimes directly responsible for some of the idiom: his definition of freedom from British rule as *Ramrajya*, for example, was widely used by party campaigners at all levels. At other levels, and sometimes by Gandhi himself, freedom from British rule was equated with the ban on cow slaughter, and the sacred cow was a recurring symbol in Congress propaganda.[44] *Swaraj* (self-rule or freedom) acquired a mystical, semi-religious connotation, with the nationalist leaders, particularly Gandhi, being credited with miraculous powers, and becoming objects of veneration.[45] In fact, as Sandria Freitag has pointed out, Hindu communal symbolism became a 'measure of success' in interpreting the Congress's all-India programme in 'locally meaningful terms'.[46] Besides, the widening of the franchise which brought new sections of society into the political arena shifted the latter's fulcrum from the club-room (where, as the Lucknow pact of 1916 showed, agreements could be reached) to the real world of the *ganjs* and *qasbahs* whose preoccupations and languages came increasingly to dominate the political agenda. Thus as the arena of mass politics came to be defined in the 1920s, the use of religious slogans and symbols, if not directly of sanctions, increased greatly in northern and eastern

and Dominance in Gujarat', in Frankel and Rao, eds., *Dominance and State Power*, pp. 74-5; Francis Robinson, 'The Congress and the Muslims', in Paul Brass and Francis Robinson, eds., *The Indian National Congress and Indian Society, 1885-1985: Ideology, Social Structure and Political Dominance*, Delhi, 1987, pp. 169-72.

[44]Mushirul Hasan, *Nationalism and Communal Politics*, pp. 219-20; Gandhi's use of religion has been evaluated differently by Ashis Nandy, *At the Edge of Psychology: Essays in Politics and Culture*, Delhi, 1980, particularly essays 2, 3, and 4, and *The Intimate Enemy: Loss and Recovery of Self under Colonialism*, Delhi, 1983, pp. 102-6; and by Partha Chatterji, *Nationalist Thought and the Colonial World: A Derivative Discourse?*, London, 1986; Richard G. Fox, 'Gandhian Socialism and Hindu Nationalism: Cultural Domination in the World System', in Sugata Bose, ed., *South Asia and World Capitalism*, Delhi, 1990, p. 246.

[45]Shahid Amin, 'Gandhi as Mahatma: Gorakhpur District, Eastern UP, 1921-2', *Subaltern Studies III*, Delhi, 1984 , pp. 1-61; also see Raja Rao's fictional account of the Congress movement in a Mysore village in his novel *Kanthapura*.

[46]Freitag, *Collective Action and Community*, pp. 237-9; the dominant 'upper-caste Hindu' aspect of the Congress movement also comes out strongly in *Kanthapura*.

India, and not surprisingly, the expansion of agitational activity on secular issues often became the spark which lit the fires of sectarian religious strife. In consequence, political mobilization, though overtly on secular issues, often became a medium for sectarian religious assertion.

The expansion of Congress activity in the United Provinces during the 1920s and 1930s is particularly instructive in these respects.[47] As the Congress Party emerged, through a series of splits and mergers, as the most important voice of an increasingly assertive 'national' movement in the late 1920s, a number of tendencies and organizations which had earlier carried on their activities largely independent of the Congress came into the folds of the party. These included members or adherents of the most overtly Hindu political and social reform movements of the period, such as the Hindu Mahasabha and the Arya Samaj. Some leaders like Madan Mohan Malaviya and Lala Lajpat Rai, for example, combined leadership of religious conversion movements and organizations set up to 'safeguard the distinct and separate interests of the Hindu community', with support for the broad Congress platform.[48] There was a significant Hindu Sabha faction within several provincial Congress committees, notably in the United Provinces, Bihar, and the Punjab, and most Congress leaders, including some with a non-sectarian reputation, were not averse to using this faction for their own ends. The religion card was also used to affect the outcome of factional disputes within the Congress movement over elections to the provincial and central assemblies, with 'pro-Muslim', 'anti-Hindu', and 'beef-eater' being some of the compliments freely exchanged in public between rival

---

[47]The following account is based on Pandey, *Ascendancy of the Congress*, and Freitag, *Collective Action and Community*; also see Mushirul Hasan, *Nationalism and Communal Politics*, pp. 209-21; because these studies focus mostly on 'communalism', caste and status assertion codes tend to be ignored; for example, often Hindu religious assertion meant also the assertion of the ritual high caste status of the local 'leader' of the Congress party; for a fictional account which brings out the popular, religious, as well as the caste and status aspects of Congress political mobilization, the reader is once again referred to Raja Rao's *Kanthapura*.

[48]Mushirul Hasan, *Nationalism and Communal Politics*, pp. 24-5, 208-9, 240-3.

Congressmen. By the early 1930s, despite growing evidence that the Congress Party was losing the support of the Muslim community at the same time as it had set its face against separate communal electorates and representation, the organization's ties with the Arya Samaj and the Hindu Sabha had grown quite close.[49]

The use of festivals and religious processions (notably *prabhat pheris*) as media for political propaganda, the more sanskritic Hindi used by some of the younger sections of the Congress leadership educated in Arya Samaj schools and colleges, the Benaras Hindu University, or the Kashi Vidyapeeth, etc. reflected the growth of a powerful 'Hindu-Hindi' cultural movement, often in connection with the Congress political movement.[50] There was considerable fluidity and movement between the ranks and leadership of Hindi promotion organizations, sectarian religious groups, and the Congress Party, and by the end of the twenties, the latter was coming increasingly under the sway of a new type of leadership, particularly at the lower levels. As the gulf between the party and the Muslim populations widened, at some places the latter began reacting to *prabhat pheris* with *tanzim* processions and *tabligh* campaigns, and not infrequently, its agitational initiatives ended in sectarian clashes.

Where its activity did not directly alienate the Muslim masses, the confident assumption held by a majority of the Congress leadership that national solidarity was inherently a quality of India's cultural heritage and the 'moral superiority' of their movement meant that the broad unity of the anti-colonial movement would not be pursued as a 'goal which had to be achieved in terms of practical politics'.[51] The resulting self-righteousness, especially when combined with the Congress Party's seeming

---

[49] Pandey, *Ascendancy of the Congress*, pp. 115-27.

[50] Krishna Kumar, 'Hindu Revivalism and Education', pp. 173-95.

[51] D. Rothermund, 'Traditionalism and National Solidarity in India', in Moore, ed., *Tradition and Politics*, p. 194; Robinson, 'The Congress and the Muslims', p. 180; Mukul Kesavan, '1937 as a Landmark in the Course of Communal Politics in the U.P.', *Occasional Papers in History and Society*, second series, no. 11, Nehru Memorial Museum and Library, New Delhi, November, 1988, pp. 20-4.

readiness to allow Hindu chauvinists to dictate terms to it, appears to have ensured that minority concerns would not be handled with any sensitivity, and that any flexibility that Muslim leaders showed in a wider cause would go unreciprocated.

For example, during the 1926-9 discussions on constitutional reforms, secular Muslim leaders showed considerable flexibility and moderation. A majority of them, including Jinnah, aware that communal electorates were widening the gulf between India's two largest religious communities and strengthening the religious sectarian elements within them, accepted the principle of joint electorates, subject to three conditions. These were: (1) that, a third of the seats in the Central Legislative Assembly would be reserved for Muslims (who constituted about a quarter of the total population); (2) that, since eligible Muslim voters under the restricted franchise then operating were a small proportion of the total Muslim population in Bengal and Punjab, for a period of ten years or until adult suffrage was introduced, whichever was earlier, Muslims would be represented in these two provincial assemblies in proportion to their population; and (3) that, residuary powers would rest with the provinces. The Congress Party, under pressure from the Hindu chauvinists within its ranks, refused to make any of these concessions, thereby gifting the initiative to the colonial government, which was able, through the so-called Communal Award of 1932, to perpetuate the principle of separate electorates.[52]

Although its nationalism continued to be characterized by its fit with Brahminical Hinduism, the party lurched, from the mid-1930s onwards, towards more overt secular postures. Influenced largely by left-wing radicalism, younger leaders, among whom Jawaharlal Nehru was the most important, tended to reject religion as an explicit factor in modern nationalism, and believing that its contemporary importance stemmed from poverty and ignorance, tried to reach out to the ordinary Muslims over the heads of their traditional leaders. They experienced some moderate success.[53]

---

[52]Mushirul Hasan, *Nationalism and Communal Politics*, pp. 271-80.

[53]Mushirul Hasan, 'The Muslim Mass Contacts Campaign: Analysis of a Strategy of Political Mobilization', in Sisson and Wolpert, eds., *Congress and Indian Nationalism*, pp. 198-22.

However, given especially the background in which this tendency came into prominence within the Congress, the republicanism of Nehru and the younger party leadership was unavoidably refracted through the reality of growing sectarian religious strife. As such neither ordinary Muslims nor a majority of their leaders could readily distinguish between what appeared to them as the assimilative Hindu nationalism of the Congress Party and the seemingly non-sectarian, but nevertheless assimilative, nationalism of a younger Congress leadership which was not fully in control of the party, and their respective support bases.[54] Hence this stratagem was only partially successful.[55]

At the same time, the Congress Party's claim to being the sole secular representative of the national movement seemed more opportunistic than principled. For example, the Congress aligned with the Muslim League to fight the 1937 elections to the U.P. legislature. But once it secured an absolute majority, all sections of the Congress Party, with the exception of Maulana Azad who thought this step a mistake, insisted that merger (and not a coalition which would concede the Muslim League's representative character) could be the only basis upon which the latter's members could participate in government. In this context it has been remarked that while Nehru's secular liberalism was undoubtedly genuine, his views sometimes merely seemed to provide respectability to those '... within the Congress fold for whom this political model was a means to the end of showing the Muslim minority in U.P. ... its place'.[56] Once in power, the Congress ministries in U.P. and elsewhere seemed insensitive towards Muslim interests. This perception, together with the growing conviction among Muslim League politicians that separate electorates and

---

[54]At several places, the Congress Party's local and district level leadership ensured that the mass contacts campaign would not get off the ground; such was their power that they also managed to sabotage a party move to disaffiliate Hindu Mahasabha members; see Mushirul Hasan, 'The Muslim Mass Contacts Campaign', pp. 213-6.

[55]Pandey notes that the objectives of the mass contact programme were extremely unclear, and that it 'offered too little too late'; *Ascendancy of the Congress Party*, p. 151.

[56]Kesavan, '1937 as a Landmark', p. 25.

representation would not be sufficient to guarantee them a share of political power, strained relations between the two most important components of the middle-class leadership of the national movement, strengthened the more extreme sections of its Muslim component, and helped push it in the direction of 'separatism'.[57]

Yet, Pakistan was not an inevitable outcome of an uncontrollable surge towards separatism by India's Muslims. For one thing, although elite conflict and religious mobilization had helped reduce the fluidity of the two categories, Muslims were no more homogeneous as a group in terms of their attributes and interests, than Hindus. The forms in which the practices of Islam were interpreted and followed varied over large regions of the country, the personalized adherence to Islamic norms which the *ulema* desired and preached with some success in the United Provinces being quite distinct from the mediatory style of Punjab's rural Islam based on Sufi shrines and the hereditary *pirs* who controlled them. In Bengal as well as in the southern parts of the country, the boundaries between Hindus and Muslims, and between their rituals and beliefs, remained quite fuzzy.[58] Above all, the political interests of the Muslim political leadership in the Muslim-minority regions (United Provinces, Bihar, etc.) and the Muslim-majority regions (Punjab, Bengal, Sind, etc.) of undivided India diverged significantly. Punjab's most powerful Muslim leaders came together under the Unionist Party which was dominated by large landowners of all communities. These leaders were extremely sceptical of Jinnah and the Muslim League leadership, and of the latter's demand for a separate Muslim state in the north-west. They saw no reason to give up their pre-eminent position in the province, which the existing electoral system had given them, for what was,

---

[57]L. Brennan, 'The Illusion of Security: The Background to Muslim Separatism in the United Provinces', *Modern Asian Studies*, 1984, pp. 237-72; Mushirul Hasan, 'The Muslim Mass Contacts Campaign', p. 212; Zoya Hasan, 'Congress in Aligarh District, 1930-1946: Problems of Political Mobilization', in Sisson and Wolpert, ed., *Congress and Indian Nationalism*, pp. 330-51; Kesavan, '1937 as a Landmark', pp. 20-4.

[58]For a discussion of rural Islam in Punjab and the attitude of the *ulema*, see David Gilmartin, *Empire and Islam: Punjab and the Making of Pakistan*, Berkeley, 1988; on South India, see Susan Bayly, *Saints, Goddesses and Kings: Muslims and Christians in South Indian Society, 1700-1900*, Cambridge, 1989.

to many of them, a fantastic idea. Even in urban Punjab, support for the Pakistan idea was, at best, equivocal.[59]

The reaction of Punjab's Muslim leadership to the Pakistan idea was critical, since the province was supposed to be at the heart of the proposed new arrangement. Hence Jinnah tried very hard, but until 1946 with conspicuously little success, to make inroads into the province. Although rising communal tensions elsewhere in the country did not leave Punjab unaffected, the province's capitulation to the Muslim League in the course of the 1946 elections did not result from a transformation in the majority Muslim population's attitude towards the idea of Pakistan. On the contrary, it reflected the factional realignments taking place in rural Punjab under the economic and social pressures arising from the war, and the changing mediatory agency of the Sufi *pirs*, particularly those belonging to the revivalist Chishti order.[60]

---

[59]It is far from clear what the concept of Pakistan meant to Jinnah and the Muslim League during the 1940s. While it is mostly assumed, particularly on the subcontinent, that the idea of Pakistan meant the same to Jinnah and the League from 1936 through 1947, Ayesha Jalal has shown that the former was quite flexible, until almost the last possible moment, about the precise constitutional arrangement which he wished to see emerging out of the demise of the British-Indian Empire. Therefore, unless otherwise stated, Pakistan is referred to in this section as an idea, rather than as a final blueprint for a separate state; see Ayesha Jalal, *The Sole Spokesman: Jinnah, the Muslim League and the Demand for Pakistan*, Cambridge, 1985; Ayesha Jalal and Anil Seal, 'Alternative to Partition: Muslim Politics between the Wars', *Modern Asian Studies*, 1981, pp. 415-54.

[60]Gilmartin, *Empire and Islam*, ch. 6; David Gilmartin, 'Religious Leadership and the Pakistan Movement in the Punjab', *Modern Asian Studies*, 1979, pp. 510-16; Ian Talbot, 'The Growth of the Muslim League in the Punjab, 1937-1946', *Journal of Commonwealth and Comparative Politics*, 1982, pp. 5-24; *Punjab and the Raj, 1849-1947*, Delhi, 1988, pp. 238-9. It is one of the ironies of the period that while having troubled political relations with the secular, non-religious Muslim leadership, the Congress platform drew on the support of the reformist *ulema*, notably those belonging to the Deoband school; the latter remained suspicious till the end about Jinnah's allegiance to Islam, while syncretic, 'popular Islam', usually distinguished by its opposition to the sectarian, inflexible, orthodox *ulema*, helped mediate between rural Punjab and the Muslim League's urban-based politics; see in this connection, Mushirul Hasan, *Nationalism and Communal Politics*, pp. 172-6, and David Gilmartin, *Empire and Islam*, pp. 52-6, 190, and 215-6; also see Gilmartin, 'Religious Leadership and the Pakistan Movement', pp. 509-10.

The overriding objective of Punjab's landlords and the province's large number of Sufi *pirs* was the preservation of the traditional rural order and their own positions within it. Both appeared to be under threat not only from the dissolution of the colonial regime with which the *pirs* and the large landowners had sought accommodation, but also from the unitary and centralist drives of the Congress Party. By allowing the provinces considerable autonomy, the 1935 Government of India Act gave Muslim-majority provinces like Punjab, Bengal, and Sind, where the party was relatively weak, a stake in a weak centre. But as had become clear since the constitutional reform deliberations of the late 1920s, the Congress Party leadership was committed to the idea of a strong centre capable of inheriting the political and military authority of the British-Indian empire in its entirety, and without having to share any of it with the provinces. In contrast, the Muslim League, walking a tight rope between a loose federal arrangement involving the provinces merging into Pakistan and India and outright separatism, but rejecting a premature commitment to either arrangement, seemed a much better bet for the Punjabi elite; though even they would perhaps have balked, had they expected it, at the prospect of a division of their province between India and Pakistan. In the end, the strong section of the effective Congress leadership which had centralist and unitarist goals, had its way. This leadership, made up by the significant unity of Jawaharlal Nehru the impatient statist and socialistic modernizer with Sardar Patel the staunch defender of a unitary Hindu order, managed to marginalize Gandhi, now more than ever a man who had helped translate India's 'national' consciousness into effective political action, but who was unwilling to pay the price which the putative 'nation-state' demanded should be paid at its birth. The triumph of the unitarists within the Congress appears to have encouraged Jinnah and the Muslim League to press for a 'partition'.[61]

---

[61]On this see Jalal, *Sole Spokesman*, and Jalal and Seal, 'Alternatives to Partition'; even Maulana Azad, respected in the Congress pantheon of heroes as a 'nationalist Muslim', publicly described the Congress party's effective repudiation of the Cabinet Mission plan for a federal arrangement, which paved the way for the establishment of Pakistan, as 'one of those unfortunate events that change the course of history'; see A.K. Azad, *India Wins Freedom*, Bombay, 1959, p. 154.

The terms in which the Congress Party's programme and propaganda were presented did not only alienate the Muslim community, but it also had the effect of confining the bulk of the support for it to the Hindu heartland of the United Provinces, Bihar, and parts of the Bombay Presidency including mainland Gujarat. Elsewhere, the party's presence was usually stronger in the cities and towns, and everywhere its leadership was seen to be dominated by members drawn from the upper castes.[62] There were important groups, such as the non-Brahmin communities in the Madras Presidency and the 'untouchables' under the leadership of Bhimrao Ambedkar, who were opposed to the Congress ideology because they saw it as an attempt to perpetuate the dominance of the upper castes. Gandhi, of course, tackled the political threat to Congress hegemony and the implicit threat to the Hindu order posed by Ambedkar and the so-called untouchable communities through the famous fast which culminated in the Poona Pact. The limitations of the non-Brahmin, anti-Congress movements were also exposed as they found themselves caught between the Congress movement and the colonial government, and several non-Brahmin leaders found it politically expedient to join the Congress Party, particularly during the last years of British rule.[63] In the event, it was not surprising that it was mainly through the arena of elite politics, rather than convincing popular mobilization, that the Congress managed seemingly to broaden its platform, though minus a majority of the Muslims. But this broadening notwithstanding, the party's nationalism remained flawed, since it drew its main strength from a narrow strata of north Indian society. Not only had the Congress Party's nationalism played the role of a midwife in the birth of Pakistan, it would also remain a source of unease to the country's religious and ethnic minorities.

---

[62]David A. Washbrook, 'Caste, Class and Dominance in Modern Tamilnadu: Non-Brahminism, Dravidianism and Tamil Nationalism', and G. Ram Reddy, 'The Politics of Accumulation: Caste, Class and Dominance in Andhra Pradesh', both in Frankel and Rao, eds., *Dominance and State Power*, for a bibliography on the different regions of India, see the essays in Frankel and Rao, eds., *Dominance and State Power*.
[63]Marguerite R. Barnett, *The Politics of Cultural Nationalism in South India*, Princeton, 1976, pp. 56-74.

IV

The loss of Muslim support during the 1946 provincial elections and the looming certainty of Pakistan only made the Congress Party in the United Provinces aggressively insensitive towards the concerns of the Muslim community.[64] 'Nationalist Muslims' found their standing within the party diminished, with the province's Congressmen turning openly hostile to the idea of accommodating them in the party's committees. The province was racked by religious rioting through and after September 1946, with the most serious of them all, the Garh Mukteshwar riots of November 1946, claiming over 400 lives. For the most part the middle level Congress response to the riots was uncaring. Congress leaders at this level were inclined to minimize the death toll, and to blame the riots on the inability of Muslims to maintain good relations with their Hindu neighbours, or on the Noakhali disturbances. As a central Congress delegation comprising Mridula Sarabhai and Maj. Gen. Shahnawaz Khan acknowledged, local Congressmen had actually played an active role in the riots.[65]

Elsewhere in the province, the Congress government allowed those involved in the rioting to be let off lightly. One of them, Babo Ragho Das, a Congressman associated with the cow protection movement and responsible for the Dadri riots of September 1946, was released from detention to be made president of the Gorakhpur district unit of the party and a member of the United Provinces Congress Committee, and known communal rabble-rousers were taken into the folds of the Congress Party and honoured as freedom-fighters.

The UP Congress remained close to the Hindu Mahasabha during these years, and sympathetic to the latter's demand to reduce Muslim representation in the armed police and the home guards, and to reserve key government positions for Hindus. Repudiating the Congress Party's announced language policy of promoting the

---

[64]Mukul Kesavan, 'Invoking a Majority: The Congress and the Muslims of the United Provinces, 1945-47', in P.C. Chatterji, ed., *Self-Images*, pp. 91-111; in the 1946 elections, the Congress Party received 1% of the urban, and 19% of the rural Muslim vote; the Muslim League got 71% and 62% respectively.
[65]Kesavan, 'Invoking a Majority', pp. 93-8.

use of Hindustani in both the Persian and the Nagari scripts, and although a decision had been deferred at the central level, the province's government legislated to make Hindi (written in the Nagari script) the sole official language of the provincial legislature. This move was intended to pre-empt a decision on the language question by the central Constituent Assembly: United Provinces being the largest Urdu-speaking province in the country, its legislators' rejection of Hindustani meant that the language would have little chance of being accepted as the 'national' language. The UP assembly's move was again justified by the province's middle-ranking Congress leadership in majoritarian terms.[66] The province's government also moved quickly to pass a bill providing for elections to village panchayats on the basis of combined electorates. Although the measure itself might seem unexceptionable given the party's attitude towards the principle of separate electorates, several Congress leaders saw this bill as a way of ensuring Hindu control over the province's villages.[67]

Nebulous at best as the Congress Party's vision of secular nationalism was, majoritarian nationalists within the party and outside it managed to make their presence felt during the framing of the constitution by the Constituent Assembly. The decision to make Hindi the national language merely formalized an initiative which had been set in motion in the United Provinces earlier.[68] The ban on cow slaughter was also included among the directive principles of state policy, although some Congressmen like Nehru believed such a step 'would appear as a concession to Hindu bigotry'.[69] 'Majoritarian nationalism' found a powerful protagonist within the Congress ranks in the form of Sardar Patel who became the Home Minister in the post-independence ministry. Patel was sympathetic to the ideology of the RSS. Impressed by the 'patriotism, motivation, and discipline' of its cadres, he managed

---

[66]Kesavan, 'Invoking a Majority', pp. 103-8.

[67]Kesavan, 'Invoking a Majority', pp. 100-2.

[68]On the language question in the Constituent Assembly, see Krishna Kumar, 'Hindu Revivalism and Education', pp. 187-9.

[69]S. Gopal, 'Nehru and the Minorities', *Economic and Political Weekly*, November 1988, pp. 2463-6.

to persuade the party's Working Committee to adopt, in Nehru's absence, a resolution which would encourage them to join the party while still retaining their memberships of the Hindu chauvinistic organization.[70]

Although majoritarian tendencies at the 'grassroots' did make life a little uncomfortable for the more secular sections of the Congress leadership, the two segments continued, as in the 1930s, to share some common prescriptions concerning the minorities. They saw eye to eye on the need for a uniform civil code, which was now included among the directive principles of state policy. The Congress Party also spoke as one on the subject of separate electorates and representation for the religious minorities. But in the hands of Sardar Patel this issue became one which represented, particularly when set in the immediate context of pre-independence politics and the partition, another opportunity for majoritarian nationalism to establish its triumph over alternative, potentially more accommodative versions of nationalism, and over a Muslim minority which had lost the bulk of its numbers and its political leadership to the new state of Pakistan.[71] Addressing the minorities sub-committee of the advisory committee of the Constituent Assembly meeting to discuss the issue of reservations, Patel is said to have spoken in the following words:

> *You* perhaps think that there will be some third power who
> will use its influence to put the minority against the majority

[70]Prakash C. Upadhyaya, 'The Politics of Indian Secularism', *Modern Asian Studies*, 1992, pp. 826-7; according to a popular middle-class Hindu nationalistic stereotype, Nehru is derisively regarded as a 'dreamer' and a 'visionary', while Patel, often referred to as the 'indomitable Sardar', was the 'iron man' of 'action'; the shift in the popular, middle-class evaluations of the two politicians partly reflects the growing yearning which this section feels for simple and authoritarian solutions to the crises of Indian nationalism; it is not also accidental that the *Sangh parivar*, in particular the RSS, refers to Patel in glowing terms and invokes him in their campaigns and propaganda material.

[71]On the abolition of separate electorates and representation for the religious minorities, see Omar Khalidi, 'Muslims in Indian Political Process: Group Goals and Alternative Strategies', *Economic and Political Weekly*, Jan. 2-9, 1993, pp. 44-5; it is significant that the strongest support for the continuation of separate electorates came from southern Indian Muslim representatives whose communities had been relatively less affected than those in the north by migrations to Pakistan.

and compel the majority to take one or two ministers according to the proportion of the population. It is a wrong idea. That conception in *your* mind which has worked for many years must be washed off altogether. *For the future of a minority it is best to trust the majority.* ....
Trust *us* and see what happens. Why are you afraid? *Make friends with others and create a change in the atmosphere.* You will then get more than your quota, *if you really feel for the country in the same manner as other people.*[72]

Conflicts within the Congress Party over what ideas like nationalism and secularism meant in practice, and over the attitude of the Indian state towards the majority community and the religious minorities were never far from the surface. They erupted at critical points such as during the passage through Parliament of a bill to amend Hindu marriage and inheritance laws, or after Nehru's political standing was gravely weakened following the Sino-Indian war of 1962. These conflicts were also palpable in the Congress Party's handling of the language agitations, in particular the *Punjabi Suba* agitation of the 1950s.

Yet, at the same time, a number of factors acted to deflect the strivings of majoritarian nationalism seemingly to the margins of the Indian political spectrum. Patel's death towards the end of 1950 helped mute debates within the party over the practical interpretation of categories like nationalism and secularism, and enabled Nehru and the more genuinely secular elements within the party to put their stamp on policy. At the same time, three other factors appear to have been critical: firstly, the considerable,

---

[72]Quoted in Omar Khalidi, 'Muslims in Indian Political Process', p. 45; emphases supplied; apart from the 'us-them' language, note the strong similarities between Patel's language and that of the present day BJP leadership; the theme of a Hindu community generous in forgiveness if only the Muslims, rather than looking to external sources of support, made amends for their historical wrongs, is common to both; likewise Muslims were expected to prove their patriotism to the Hindu majority, and upon them lay the onus of creating an atmosphere conducive to their well-being; similar attitudes also prevail among Catholics in the Irish Republic; see Graham Walker, 'Irish Nationalism and the Uses of History', *Past and Present*, 1990, no. 126, pp. 203-14.

but little noticed, employment mobility and political space which the departure of the British from India and the administrative Muslim elites from U.P. and Bihar entailed for this region's Hindu upper-caste elites; secondly, unitarianism being common to both strains of Indian nationalism, the success of the ideology of a strong, centralized state embodying the nation, and giving organized political expression to it; and thirdly, the role of this state in the sphere of the economy, because of which it could emerge as the largest employer in the organized sector and the biggest single avenue for mobility for the educated middle classes, the bulk of whom belonged to the Hindu upper castes.

In general, an 'over-developed state' with a relatively independent bureaucracy has been regarded as a major characteristic of post-colonial societies.[73] Yet, caught in social conflicts stemming primarily from disputes over the distribution of power and patronage, the state in several of these societies has also, all too easily, been riven asunder by contending groups. In India too, the overwhelming role of the state has meant that some existing and emerging cleavages within society could, when they became sharp enough, pose a grave challenge directly to its integrity. Secondly, far from being decisively engaged and defeated, majoritarian nationalism in India has been able to preserve itself as a *structural* feature of the system, cloaked in passivity, as long as avenues for rapid employment mobility existed or the unitarian political order was not under any palpable threat, by the rhetoric of building a strong, independent, self-reliant nation, but reappearing, once these avenues ceased or the centralization of power at the centre was challenged, as an attractive alternative to any meaningful attempt to reckon and deal with the deep cleavages within Indian society.

V

The political economy of Indian development, in particular the

[73]Hamza Alavi, 'The State in Post-Colonial Societies: Pakistan and Bangladesh', *New Left Review*, 1972, pp. 59-80.

role of the state, has been the subject of much study and debate. In general, there has been some unanimity on the issue of the independence of the state and its institutions *vis-a-vis* the dominant classes, with the bureaucracy in particular being regarded as a class on par with the other dominant propertied classes, but whose strategic role is greater because it mediates between the various classes, and between the latter and the state.[74] Moreover, caught in the enlightenment rhetoric of nationalism, and having to take recourse to the state to telescope both the economic and social processes of modernization in a few decades, the Indian elites have, by and large, tended to privilege the nation and the state over its people. Not accidentally, the state has been the major source of employment and mobility, most notably of all for the Hindu upper-caste elites.

During the last thirty years, the public sector has expanded greatly. It accounted for about 26.5% of the gross domestic product in 1990-1, as against some 10% in 1960-1. Over roughly the same period, public sector employment has risen from about seven million to more than 18 million, its share of total employment in the organized sector having gone up from about 58% in 1961 to 71% by the end of the 1980s.[75] Moreover, more than half of those employed in the public sector hold white-collar jobs.[76]

---

[74]P. Bardhan, *The Political Economy of Development in India*, Delhi, 1984; 'The Third Dominant Class', *Economic and Political Weekly*, January 1989; Baldev Raj Nayyar, *India's Mixed Economy: The Role of Ideology and Interests in Development*, Bombay, 1989; O. Törnquist, *What is Wrong with Marxism? On Capitalists and State in India and Indonesia*, Delhi, 1989; for a brief survey, see J.D. Pedersen, 'State, Bureaucracy and Change in India', *Journal of Development Studies*, 1992, pp. 616-39.

[75]Government of India, Ministry of Planning, Department of Statistics, Central Statistical Organization, *National Accounts Statistics, 1992*, New Delhi, 1993, p. 75; employment data from Government of India, Department of Industrial Development, Office of the Economic Adviser, *Handbook of Industrial Statistics, 1989*, New Delhi, 1990, pp. 203-4; the 1961 data is from Pedersen, 'State, Bureaucracy and Change'; employment in the organized sector accounts for nearly a quarter of all wage employment, and the latter for nearly 40% of the total work-force.

[76]Pedersen, 'State, Bureaucracy and Change', pp. 621-3.

Reliable data on the religious and caste composition of India's government employees, particularly those employed by state governments, local bodies, and quasi-government undertakings is hard to come by. Official sources do not report data on the representation of individual communities other than the 'scheduled castes' and 'scheduled tribes' who are entitled to statutory quotas. One has therefore to rely upon private studies and reports of official commissions and committees appointed to look into the grievances of the 'backward classes' and the minorities;[77] and the methods adopted by these studies have necessarily been rather ad hoc and controversial. Nevertheless the conclusion is inescapable that the bulk of the better paid jobs at the higher levels of government are held by those belonging to the upper castes among the Hindus (about 8% of the total population according to some estimates), and that public sector employment has been a major source of mobility for these sections.

Of the Indian Administrative Service (IAS) officers serving in 1985 who were identifiable as 'Hindus', Brahmins, Kayasths, Kshatriyas, and Vaishyas (including Marwaris) between them accounted for nearly 70% of the over 3,200 appointments. Members of the intermediate castes held a mere 66 appointments. Two-thirds of the latter were held by those hailing from Andhra Pradesh, Kerala, Tamil Nadu, Maharashtra, and Karnataka which have had a history of 'backward class' movements, or states like West Bengal where caste oppression was not particularly severe. Clearly, members of the intermediate castes in the Hindu-Hindi heartland region of Uttar Pradesh, Bihar, Madhya Pradesh, Rajasthan, and Haryana have not done outstandingly well, accounting as they do for only about one per cent of the appointments from these states.[78]

---

[77]Government of India, Ministry of Home Affairs, *Report of the Backward Classes Commission*, New Delhi, 1980; Government of India, Ministry of Home Affairs, High Power Panel on Minorities, Scheduled Castes, Scheduled Tribes, and Other Weaker Sections, *Report on Minorities*, New Delhi, 1983.
[78]Santosh Goyal, 'Social Background of Officers in the Indian Administrative Service', app. II in Frankel and Rao, eds., *Dominance and State Power*, pp. 429-32; the caste affiliations of over 28% of the IAS officers identified as 'Hindus' could not be ascertained.

The position of the intermediate castes in other areas of public sector employment, as Table 1 below shows, is only slightly better:

	Class 1	Class 2	Classes 3&4	All classes
Total no. of employees	174026	912925	484687	1571638
SCs/STs	5.68%	18.18%	24.4%	18.72%
OBCs	4.69%	10.63%	18.98%	12.55%

Table 1: Representation of Scheduled Castes and Scheduled Tribes (SCs/STs) and Other Backward Classes (OBCs) in Central Government Services[79]

Nor is the position of the Muslims (some 11% of the population) very much better. In 1971 they accounted for less than two per cent of those employed in the central government's secretariat in Delhi; they held about two per cent of the appointments in the IAS in 1985, and about three per cent in the Indian Police Service in 1983.[80] According to the survey conducted by the High Powered Panel on Minorities, Scheduled Castes, Scheduled Tribes, and Other Weaker Sections, members of minority

[79]Source: *statement no. 1, app. vii*, in Government of India, *Report of the Backward Classes Commission*, New Delhi, 1980, part 1, vol. 2; the employees covered include those of ministries and departments of the Government of India, autonomous bodies attached to the government and subordinate bodies, and public sector undertakings; according to the commission, the 'backward classes' make up nearly 52% of the Indian population; there is a statutory 22.5% quota for SCs and STs in central government employment. Unfortunately, similar data on employment in the state governments and their undertakings, etc. is not available, but the initiatives taken in recent years by several state governments to reserve jobs for the 'other backward classes' suggest that these communities felt 'under-represented' in the public services.

[80]Figures for employment in the central secretariat and appointments to the Indian Police Service are from Mushirul Hasan, 'In Search of Integration and Identity: Indian Muslims since Independence', *Economic and Political Weekly*, November, 1988, pp. 2471-4; figures for appointments to the IAS are from Goyal, 'Social Background', p. 429; bias being greater at this level, it is likely that Muslim representation in the lower ranks of public employment would be even smaller; in the central secretariat certainly, as Mushirul Hasan, p. 2473, shows, the proportion of Muslim employees falls in the lower ranks.

religious groups (Muslims, Sikhs, Christians, Buddhists, and Parsees who together comprise nearly a fifth of the total population) accounted for about 9% of central government employment and about 16% of the employment in central public sector undertakings.[81]

There can thus be no doubt that the direct employment effects of a major role for the state in Indian society have, in general, been such as to ensure greater job mobility for members of the Hindu upper castes than for other sections of the population. But the available data does not allow us to judge whether or not upper-caste Hindu domination of public sector jobs has declined over time. Besides, except in so far as successive governments have failed to invest adequately in elementary and secondary education, the charge that the *system* allows or encourages discrimination against those who do not belong to Hindu, upper-caste communities, particularly in the northern Indian states, may not be easy to sustain. Moreover, there is merit in the argument that civil service employment should not be viewed as a form of public sector intervention with distributional objectives; and that even when regarded in that light, the former has to be set against the impact of other forms of state intervention (or non-intervention) with more explicitly distributional aims. One may also validly argue that the demand for preferential access for intermediate caste elites to civil service employment originates in a notion of the latter as a source of power or patronage which militates against the true role of civil servants in modern society.

The above arguments are valid in their own contexts. Yet it may be worth pausing to consider that intermediate caste elites, in particular, *perceive* the system to have functioned in such a way as disproportionately to benefit upper-caste elites, and that the ideology of liberal, overtly non-sectarian nationalism seems unacceptable even to those who might otherwise be said to have done well under its regime. Above all, the political response of India's upper-caste leaders to the challenge which the intermediate caste elites have posed to their domination of public sector

---

[81]The estimates are for sample districts with minority population proportions well above the national average; see *Report on Minorities*, pp. 58-66, 78-82.

employment gives the latter a significance which is impossible to ignore. The nature of this political response also raises important questions about the practice of unitarian nationalism in India.

VI

On the face of it, India's political leadership has tried implicitly to deflect the thrust of majoritarian nationalism by replacing religion with territory as the basis of nationalism. But in an overwhelmingly religious society in which even the most clear-sighted leaders have found it impossible to distinguish romanticism from history and the latter from mythology, this distinction is often not clear-cut. Further, if the idea of India is suffused with religious and mythical meanings, so is the territory it covers. Indeed, in the minds of her bureaucratic and political elites, the sanctity of India's borders derives not from their immediate past history including that of the consolidation of the British Indian empire, but from mythology. In 1959, for example, Prime Minister Jawaharlal Nehru and the Government of India argued, in the course of rejecting the Chinese government's contention that the borders between the two countries were arbitrarily drawn by the colonial authorities, that India's boundaries had been part of her 'culture and tradition for the past two thousand years or so'. A White Paper prepared by the Foreign Ministry invoked support from the Vishnu Purana, the Rig Veda, the *Mahabharata*, and the *Ramayana* for its view that the country to the south of the Himalayas and north of the ocean was called Bharat. Thus the 'Bharat of the Brahmanical ideology' was not only 'made congruent', as we saw above, with the 'India of the West's imagination', but also with the actual boundaries established at the end of Britain's nineteenth century conquest of the subcontinent.[82]

In practice as well, territorial nationalism in the Indian context is often indistinguishable from religious nationalism. The presence of Islamic states in the neighbourhood was bound to give a religious edge to territorial nationalism. Similarly, the presence of a substantial Hindu or Muslim minority community in some of

---

[82]Embree, *Imagining India*, p. 16.

116

India's border states has meant that religious sectarian slogans and ideas have always implicitly characterized electoral mobilization and the integrationist politics of centrist and right-wing nationalist political parties in these states.

Since the early 1980s, the distinction between territorial and religious nationalism has become even more blurred. To a great extent, this blurring accompanied the response of India's unitarian political and bureaucratic elites to the twin challenges they faced since the late 1960s.

The first of these challenges was the collapse of the political-organizational basis of centrist nationalist politics in India. The inability of the Congress Party to suitably accommodate the secular demands of the upwardly mobile peasantry belonging to the intermediate castes who were consolidating their political presence in large parts of India eroded the party's earlier domination of the country's politics. In the Hindi heartland states, the party's position came under challenge from parties representing the interests of these newly mobile sections. In Tamil Nadu and Punjab, and later in Andhra Pradesh, the challenge came from regional parties whose base also lay with the middle and rich peasantry, while in West Bengal, the Communist Party of India (Marxist) led a Left Front coalition to power in 1977.[83]

Mrs. Gandhi's personal predilections combined with the Congress Party's inability to address this challenge adequately at the level of organization. With the latter virtually ceasing to exist and the interdependence between the party and the government a thing of the past, national power came to lack a firm institutional base independent of the government.[84] Mrs. Gandhi's characteristic response to the challenge which the rise of regional parties posed to her party's position and her personal position within it was to 'nationalize' issues on which elections to Parliament were fought, hoping thereby to create a 'wave' which would override the relative autonomy of the local structures through which electoral

---

[83]See Frankel on Bihar, Zoya Hasan on Uttar Pradesh, David Washbrook on Tamil Nadu, Ram Reddy on Andhra Pradesh, Paul Wallace on Punjab, and Atul Kohli on West Bengal in Frankel and Rao, eds., *Dominance and State Power*.
[84]Paul Brass, 'National Power and Local Politics in India: A Twenty-year Perspective', *Modern Asian Studies*, 1984, pp. 89-118.

mobilization took place in India. Although local networks of influence such as those based on land, caste, kinship groups, lineage, etc., did not cease to exist, increasingly these were being articulated in the process of vertical affiliations either in support of, or in opposition to Indira Gandhi and the party she led. Mrs. Gandhi's emphatic victory in the 1971 elections which she fought on the slogan of '*Garibi Hatao*', and which helped her for the first time to appeal to the voters over the heads of their traditional leadership and thereby to overcome the looming fragmentation of India's party political system, represented an early success of this strategy.[85]

By the time of the 1979-80 elections which saw Mrs. Gandhi regain power after nearly three years in the opposition, the fragmentation had become real. The 1977 elections saw the intermediate caste elites of the Hindi heartland and regional elites from Punjab and Tamil Nadu share power for the first time at the centre. In Bihar, Uttar Pradesh, Punjab, and Tamil Nadu, intermediate caste leaders or regional parties also came to power with comfortable majorities. Although the C.P.I.(M.)-led Left Front which came to power in West Bengal in the 1977 elections was more overtly 'national' in outlook, the compulsions of political survival in an environment dominated by a powerful central government forced it to make common cause with regional parties on a number of issues.

As Indira Gandhi was well aware, rather than a united all-India party organized in the mirror-image of the Congress, the immediate challenge to her personal dominance and that of her party was likely to come from regional and left-wing parties in alliance with politicians representing the peasant castes of the Hindi heartland states. Further, this alliance had been able to propel itself to power with the support of the Bharatiya Jana Sangh (the progenitor of the present day Bharatiya Janata Party) which had significant pockets of influence in Madhya Pradesh, Rajasthan,

---

[85]It is not a coincidence that during the Emergency (1975-7) some leaders of the Congress Party actively campaigned in favour of switching over to a presidential form of government; such a system would have led to elections being more sharply focused on 'national' issues, and helped divide or disorient more local or provincial bases of power.

Delhi, the Jammu region of Jammu and Kashmir, and Punjab; and which though possessing a unitarian Hindu upper-caste perspective, had been compelled by the exigencies of India's electoral politics to throw its weight behind the broad alliance of political parties representing the intermediate castes and the regional parties.

By the late 1970s, the political programme of a section of the anti-Congress coalition had also evolved sufficiently to reveal the latter's ability to threaten Hindu upper-caste dominance of the government and its unitarian basis. The most controversial initiative taken by the ruling Janata Party's intermediate caste leadership in Bihar and Uttar Pradesh, in the teeth of opposition from the upper castes represented by the opposition Congress Party and the former Jana Sangh component within the newly-formed ruling Janata Party, was the decision to implement the reports of their respective backward class commissions providing for job and educational reservations for members of the intermediate castes.[86] But not content with securing their positions at the state level and establishing horizontal alliances, leaders of the intermediate castes also began assiduously to address the task of converting their political strength into systemic clout at the centre. The appointment of a backward classes commission (Mandal Commission) by the Janata Party government brought the issue of job reservations in the central government, and threats to upper-caste mobility, to the fore.

The second challenge to Mrs. Gandhi, the Congress Party, and her unitarian platform came from parties with strong regional bases of support. From the late 1970s, the Left Front government in West Bengal, the Akali Dal in Punjab, and the Dravida Munnetra Kazhagam (DMK) in Tamil Nadu began to campaign for a redistribution of power between the centre and the state governments.[87] In particular,

---

[86]For a caste-based analysis of successive governments in Uttar Pradesh and Bihar, see Zoya Hasan, 'Patterns of Resilience and Change', pp. 170-88, and Frankel, 'Caste, Land and Dominance in Bihar', pp. 99-119.

[87]There are two views on whether the 1960s and the 1970s saw a greater centralization of power in Delhi's hands. While the centralization argument is well known, the contrary view, of an evolving pluralism, has hardly been put forward with any seriousness. An exception in this respect is Paul Brass, 'Pluralism, Regionalism, and Decentralizing Tendencies in Contemporary Indian Politics', in A. Jeyratnam Wilson and Dennis Dalton, eds., *The States of South Asia: Problems of National Integration*, New Delhi, 1982, pp. 223-64.

they sought a renegotiation of centre-state financial relations, and limits on the powers of the central government to dismiss popularly elected state governments.

Mrs. Gandhi chose not to face either of these two challenges directly. Instead, she focused on the secular agitation launched by the Akali Dal demanding the long-promised inclusion of the Union Territory of Chandigarh in the state of Punjab and a greater share of river waters for the state, and succeeded in giving it a religious colour. In general, since the 1950s, the Congress Party's pre-eminence in Punjab had come to depend on its ability to split the Akali Dal. In the 1950s, and till the mid-1960s, this tactic had succeeded handsomely. But the alliance between the Akali Dal and the Jana Sangh, which briefly held office in the state in the late 1960s and again in the late 1970s, meant that the Congress hopes of staying in power came to rest upon splitting the Akali vote in such a way as also to consolidate and capture the 'Hindu vote'. If effected successfully, such a capture would help expose the ideological fragility of the anti-Congress alliance of the left parties, regional elites, middle-peasant parties, and the Hindu, right-wing Bharatiya Janata Party. By exposing the vacillatory character of the latter's upper-caste support base, the strategy would also have implications well beyond the narrow confines of Punjab. And by the late 1970s the Congress Party leadership had picked an obscure fire-spouting religious preacher, Jarnail Singh Bhindranwale, to achieve this for them.

Much has been written about the role which the Congress Party, particularly Giani Zail Singh and Sanjay Gandhi, played in helping to create the monster which Bhindranwale eventually became.[88] But while the Congress Party's manipulation of

---

[88]There are a number of surveys dealing with different aspects of the Punjab crisis, but a surprising degree of unanimity regarding the political machinations of the Congress Party leadership; the following account is based on Robin Jeffrey, *What's Happening to India? Punjab, Ethnic Conflict, Mrs. Gandhi's Death and the Test for Federalism*, London, 1986; Richard G. Fox, *Lions of the Punjab: Culture in the Making*, Berkeley, 1985; Rajiv Kapur, *Sikh Separatism: The Politics of Faith*; J.S. Grewal, *The Sikhs of the Punjab*; New Cambridge History of India, II.3, Cambridge, 1990; Amarjit Kaur, Shekhar Gupta, J.S. Aurora, *et al.*, *The Punjab Story*, New Delhi, 1984; Mark Tully and Satish Jacob, *Amritsar: Mrs. Gandhi's Last Battle*, London, 1985; Dalip Singh,

Bhindranwale took place within the context of Punjab's politics, it also gave the party a very useful weapon with which to fight the gathering internal threats to the unitarian, centralized, upper-caste dominated order of which it was the principal champion.

The Congress leadership's successful efforts to use the Akali agitation to defeat the wider challenge to its dominance represents perhaps the most cynical display of *realpolitik* in modern India. Firstly, Indira Gandhi refused seriously to address any of the secular demands raised by the Akali Dal. Several rounds of talks held between the Akali leadership and representatives of the central government during 1980-84 proved abortive, largely because the Akali agitation was a potential asset which the Congress Party was not about to let go.[89] Simultaneously, it encouraged the growth of a militant-religious dimension to the Akali Dal's agitation. This was accomplished on the one hand by conceding some religious-sectarian demands, not formally part of the Akali agitation but raised by the extremist fringe of the movement, to amend Article 25 of the Indian constitution to enshrine the religious distinctiveness of the Sikhs, ban the sale of tobacco near the Golden Temple, etc.; and on the other by boosting the prestige and stature of Bhindranwale and other extremists within the Sikh religious leadership. As extremism gained ground, the Congress Party and its supporters, with help

Dynamics of Punjab Politics, New Delhi, 1981; Avtar Singh Malhotra, *Save Punjab, Save India*, New Delhi, 1984; Kuldip Nayar and Khushwant Singh, *Tragedy of Punjab: Operation Blue Star and After*, New Delhi, 1984; Paul Brass, 'The Punjab Crisis and the Unity of India' and 'Socioeconomic Aspects of the Punjab Crisis', both in Paul Brass, *Ethnicity and Nationalism: Theory and Comparison*, New Delhi, 1991; Sucha Singh Gill and K.C. Singhal, 'The Punjab Problem: Its Historical Roots', *Economic and Political Weekly*, April 1984; Gopal Singh, 'Socio-Economic Basis of the Punjab Crisis', *Economic and Political Weekly*, January 1984; Dipankar Gupta, 'The Communalizing of Punjab: 1980-1985', *Economic and Political Weekly*, July 1985, pp. 1185-90.
[89]On one occasion (February 1984), an anti-Sikh riot in the Congress-ruled state of Haryana helped break up negotiations between an Akali delegation and the central government; the fact that Congress activists took part in the riots and that the state government did nothing to control it supports the widely-held view that the riot was *staged* to prevent a possible settlement; see, more generally, Tully and Jacob, *Amritsar*, pp. 73-83, 89-91.

from a largely uncritical media, succeeded in portraying the Akali agitation as a religious-secessionist movement for the creation of a Sikh theocratic state of Khalistan.[90] The 'manner in which the Centre reacted to ... Akali demands, which were initially secular, ... mnemonically revived tradition as an ideological rationale for activism';[91] and from looking to the government's demonology to define their goals and objectives for them, the extremists soon graduated to setting their own agenda.

As extremism gained ground and the moderates, abandoning earlier postures, began talking the language of the militants, the central government could point to the justice and correctness of its initial characterization of the Akali movement. And with the religious extremists in Punjab 'posing a threat to the country's unity and integrity' and the unresolved problem in Kashmir also rearing its head, Mrs. Gandhi and the Congress leadership could play the ethnic/religious card in the guise of upholding secularism and 'national unity'.[92] Territorial nationalism and religious nationalism, if they were ever distinct, merged; religious consciousness and 'nation-state consciousness' were once again co-terminous in the Congress agenda, and the 'unity' of India had seemingly come to depend on the unity of the Hindus behind Mrs. Gandhi and the Congress Party.[93]

---

[90]The central government's demonology about 'bloodthirsty Sikhs' was so successful that even army officers heading predominantly Sikh units succumbed to it; as a result, immediately after the army's storming of the Golden Temple in June 1984 ('Operation Bluestar'), Hindu army officers heading these units deserted their posts without carrying out routine unifying practices such as attending the weekly gurudwara or holding *durbars* to explain the operation; see Gupta, 'The Communalizing of Punjab', p. 1189.

[91]Dipankar Gupta, 'The Communalizing of Punjab', pp. 1187-8.

[92]Mrs. Gandhi also used the mass conversion to Islam of nearly a thousand members of the 'scheduled castes' in a small town called Meenakshipuram (Tamil Nadu), to mobilize Hindu opinion; see Engineer, *Politics of Confrontation*, p. xiv.

[93]Dipankar Gupta, 'Communalism and Fundamentalism: Some Notes on the Nature of Ethnic Politics in India', *Economic and Political Weekly*, Annual Number 1991, pp. 573-82; the Congress Party's drive towards sectarian nationalist mobilization may also have been due partly to the the fact that an assertive new generation of Muslims was coming into public life independent of the Congress; the events of the Emergency and its aftermath may also have had the effect of shifting the base of the non-Congress Muslim leadership from southern India to Uttar Pradesh and Bihar.

Thus the 'Hindu card' which Mrs. Gandhi played with such devastating effect during the 1982-3 state elections in Jammu and Kashmir and the local elections in Delhi was not an accidental or one-off tactic. It was a carefully considered and rehearsed tactic which gave her both a 'national' and a 'nationalistic' platform during the last five years of her life, and enabled her son to lead the Congress to victory in the 1984 elections to Parliament. It also succeeded in temporarily seeing off the threat to India's unitarian order from the regions, and the challenge to upper-caste dominance from the middle peasants of the Hindi heartland states. The fall in the Bharatiya Janata Party's representation to a mere two seats in Parliament after the 1984 elections illustrated just how adroitly the Congress had walked away with the former's clothes. As the Congress Party underlined the identity of nationalist and Hindu religious mobilization, the BJP learnt to its cost that religious mobilization succeeded best when it was combined with nationalism. Thanks to the mobilizations of the 1980s, the intertwining of religion and nationalism, never far from the surface, returned openly as a dominant feature of Indian politics.

The Congress Party could not, even if it wished to, easily undo the kind of sectarian Hindu mobilization which it had sought to effect between 1980 and 1985. At the same time, the assassination of Mrs. Indira Gandhi by her bodyguards highlighted the high costs of the gamesmanship which had been the stuff of the party's politics during the preceding years. Moreover, since 1977, northern Indian Muslims had turned away from it and were beginning to develop an independent political leadership. It was vital to arrest this erosion. Caught between contradictory pulls and pressures, the party's central leadership, now without the tactical acumen of Mrs. Gandhi to guide it, attempted to defuse the Punjab crisis by signing an agreement with a section of the moderate Akali leadership.[94] At the same time, in another display of its readiness to make concessions to the minority religious leadership,

---

[94]But its fear of losing the 'Hindu vote' outside Punjab led the Congress Party to go back on its commitments under the Rajiv-Longowal accord for signing which the latter paid with his life; the accord broke down following the dismissal of the elected Akali government in 1987, ostensibly because of its failure to curb terrorism, to coincide with elections to the assembly in the neighbouring Hindu-dominated state of Haryana.

the Congress Party sought to placate Muslim clerics by passing a constitutional amendment to overturn a Supreme Court ruling upholding the right of divorced Muslim women to claim maintenance from their husbands, a ruling which according to the clerics struck at the root of Muslim personal law. And thirdly, to sustain its efforts at Hindu religious mobilization, Rajiv Gandhi's government threw open for worship the Babri Masjid in Ayodhya, which a section of the town's Hindu religious leadership claimed was built on the ruins of a temple at the precise spot where Ram was supposedly born, and which had been closed to the public since 1949 after some idols were forcibly installed within it.

Notwithstanding these gestures and despite inaugurating its campaign from Ayodhya with the promise of a *Ramrajya*, the Congress Party lost the 1989 elections. The election outcome was far from decisive, but it enabled the return to power of the alliance of intermediate caste and regional elites in the form of the Janata Dal-National Front, with support from the Bharatiya Janata Party which saw its parliamentary representation jump from a mere two seats in 1984 to nearly eighty seats in 1989, and the left parties. Within a year of assuming office, a section of the Janata Dal's intermediate caste leadership managed to use Prime Minister V.P. Singh's vulnerability to challenges from within his party to manoeuvre him to accept the recommendation of the Backward Classes Commission (Mandal Commission) reserving jobs both at the central and state levels for members of the intermediate castes. Protests by upper-caste youth, with the backing of a large section of the print and the newly emerging video-news media, erupted in a big way.[95] As the situation in Punjab and Jammu and Kashmir also seemed to get out of hand, history appeared to repeat itself. Only this time, the BJP, after bringing down V.P. Singh's government, managed to use the issue of a Ram temple at Ayodhya to catapult itself to the leadership of the upper-caste unitarist elite, and mobilize against the renewed challenge of the intermediate castes, and against the so-called 'appeasement of secessionists' by

---

[95]For an excellent account of the attitude of Delhi's English language press to the anti-Mandal agitation, see S. Muralidharan, 'Mandal, Mandir *aur* Masjid: "Hindu" Communalism and the Crisis of the State', in K.N. Panikkar, ed., *Communalism in India*, pp. 196-218.

the Janata Dal government.[96] The Congress Party, despite returning to power as a minority government in the 1991 elections, found to its cost that majoritarianism being a structural feature of India's political system with a pivotal role in its unitary apparatus, cannot as easily be manipulated or suppressed as the earlier genie it had let out, of Sikh religious extremism. More emphatically than the Congress Party, and with greater consequences for the future of the Indian republic, the BJP has succeeded in fusing nationalism with militant Hinduism, and if its invoking the language of the freedom struggle, in particular the Quit India movement, is any indication, looks set to claim the heritage of the unitarist nationalist platform which was so important a part of the Indian anti-colonial movement.

VII

Perhaps the most ominous social and political development in India in recent times is the rapid growth of aggressive Hindu chauvinism. To most appearances, this growth has been rather sudden, even unexpected. The BJP, the principal *political* expression of Hindu chauvinism, won a mere two seats in a house of nearly 550 members in the 1984 parliamentary elections, and it was not in power in any state. In the 1989 elections, however, the party's parliamentary representation shot up to nearly 80 seats, and to over 120 in 1991, by which time it had also come to power in several states of northern India. Although it lost all but one of these states in the mid-term elections held in 1993, the BJP's electoral fortunes have recently shown signs of revival, with the party having formed governments in the key western Indian states of Gujarat and Maharashtra. In the latter, it is a junior partner of the even more aggressive Shiv Sena which became notorious for its open involvement in the attacks on Muslims in Bombay in the early weeks of 1993.

Electoral gains are merely one sign of the rapid growth of aggressive Hindu chauvinism. By far the more ominous portent is

---

[96] See L.K. Advani's interview to the *Sunday Times of India*, 14 October 1990.

the relative success of the BJP, and more generally of the *Sangh parivar*, in defining the agenda and discourse of Indian nationalism and forcing other parts of the country's political spectrum to react to this agenda, and couch their responses in terms of its discourse. The most important reason for the inroads the Bharatiya Janata Party has made, particularly among the educated middle classes, is that it has managed to eliminate the thin distinction between majoritarian nationalism and the liberal, secular nationalism which has so far been part of the staple, modernizing, nation-building discourse of the Indian elite. Both models are alike in stressing the homogenizing effects of modernization, and in seeing it as a desirable outcome of the process. While the temple agitation focused attention on the religious basis of the *Sangh parivar's* homogenization outlook, its emphasis on *civil* issues such as the principle of equality of India's citizens, as individuals, in relation to the state and a common civil law has helped mobilize those sections of the middle classes, who even while being self-consciously 'Hindu' in their religious beliefs, are not easily moved by religious appeals. In this sense, each campaign complemented the other, and together they reinforced the BJP's claim to be *the* party of modern Indian nationalism. Although not all sections of the *Sangh parivar* share the BJP's liberal pretensions and members of the 'family' have mastered the art of speaking in several voices at once, important sections among India's middle classes have been seduced by the BJP's claim to have 'secularized' the religious demand to build a Ram temple at the site of the 16th century mosque. At the same time, to stress the essential 'moderateness' of its programme, the BJP has drawn upon a common assumption, which however is not shared by the more extreme sections of the *Hindutva* fraternity, that India's religious syncretic traditions would never permit the creation of a Hindu theocratic state.

It is an interesting paradox that while the BJP has appropriated the language of secularism from the other political parties, the latter have responded to the success of the BJP's multi-pronged initiative by moving some distance in the direction of its platform and by borrowing some of its nationalist vocabulary. This movement is most pronounced in the case of the ruling Congress Party's studied espousal of a so-called 'soft' *Hindutva*. Secular intellectuals and India's influential communist parties too have begun to proffer and publicize versions of a 'purer' and 'truer' Hinduism closer to popular religion as they understand it.[97] In doing so, however, they seem merely to be occupying the ground which the BJP relinquished less than a decade ago. Moreover, it is moot whether the variety and the open-ended character of popular religion can survive the centralizing political mobilization which in recent years has become an essential part of the ideology of Indian nationalism.

More explicit recognition of the importance of the Hindu identity in contemporary Indian politics is only one reflection of the political bind in which India's left and secular parties and intelligentsia find themselves. The BJP/RSS's seemingly liberal line of argument on civil issues also poses them acute problems, because while being uneasy with group identities, they cannot see their way to overcoming them in the near future. Hence they are undecided whether particular forms of intervention defend legitimate group interests or, by accentuating sectarian identities, help their ideal of a liberal, secular, modern nation-state recede even further into the future. The deepening teleological tunnel has led to a schizoid approach which defends 'divisive' initiatives on short-term 'tactical' grounds of practical politics, but which is not clear about the longer term (or 'strategic') implications of such initiatives for their liberal vision. Secondly, in combating the BJP's mobilization on the issue of civil rights, they are forced to highlight the former's sectarian sub-text; and in doing so, and even when refuting stereotypes about Muslims which most middle-class Hindus hold, *they* are forced unavoidably to 'communalize' a seemingly liberal and 'secular' demand! Their ability thereafter to resist the *Sangh parivar's* overtly religious campaign is gravely hampered. So complete is majoritarian nationalism's liberal disguise for those who do not care to perceive it, that genuinely non-sectarian nationalists seem to have little room for manoeuvre. This poses a serious problem for the latter, one which moreover cannot be resolved purely on the basis of tactical adjustments to their positions

---

[97]S. Yechury, *Psuedo-secularism Exposed: Saffron Brigade's Myths and Reality*, Communist Party of India (Marxist) publication, New Delhi, 1993; also see C.P. Surendran, 'BJP Rule: What Kind of India will it be?', the *Illustrated Weekly of India*, March 1993.

without prejudicing the integrity of their non-sectarian outlook, or the distinctiveness of the latter from that of 'moderately' chauvinistic or hegemonistic elements within the Congress and the *Sangh parivar*. Indeed, the longer-run appeal of *Indian* nationalism for the country's religious, linguistic. and ethnic minorities, and other disadvantaged sections of her population may well come to depend upon the ability of genuinely non-sectarian nationalists in India, who comprise chiefly the left parties, to resolve these dilemmas, rescue the ideology of nationalism from the grip of national and religious chauvinists and strengthen its democratic content.

The Demographics of Religious Fundamentalism

Alaka M. Basu

THE TENDENCY for a numerically or politically dominant group to feel threatened by a real or imagined increase in the numbers of a minority group is well documented in history and in a number of contemporary populations. A little less frequently documented is the tendency for representatives of a dominant group to exploit these fears by calling for increased restraints on or interventions in the lives of a minority, ostensibly to keep its numbers in check but usually also to consolidate its minority or suppressed status independently of its numbers. This tendency is greatly facilitated by the ease with which an entrenched majority can be made to feel threatened by the simplest kind of pseudo-scientific reasoning and backed by the minimum of information.

This paper looks at numbers as the basis of the rising tide of Hindu fundamentalism in India. The focus is on the nature and validity of the demographic argument advanced to justify an anti-minority stance in the Hindu community. The title of the paper is, therefore, perhaps more aptly, albeit more convolutedly, captured by something like 'The Minority Demographics of Hindu Fundamentalism'. That is, the focus is on the demographic behaviour of the minority, by which one usually means the Muslim, community. It is true that rising identity consciousness and fundamentalism may be partly explained by overall rising population densities – Hindu and Muslim – which in turn generate the pressure on resources and the struggle for survival which have characterized several fast-growing populations historically, and have often led to increased attempts to distinguish between 'them' and 'us' as rightful heirs to a shrinking world.

But such a broader 'population growth and political stability' argument is not the focus of the present paper. Instead I look at the population related basis of Hindu-Muslim tensions at two levels. First, there is the perception of the reality. What are some of the expressed fears of the majority about the size, growth and distribution of the Muslim minority in the country? I look at some of the ways in which population based arguments are used to legitimize calls for greater intervention in Muslim life by the Hindu revivalist movement. And, secondly, there is the level of reality. Does the size, growth and distribution of the Muslim population actually threaten the Hindu majority in any objective way? I also get briefly diverted into a discussion of some of the ways in which such 'politicization'[1] of the demographic argument is in turn used by the minority community to resist changes in its make-up which could only be beneficial to itself, a case of cutting off the nose to spite the face. The net result seems to be a marked growth in interreligious strife, and a hardened resolve to maintain demographic and political differences, to the detriment of both sides of the impasse.

What are the components of Muslim demographic behaviour? They are the same as the components of the demographic behaviour of any population group. Such behaviour is defined at its broadest level by the population growth rate. But the growth rate in turn is composed of the net balance between three demographic parameters – births, deaths and net migration. The politicization process is well aware of all these measures of demographic behaviour and refers primarily to two of them in its anti-Muslim message – migration and fertility – as the primary determinants of this population growth. But it is for the large part suspiciously

[1] By the term 'politicization' of fertility, I refer to the use of fertility related arguments by any special interest group to push for interventions which are already a part of its own political agenda and which may or may not actually have an indirect bearing on fertility itself (see Basu, 1995). In the present case, the hypothesis is that the Hindu communal groups are politicizing the issue of Muslim fertility to strengthen their larger political agenda.

disinterested in the fact that births, deaths and migration are in their turn a function of a host of other 'proximate determinants', of which religious identity is but one, and an ambiguous one at that. And when it does acknowledge the wider influences on demographic behaviour, it again restricts itself to purely religion-derived practices and beliefs as if these have no larger context and as if these are definitively related to higher birth and population growth rates.

II. Size and Growth of the Muslim Population

At the time of the 1981 census, Muslims made up 11.4% of the Indian population, up from 11.2% at the time of the 1971 census. Figures for the 1991 census are not available, but indirect sources, such as national surveys, suggest that the situation is still more or less the same. For example, the Operations Research Group's (Operations Research Group, 1990) all-India representative survey of family planning practices conducted in 1989 estimated that 10.6% of couples in India were Muslim. But this figure is admittedly not strictly equivalent to the percentage of the population that is Muslim, which may well be somewhat higher.[2] However the main point is that there is little reason to believe that the rate of growth of the Muslim population has led to drastic changes in their proportions in the country.

When one looks at their distribution, any political case about their 'swamping' the nation becomes even more untenable (independently of the fact that as individual citizens they have as much right to this nation as any other citizens). Muslims constituted a higher proportion than this national average in only five states in the 1981 census – Bihar, Jammu and Kashmir, Kerala, Uttar Pradesh and West Bengal; and if one excludes the outlier (Jammu and Kashmir, which was 64% Muslim in 1981), the national average falls further. But it is true that the Muslim population of the country is more urban than the Hindu population, and if one

---

[2] It may be higher for two reasons. First, given the later age at marriage among Muslims, there may be fewer couples proportionately to the total population. And secondly, given their higher fertility, they have a younger age distribution so that there are more absolute numbers of Muslims per household.

looks at the urban areas alone, Muslims make up a higher proportion than the national average in the states of Madhya Pradesh and Maharashtra as well. And perhaps that is where the demographic problem lies – in their greater visibility in the political hotbeds; that is, the towns and cities (but once again, only in seven states).

But perhaps these figures based on 1971-81 events cannot tell us enough about the present. Perhaps the Muslim growth rate is actually much higher currently, not because fertility has risen, but because in-migration has increased.[3]

III Migration

Illegal migration of Muslims into India has indeed been a major political plank on which Hindu parties have sought to consolidate their own identity. In one sense this is a replay of the sons-of-the-soil movements of the 60s and 70s when the threat was perceived as emanating from migrants from other parts of the country rather than those from outside. It is difficult not to feel that the obsession with illegal foreign migration is a more politically expedient, and 'legitimate', way to whip up similar emotions against the legal Muslim community in the country. After all, just as poor, illiterate, Muslim households cannot be blamed for not being able to prove their legal status very easily, the anti-migration extremists cannot be blamed for not being able to distinguish between Indian and

---

[3] Since this paper was written, the 1991 census report on the religious breakdown of the Indian population has been released (Government of India, 1995). It confirms that during the 1981-91 decade, the Muslim population of the country did grow faster than the Hindu. Since then, there has been a flurry of popular political writing on the subject, with the difference in growth rates being ascribed by different groups to illegal migration from Bangladesh or to the higher fertility of Indian Muslims, depending on the interventions sought. But the tone of these comments is invariably antagonistic. I have not come across any article which notes that a rise in the proportion of the Muslim population from 10.88% in 1981 to 11.67% in 1991 represents an increase in proportion of 0.08% per year which, given the low base level to begin with, does not seriously threaten Hindu supremacy in any way. It is especially non-threatening because it is unlikely to continue – illegal migration is facing increasing vigilance, and religious fertility differences, as discussed in this paper, are narrowing.

foreign Muslims in their drive to evict the latter; such a drive perforce ends up harassing the former. Such a situation certainly seems to have been reached in Maharashtra in recent times.

In any case, do we have any numbers on illegal migration? By its very nature, illegal migration is almost impossible to estimate with any confidence. To illustrate, I take up one possible and common line of reasoning. This is the changing nature of the population in the border districts of the country. But even here, the data to do any kind of robust analysis are just not available. If one looks at West Bengal, for example, it is true that between 1981 and 1991 population growth rates in the districts adjoining Bangladesh have been well above the average growth rate for the state as a whole (see the figures in Bose, 1991). The sex ratios of these border districts have also become distinctly more masculine, in contrast to the rest of the state where the sex ratio has changed in favour of females, consistent with the tendency of poor males to migrate out of their region of origin more readily than females or even entire families.

But then there is the other side of the picture which gives one pause. These same border districts have always had higher than average growth rates.[4] Secondly, they have a number of characteristics which suggest that these higher growth rates are as likely to be an outcome of higher fertility (that is, higher rates of what demographers call natural increase) as of higher in-migration. For example, their literacy rates (and literacy is now universally acknowledged to be a powerful indicator of fertility) are substantially lower than the state average. Thirdly, there is no reason to expect the migrants into these border districts to have remained there; once they have penetrated the borders of the country, there is no real reason for illegal migrants not to move on to better opportunities.[5] People who do not brook borders would surely not brook non-borders.

---

[4] Unless, of course, one wants to argue that this only means that they have always faced higher than average in-migration as well.

[5] Although there is one real reason for them to linger for a while; presumably, the closer the migrant is to his original home, the greater is his access to the relations and friends who help his initial efforts to find a place under the sun.

A more problematic fact is that since we can only infer their numbers from such indirect means, we cannot know much more about their other characteristics. Most importantly, are the illegal migrants predominantly Muslim? The Bangladeshi migrants who entered India during the early 1970s were about 90% Hindu (Weiner, 1993) for a variety of political reasons, not least being that the suppression they faced at the hands of the Pakistani army was even greater than that faced by the Bangladeshi Muslim insurgents. The religious composition of today's Bangladeshi migrants is less certain if only because it is more likely to be driven by economic rather than political factors, except at specific times such as during the backlash in Bangladesh after the Ayodhya events. But there is no reason to suppose that it is Muslim dominated even if it is not overwhelmingly Hindu.

All this is not to suggest that illegal migration into India is not a very real issue. It is instead to point out that there is much political mileage being gained by our ignorance about anything more than the fact that there is such migration, perhaps on a fairly large scale. The vastly different figures used by the same politicians at different times suggest strongly that there is substantial politicization of the issue. For example, before the Maharashtra elections, Bal Thackeray, speaking about the influx into the state, 'reportedly spoke of 43,000 foreign nationals, while the BJP raised a hue and cry first about 3 lakh foreigners, then 1.75 lakh and finally 50,000' (*India Today*, 30 April 1995).

In addition, this is obviously not just a question of illegal migration; there is no evidence at all of any attempt to identify and deport Hindu illegal migrants so far and, as already stated, there must be a fair number of these as well. Secondly, there is much evidence that the drive to identify illegal migrants is focussed so exclusively on Muslims that it seems to be serving primarily to legitimize the terrorization of Muslims from West Bengal and Bihar living in places like Bombay and Delhi. That is, it is one more demographic bogey created to victimize the minority groups, most of whom are naturally as unable to prove their legal status as most of the members of the majority community.

Finally, perhaps there is a need to make an ethical point about the hysteria being whipped up about illegal migration into India by *all* political parties. Given our inhospitable political welcome, and given the limited economic opportunities we can offer, it is surely only those with even less at home who have dared to make the move into India. While they do not for that reason deserve to be willingly absorbed given the current global geopolitical situation, they do certainly deserve more compassion than any of the political parties have been willing to show. And they certainly do not deserve the brutal harassment that they are currently promised (once we have located them and brutally harassed thousands of other defenceless Indians on the way, that is). Not only is the current political rage not the mark of any civilized society, it should be particularly anathema to the Hindu culture that the Indian fundamentalists want to restore.

But perhaps this association of civilization with humane treatment of outsiders is not correct. The anti-immigration plank has historically been the favourite weapon of groups that feel threatened in any way. The United States population debates in the early twentieth century, for example, seemed to spend much of their time discussing ways to prevent the dilution of the superior Anglosaxon and Nordic streams of migrants by overenthusiastic and unstoppable migrants from Southern and Eastern Europe (Hodgson, 1991). The venom being expended by many official and non-official agencies upon a variety of migrants from poor backgrounds – be they illegal migrants from Mexico, 'guest workers' from Turkey or labourers from Algeria – in the contemporary developed world are all perhaps indications that the acquisition of self-confidence and esteem require the presence of a weaker enemy who can be crushed.

IV Fertility

The fear that the Muslims in India are growing intolerably fast is not new. Indeed it seems to be associated with the very processes which began the counting and categorizing of religious communities in the first place. I refer of course to the introduction of the census in colonial India, an instrument of administration, but extremely susceptible to politicization as well. For example, based on the censuses of 1872 to 1902, U.N. Mukherji wrote a series of articles in which he classed the Hindus as a dying race and sought to demonstrate that they would soon disappear from the face of the country (Jones, 1984).

The seventies and early eighties also saw a spate of articles in the academic literature discussing the higher fertility of Muslims than of Hindus in India, speculating on the causes of this fertility differential and often concluding that there was a strong religious element involved. This literature partly arose to address and in turn contributed to the Hindu concern with unacceptably high Muslim growth rates. Some of these studies were Visaria, 1974; Srivastava, 1979; Ghosal, 1981; Pakrasi and Halder, 1981, and using sometimes very simple analyses, but often adding some socioeconomic controls as well, their general conclusion was consistent. However, it must be mentioned that it was not unanimous (for example, it was found to be less relevant in south India; see, for instance, Reddy 1981) and when it actually looked at the mechanisms for high fertility it found that Muslims were perhaps not so much for high fertility as against birth control or at least less able to practice effective birth control (see, for example, Khan, 1978; Khan, 1979; Chatterjee, 1979).

While this literature must have entered the Hindu political consciousness, and perhaps precisely because it soon became an unsavoury political issue, the later eighties and early nineties did not see much research on the influence of religion on fertility. But this silence was extremely unfortunate because it meant that newer methods of analysis could not be applied to the problem and, more importantly, it did not upgrade our information to take into account the rapidly falling religious differentials in fertility in many parts of the country, as I discuss a little later on. This meant that the public view on this question continued to be based on information which was relatively incomplete[6] and which ignored the fact that all communities are partaking of the significant falls in fertility that are now finally underway in India. That is, while it is true that during the period up to the seventies, the high fertility regime of India included significant religious differentials, in the period in which Hindu fertility began to fall decisively, Muslim fertility did not remain static.

---

[6] This is not to imply that information is at all satisfactorily complete today.

Today, the general fertility argument against Muslims in the country includes the following assertions: Muslim fertility in India is significantly higher than Hindu fertility; Muslim fertility is higher than Hindu fertility because of the legal ability of Muslim men to have several wives; Muslim fertility is also higher than Hindu fertility because Islam is against family planning.

All three assertions have been made *ad nauseam* by a number of influential individuals and are now faithfully repeated by many more ordinary individuals to legitimize their own religious prejudices, prejudices which may in fact have been created by this kind of indoctrination. Take, for example, this hysterical and influential outburst by Sadhvi Saraswati in one of her audio cassettes doing the rounds. 'For every five children the Hindus have, the Muslims have fifty. And who feeds these fifty children? Hindus do! After Muslims divorce, then the waqf boards support the children with taxes that we pay ... Within twenty-five years you will be living like a poor minority in this country.'

Fortunately, recent years have seen some large scale data sets which do allow one to reexamine the current status of the religious difference in fertility, although, as already mentioned, there is as yet little micro-level study of the question. But before I look at some of the new data, I briefly discuss the grounds for inferring higher Muslim fertility from information about legally allowed polygyny and the Islamic view on family planning.

Muslim Polygamy and Fertility

The resentment about legal polygyny and its role in higher Muslim fertility in the country is open to a number of challenges, although, given the complicated nature of much of the evidence, these challenges would admittedly often be another form of politicization of the issue. But some of these counterpoints are nevertheless worth laying out, if only to strengthen the hands not so much of a defensive Muslim minority as of the few 'secularists' who seek to reduce the number of sources of potential communal tension.

To begin with, we have hardly any data on the impact of this legal freedom on actual polygyny levels. This is at least partly because until it became a political issue, the question of polygyny

137

in India was a non-issue. The last available large-scale data set, that from the census of 1971, found in fact that polygyny levels were slightly higher among the Hindus (5.8% as compared to 5.7% among the Muslims) and that this gap was larger for more recent marriages (5.06 among the Hindus compared to 4.31 among the Muslims) (Government of India, 1975). This similarity is hardly surprising. Quite apart from the strong cultural similarities between the two religious groups in the country, the Muslim population is not often in a social or economic condition to actually take advantage of its more 'liberal' personal laws.

In any case, the Hindu personal code is not very much more restrictive. For example, bigamy is not a cognizable offence even among the Hindus. The Hindu bigamist is only breaking the law if his first wife (or someone from her immediate family) dares to lodge a formal protest. Besides which, the onus is on her to 'prove beyond reasonable doubt' that her husband has contracted a second marriage by performing the ceremonies required under section 7 of the Hindu Marriage Act of 1955. The Supreme Court held in the now famous Priya Bala vs. Suresh Ghosh case that 'since the first wife could not prove beyond reasonable doubt that Suresh had contracted a second marriage with Sandhya Rani according to customary rites and ceremonies, only on Suresh's admission that Sandhya Rani is his second wife, we cannot hold him guilty of bigamy' (Priya vs. Suresh, 1971. S.C. 1153).

Given the few numbers involved, it therefore cannot be suggested that Muslims have higher fertility because their personal law permits polygyny. But it is still of more than academic interest to address this question – Does polygyny increase fertility? Once again, there are few studies of the issue in India, but the little evidence from surrounding regions suggests that in fact women in polygynous unions have fewer births than women in monogamous marriages (see, for example, Shaikh, Aziz and Chowdhury, 1987, on Bangladesh). The same general conclusion is reached by a much bigger body of research on the subject in Africa (see, among others, Benefo, 1991; Pebley and Mbugua, 1989; Pebley, Mbugua and Goldman, 1988) although it is true that there is also some indication from this literature that polygyny may have no relationship to fertility and sometimes even have a positive relation to fertility.

Among the explanations offered in the literature for the lower fertility of women in polygynous unions is the fact that often the second wife comes in to make up for the barrenness of the first, the relative sexual neglect of some wives over others, and an overall lower frequency of exposure to sex and pregnancy per woman even when the man divides his attentions equally among his various wives. Longer birth intervals among wives in polygynous marriages confirm the possibility of their lower fertility. The demographic literature even suggests that one outcome of modernization and reduced polygyny in previously polygynous societies may well be an increase in fertility (see, for example, Page and Lesthaeghe, 1988; Hern, 1988; Lesthaeghe and Eelens, 1989).

One reason for the popular belief that polygyny must lead to higher fertility and higher population growth rates is the fact that for most of these communal groups the man is the unit of analysis. The argument therefore is that even if the average woman in a polygynous situation has fewer births, each man ends up with a total of several more than the man with only one wife. This logical reasoning is then extended to imply a larger number of total births in a polygynous society. But given the sex ratio of human populations, the female deficient sex ratios of South Asian populations, and the fact that in this region few second wives are previously widowed or separated, every man who has four wives is leaving three men unable to have even one.

Islam and Family Planning

What about the regularly expressed fear that the Hindu majority will be swamped by the faster growth rate of the Muslim minority because Islamic teaching is against birth control? While it is true that average birth rates in the Muslim population of India are currently higher than those among the Hindus, the religious basis of this difference[7] is contradicted by several concrete examples as well as by a more careful review of the Islamic position on birth control.

The two showpieces at the recent United Nations conference on population and development held in Cario – Indonesia and

[7] At least in the past; as I discuss later on, in the future, religion may well become an increasingly important influence on fertility behaviour.

Bangladesh – may be denigrated because they may not represent the best side of fertility control and there already exists a minor demographic industry trying to explain the 'success' of the two countries' family planning programmes in terms which are often unflattering. But the fact remains that both countries have experienced a definite and significant decline in the birth rate and that both countries are overwhelmingly Muslim in their populations, and in one case also unabashedly Muslim in political ideology. Any religious barriers to birth control seem to have been successfully surmounted, whether by political will, structural circumstances, or even reinterpreted religious injunctions.

Even within India, there is hardly any such thing as 'Muslim fertility'. Birth rates among this community are as differentiated as they are among the other religious groups with differentials across socioeconomic or regional groupings often being larger than those between the two religions. The fertility of Muslims in Kerala, for example, is not only appreciably lower than the fertility of Muslims in Uttar Pradesh, it is also noticeably lower than the fertility of Hindus in Uttar Pradesh. In turn this implies that there is not an overwhelming hold of religion on reproductive behaviour in practice.

Nor is there such a hold in principle. Although religious restrictions are sometimes stated by surveyed Muslims as the reason for their lower levels of contraceptive use (for example, Operations Research Group, 1990), these restrictions are more a result of the politicization of the fertility issue by the Muslim leadership in a vein complementary to its politicization by the vocal Hindu communal leadership. A review of the literature on the subject of Islam and family planning in general (that is, not restricted to the Indian subcontinent) finds an active movement reinterpreting the scriptures to identify the elements in favour of birth control. Often, even such a reinterpretation is not necessary; although several conditionalities exist, there is nothing in traditional Islamic religious discourse which directly prohibits contraception (Guend, 1993). Most of the injunctions, especially those related to the rights of the child, and those that endorse the exercise of individual judgement or *ijtihad*, can be, have been and are increasingly being fruitfully interpreted as favourable to birth control (Musallam, 1983;

Guend, 1993; Sachedina, 1990; Dardir and Ahmed, 1981; Omran and Roudi, 1992; Jacobson, 1994; Obermeyer, 1994; Engineer, 1994), almost always with the active consent of at least a substantial proportion of the religious leaders in several parts of the Islamic world.

Indeed, when there is effectively active Islamic opposition to family planning, closer analysis reveals that the roots are usually non-religious and political, although in ways which are different from those current in India – for example, based on opposition to specific methods of birth control (sterilization and abortion in particular), opposition to changes in marital structures and the patrilineal extended family (Guend, 1993), or opposition to what is perceived as Western influence, or fear of an adverse shift in the delicate balance of power in the case of West Asia (Jacobson, 1994) and so on.

Hindu-Muslim Differentials in Fertility

Even if, as the last two sub-sections attempted to demonstrate, one cannot indirectly infer that Muslim birth rates will be higher than Hindu birth rates because Muslims have access to polygyny and/or because Islam is against family planning, there can be important differentials in fertility by religion, for other kinds of reasons, some of them even religion based. It is therefore worthwhile to examine some of the direct evidence on religion and fertility and this sub-section attempts such an analysis. But it must be mentioned that the data to do a really sophisticated analysis do not exist currently in any easily accessible form, and I am therefore dependent on a somewhat convoluted method of understanding interrelationships.

First, birth rates are and have been somewhat higher for Muslims than for Hindus. The mean number of live births borne by the average woman in the national survey conducted by the Operations Research Group in 1988-89 (Operations Research Group, 1990) was estimated at 3.09 for Hindus and 3.51 for Muslims.[8]

---

[8] Incidentally the corresponding figure for women of other religions was, at 2.83, significantly lower than for either of these groups, a finding that received much less emphasis and discussion in the ORG report than did the Hindu-Muslim differentials.

A part of this difference may be mechanical. If the Muslim sample is weighted more towards older women than is the Hindu sample, average Muslim fertility measured will be higher simply because older women have more children than younger women. The ORG report does not provide age distributions of the sample women by religion, so this error cannot be checked; but the fertility measures to be truly comparable should have been standardized by age. However, the report does present fertility tables by age and one does find that Muslim fertility is higher than Hindu fertility in all age groups. However the difference seems to be larger for the older age groups. That is, over time, there seems to be a convergence in fertility rates between the two religious groups.

In any case, what do these fertility differences reflect? Is there really such a thing as 'Muslim Fertility'? When one looks at other data sources (it is unfortunate that no one data set allows one to look at all aspects of the religious differential), one is confronted with a range of fertility rates even within the Muslims, so that if it is religion that explains their reproductive behaviour, then religion must be having very different impacts in different socioeconomic settings. Newly emerging results from the National Family Health Survey conducted during 1991-92 (International Institute for Population Sciences, 1994) strongly suggest that fertility differentials among the Muslims are as marked as among the Hindus, with Muslims in Tamil Nadu, for example, being as different from Muslims in Uttar Pradesh as the Hindus in Tamil Nadu are different from those in Uttar Pradesh.

Moreover, religious differentials also vary greatly from place to place. For example, in Tamil Nadu the Total Fertility Rate (which is an estimate of the number of children a woman will have over her reproductive life if she follows the current child-bearing rates of women of different ages) for Muslims and for Hindus is identical at 2.5, whereas Muslim fertility in Uttar Pradesh is about 10% higher than Hindu fertility.

Why should there be such variations? Because the Muslim community is as socioeconomically diverse as the Hindu community and because socioeconomic factors have a strong bearing on reproductive behaviour. And because reproductive behaviour in turn is an outcome of several things – the ability to bear children, the desire for children, and the ability to control childbearing, all of which are independently influenced by a host of socioeconomic factors, religion being only one of these. I illustrate these caveats by looking in greater detail at the Hindu-Muslim differential in three states in the country – Uttar Pradesh, Tamil Nadu and Maharashtra. I choose these three to represent a range of socio-economic conditions – Uttar Pradesh because it is demographically still somewhat backward, Tamil Nadu because it is well on its way to achieving a demographic transition, and Maharashtra because it is currently seeing an unexpectedly large amount of interreligious hostility which is at least partly justified with demographic reasoning.

Table 1. Statewise Differentials and Trends in Fertility

		All India	Maharashtra	Uttar Pradesh	Tamil Nadu
Total Fertility Rate	Total	3.37	2.86	4.75	2.48
	Urban	2.70	2.54	3.51	2.38
	Rural	3.64	3.12	5.12	2.54
Number of Births to Women Aged 45-49	Total	5.11	4.56	6.12	4.51
	Urban	4.46	4.14	5.48	4.63
	Rural	5.35	4.87	6.27	4.45

Source : Various Volumes of the National Family Health Survey, 1992-93.

Table 1 presents some fertility measures for the three states. The great range of fertility experience is obvious. On closer examination, so is the cross-sectional and secular variation within each state. Rural Uttar Pradesh definitely has the longest to go to achieve a stable population, whereas urban Tamil Nadu is very nearly there. The rest of the possible configurations fall in between. There is also reason for optimism in the story when one looks at the last three rows of Table 1. While the Total Fertility Rate is a measure of *current* fertility, the last row looks at the completed family size of only women aged 40 to 49 years; that is, women who have had their childbearing in the past. For all groups, these family sizes are substantially larger than current fertility rates, suggesting that a fertility decline is definitely under way across the board, although the speed of this decline naturally differs from one situation to another.

Table 2. Religious Differentials and Trends in Fertility

		Maharashtra	Uttar Pradesh	Tamil Nadu
Total Fertility Rate	Hindu	2.69	4.75	2.46
	Muslim	4.11	5.26	2.48
	(M-H)	1.42	0.51	0.02
Number of Births of Women Aged 40-49 years	Hindu	4.12	5.93	4.17
	Muslim	5.20	6.43	5.37
	(M-H)	1.08	0.50	1.20

Source : As in Table 1.

Table 2 looks at Hindu-Muslim differentials in these same fertility indicators – current fertility, as measured by the Total Fertility Rate and past fertility, as measured by the number of children born to women aged 40-49 years at the time of the survey.[9] The actual gap in fertility between the two religious groups is

[9] The 40-49 age group being used here as opposed to the 45-49 year group in Table 1 is due purely to the idiosyncrasies of data availability.

also presented. Several points emerge from these figures. The most important is the finding that there is no such thing as a level of 'Muslim fertility' which operates across the board. Total Fertility Rates for Muslims even in this sample of only three states range from 5.26 in Uttar Pradesh to 2.48 in Tamil Nadu. Secondly, Muslim fertility has been declining in just the same way as overall Indian fertility in all three regions (this decline is represented by the difference between children ever born to older women and the Total Fertility Rate). And most important of all, there is no consistent difference between the fertility levels of Hindus and Muslims in the three areas. Looking at current fertility, for example, Hindu and Muslim Total Fertility Rates are virtually identical in Tamil Nadu, while in Maharashtra there is a difference of about 1.42 births between the two groups. The demographically most backward state, Uttar Pradesh, in fact displays a smaller religious difference in fertility than Maharashtra.

Even more revealing is an examination of trends in religious differentials in fertility The gap between the two groups has narrowed enough to be virtually wiped out in Tamil Nadu over time (once again, I am looking at the level of the fertility difference between children ever born to older women and current fertility). Uttar Pradesh seems to have retained its religious difference in fertility, with Muslims having had in the past and continuing to have today an average of half a birth more than Hindus. But in Maharashtra, the fertility gap between Hindus and Muslims has actually *increased* over time.

What is one to make of all this variation? Is religion really the immutable force that it is made out to be? Table 3 presents one possible confounding factor. There is a large literature now on the impact of education in general and female education in particular on reducing fertility and if this literature is valid, Table 3 suggests that the religious difference in education may explain at least a part of the religious difference in fertility. The relevant educational differences are those for the urban areas, since the bulk of the Muslim population is urban in all three states.[10] In

[10] For the same reason, it would have been nice to look at urban fertility rather than state averages in Table 2, but, once again, the data available do not allow such a disaggregation.

both Maharashtra and Uttar Pradesh, Muslim female illiteracy levels are markedly higher than Hindu, while in Tamil Nadu, the Muslim women do, if anything, better than the Hindu women.

Table 3. Religious Differentials in the Education of
Respondents

| | | Percent of Women Illiterate | | |
		Maharashtra	Uttar Pradesh	Tamil Nadu
Urban	Hindu	28.1	37.4	29.1
	Muslim	43.8	74.7	27.5
	(M-H)	15.7	37.3	– 1.6
Rural	Hindu	62.9	81.3	64.0
	Muslim	62.9	92.2	40.8
	(M-H)	0.0	10.9	–23.2

Source : As in Table 1.

But female education cannot of course explain the whole Hindu-Muslim fertility difference. This is hardly surprising. While female education is a powerful predictor of fertility and rises in female education are strongly associated with falls in fertility, there are, of course, a number of other socioeconomic factors that impinge on fertility. These are well dissected in the demographic literature and it would be fruitless to detail them here because we do not have the data to test their importance in the present case. From all accounts, the Muslim community in India is socioeconomically more depressed than the Hindu community (see, for example, Sharif, 1993; Balachandran, 1995, in this volume), but we do not know if such socioeconomic differentials are sharper in Maharashtra than in Uttar Pradesh and thus explain the lower religious fertility difference in the latter. They could be, if it is true that differentials tend to widen at the early stages of development (which Uttar Pradesh has yet to reach). The only trouble with this hypothesis is that Tamil Nadu, which is less advanced, at least economically, than Maharashtra seems to have smaller socioeconomic differences by religion.[11] All this emphasizes the importance of larger political forces to decrease socioeconomic differences which may get accentuated with certain kinds of development.

But as even very simple binary tables (see, for example Operations Research Group, 1990) suggest, many of the religious differences in fertility do narrow considerably when one takes into account the lower levels of development in the Muslim community. Female education and income are the two variables considered by the Operations Research Group, for example, and in both cases, the gaps are considerably narrowed. At the same time, they are not completely wiped out and much further analysis is needed to decide on how much religion *per se* contributes to this continuing difference. But it is worth noting.

In addition to sociocultural factors being thus important, there is some suggestion that minority status matters – in the one state where Muslims have a majority, Jammu and Kashmir, Muslim fertility at the time of the 1981 census was in fact lower than Hindu fertility (Goyal, 1990). Besides the political stability conferred by not being a minority, the feeling of stability instilled in a less hostile environment may also be important; perhaps this is why the fertility gap by religion is higher in Maharashtra than in Uttar Pradesh even though female illiteracy gaps by religion are lower in Maharashtra than in Uttar Pradesh.

The first two rows of Table 4 are consistent with the state difference in the religious variations in fertility. Contraceptive use differences by religion are similarly most marked in Maharashtra, less so in Uttar Pradesh and much more muted in Tamil Nadu. But can one infer from this that Muslims in Maharashtra *want* much higher fertility than the Hindus, than they do in the other two states? Table 5 speaks otherwise. Row 2 of Table 5 presents what demographers call the unmet need for contraception. This is the proportion of couples who do not want another child (either immediately in the case of the unmet need for spacing, or ever in the case of the unmet need for limiting births) but are still not using any effective contraception to thus defer or stop further births. The religious gap in the total unmet need for contraception

---

[11] And smaller socioeconomic differences in general perhaps. Note for example the much smaller gaps in urban-rural fertility in the state in Table 1.

Table 4. Religious Differentials in Contraceptive Use

		Maharashtra	Uttar Pradesh	Tamil Nadu
Per cent couples currently using Any Method	Hindu	56.6	21.2	50.2
	Muslim	36.1	10.5	45.8
	(H-M)	20.5	10.7	4.4
Any Modern Method	Hindu	55.3	20.0	45.8
	Muslim	35.2	9.5	41.4
	(H-M)	20.1	10.5	4.4
Pills	Hindu	0.9	1.0	0.5
	Muslim	3.6	1.0	0.9
	(H-M)	−2.5	0.0	−0.4
IUD	Hindu	2.4	1.2	3.2
	Muslim	2.3	0.9	8.9
	(H-M)	0.1	0.3	−5.6
Sterilization	Hindu	49.6	14.6	40.8
	Muslim	26.6	4.3	27.7
	(H-M)	23.0	10.3	13.1

Source : As in Table 1.

in Maharashtra is almost as high as the religious gap in the current use of contraception – indeed the latter is almost fully explained by the former. That is, the religious difference in the *demand* for contraception is much smaller than would be suggested by figures on the religious difference in fertility or in actual contraceptive use. The last row of Table 5 confirms the culprit – the much lower proportion of the demand for contraception that is satisfied among the Muslims as compared to the Hindus. In the case of Uttar Pradesh and Tamil Nadu, on the other hand, religious differentials in the unmet need for contraception are much smaller, as are religious differences in the percentage of the demand for contraception that is being currently being met, with the main distinction being that on all these scores, Tamil Nadu does much better than Uttar Pradesh for its total population as well as for its religious sub-groups.

Table 5. Religious Differentials in the Unmet Need for Family Planning

	To Space Births		To Limit Births		Total	
	Hindu	Muslim	Hindu	Muslim	Hindu	Muslim
A. Maharashtra						
1. % couples currently using contraception	2.9	3.2	53.6	32.9	56.6	36.1
2. % couples with unmet need for contraception	6.9	10.8	5.8	13.1	12.7	23.9
3. % total demand for contraception (1+2)	9.8	14.0	59.4	46.0	69.3	60.0
4. % demand satisfied	29.6	22.9	90.2	71.5	81.7	60.2
B. Uttar Pradesh						
1. % couples currently using contraception	2.0	1.6	19.2	8.9	21.6	10.5
2. % couples with unmet need for contraception	17.0	14.8	13.0	16.1	30.0	31.0
3. % total demand for contraception (1+2)	19.0	16.4	32.2	25.1	51.2	41.5
4. % demand satisfied	10.5	9.8	59.6	35.5	41.5	25.4

Table 5 *continued.*

	To Space Births		To Limit Births		Total	
	Hindu	Muslim	Hindu	Muslim	Hindu	Muslim

C. Tamil Nadu

1. % couples currently using contraception	3.0	5.7	47.2	40.1	50.2	45.8
2. % couples with unmet need for contraception	7.6	11.0	6.7	6.6	14.4	17.6
3. % total demand for contraception (1+2)	10.6	16.7	53.9	46.7	64.6	63.4
4. % demand satisfied	**28.3**	**34.1**	**87.6**	**85.9**	**77.7**	**72.2**

Source : As in Table 1.

Note : In Tables 5A, B and C, line 4 is computed by multiplying line 1 by 100 and dividing by line 3.

Why is this gap between the demand for contraception and the actual level of contraceptive use so much worse for the Muslims in Maharashtra (and to some extent those in Uttar Pradesh)? The Indian government is justifiably proud of the paramount role of its family planning programme in being responsible for most of the birth control practice in the country; so it must also accept some responsibility when birth control levels are low and especially when they are lower than the demand figures indicate. As several research studies point out (see, for example, Bongaarts and Bruce, 1995; Bertrand et al., 1995), the unmet need for contraception is fashioned by a number of factors – *information* about contraception, the *accessibility* of contraceptive services, the *quality* of family planning services available, and the *cultural acceptability* of available services.

This is not the place to go into the pluses and minuses of the Indian family planning programme. But a few factors relevant to the present debate may be laid out. Most data sets agree that, at least at a superficial level, there is now some knowledge of contraception and the family planning programme in all sub-groups of the Indian population, urban or rural, Hindu or Muslim, rich or poor, educated or illiterate. In principle, availability of or access to contraceptive services *per se* is also not a major issue. The main problem seems to lie in the quality of services provided and in the range of contraceptive methods available in the field (as opposed to available on paper, where the family planning policy is very conscious of the need to offer what is called a 'cafeteria' of birth control methods).

The Muslim community obviously faces greater obstacles to contraceptive use than the Hindu community if the levels of unmet need in Table 5 are valid. Some of these obstacles are common to those faced by poorer, socioeconomically disadvantaged groups in general – problems related to quality of care (including simple measures such as courtesy, something greatly lacking in the formal health care sector in our country), follow-up services, and a balanced explanation of the advantages as well as possible side-effects of various methods.

But, in addition, being Muslim entails two important, unique hurdles which the government family planning programme does not seem to address sufficiently. The first of these is the question of the greater conservatism of Muslim women. Family planning services focussed on this community therefore need to either concentrate on the men or to provide services to women in the kind of private and male-free atmosphere that the system of purdah demands. As far as providing male contraception is concerned, the programme has fared miserably in all parts of the country; except for a brief period before the Emergency (Basu, 1977), the emphasis has always been and continued to be on female methods of birth control and on women's responsibility for birth control. This, naturally, must change, not only for reasons of egalitarianism, but also because male methods of contraception are much safer than female methods, and because temporary male methods like the condom offer the additional advantage of protection from sexually transmitted diseases.

As for the providers of contraceptive services, Muslim women (as well as women in north India in particular) have demonstrated the need for much greater cultural sensitivity in the location of services and the sex of the provider. For example, one reason why the abortion and family planning services of voluntary agencies such as the Parivar Seva Sanghtha are so much more popular than those provided by the government (even in conservative Muslim areas) is that they are provided in relative discretion and privacy (through the simple device of being located in a busy marketplace, for example, so that the woman seen in the area is not automatically assumed to be seeking birth control), and because their medical and paramedical staff are overwhelmingly female when the clients are female. In comparison, look at the staff position of health workers in rural areas. According to the yearbook of the Ministry of Health and Family Welfare for 1990-91 (Government of India 1992), Uttar Pradesh had 144 posts of obstetricians and gynaecologists (as one indicator of female medical staff) sanctioned for the rural areas, and only 26 of these posts had actually been filled. In Tamil Nadu, the two corresponding figures (posts sanctioned and posts filled) were 30 and 30 (figures for Maharashtra were not available).

But perhaps the most uniquely Muslim problem concerns the choice of contraceptive methods available in the national programme. As already stated, in principle the government is committed to the cafeteria approach. But in practice, sterilization is the overwhelmingly important method available and pushed, which explains at least a large part of the fact that about 70% of acceptors of contraception are acceptors of sterilization. Non-terminal methods of birth control account for a growing but still small proportion of all contraceptive practice in the country. While this emphasis on sterilizations has been criticized in the literature for a number of reasons to do with safety as well as efficiency (among them that the typical sterilization acceptor is older and has more children than the acceptor of modern temporary methods of birth control), an important criticism to include should be the common Islamic opposition to sterilization even in the absence of a general Islamic opposition to family planning[12]. The figures in

---

[12] The recent decline in fertility in Bangladesh, for example, has been achieved with very low levels of sterilization acceptance and an overwhelming reliance on non-terminal methods of birth control.

Table 4 certainly suggest that this is a valid criticism. Even though the official programme is so hung up on sterilization, Muslim women seem to feel much more comfortable with temporary methods like the pill and the IUD and indeed in Maharashtra the use of the pill is significantly higher for Muslims than for Hindus, and in Tamil Nadu, IUD use is higher for Muslims.

This preference for temporary methods does not mean that the Muslim community is interested only in birth spacing and not in limiting the total number of births. As Table 5 shows, the demand for contraception to limit the number of births is not much lower for the Muslims than the Hindus in any of the three states under consideration. The difference seems to be that Muslims prefer to cease further childbearing with more reversible methods of birth control.

But as the argument of this paper states, this may well change as the majority focus on minority fertility results in a greater opposition to birth control *per se* by the leaders of the Muslim community and a consequent decreased demand for family planning services in this community. This situation certainly seems already plausible in Maharashtra.

V Some Implications

Such a communal politicization of fertility has many unwholesome implications for both communities. It is self-fulfilling because it hardens differences and hardens the resolve to maintain these differences. The absence of the Muslim religious leadership's endorsement of family planning in India has already been mentioned. But this digging in of heels extends to much more than family planning. It extends in particular to any attempt from outside, but also from within, the Muslim community to reform the personal code, often by doing something as innocuous as highlighting already existing provisions in Islam which could promote such reform. Nothing exemplifies this more than the Shah Bano case in 1986-87 which inflamed so many religious passions, made strange bedfellows such as the women's groups and the Hindu communal organizations, and drove such a rift between the Muslim identity and the gender identity of Shah Bano and her compatriots.

153

At the same time, it legitimizes the resistance to further change in the Hindu community, change which can hardly be said to be unnecessary. More dangerously, it legitimizes a regression of social progress. For example, a ban on widow remarriage is now openly espoused by various politico-religious publications now floating around about the rights and responsibilities of Hindu women; a progressive feature of Muslim life, one that a secular state has thought fit to incorporate into a mainstream law as well, is now alluded to as an immoral practice. Similarly, some BJP leaders have reportedly pleaded for a return to the good old days of Hindu polygyny. Instead of choosing the best that both systems have to offer, the communal move is towards converting Muslim personal law entirely into a form of existing Hindu law or else seeking to promote among Hindus the most reactionary aspects of Islamic personal life.

The overall conclusion therefore is that demographic perceptions about communities can lead to exactly the kind of political and social instability that demographic events themselves can. At the same time, demographic arguments in favour of communalism are easy to invoke, not because they are true, but because we so know so little about the truth of the matter. Very often, the data and the theory are not available precisely because this is believed to be a sensitive subject; what such research sensitivity may end up doing however is giving free play to the imagination or rhetoric of much uninformed ideology.

References

Balachandran, G. (1995), 'Religion and Nationalism in Modern India', this volume.

Basu, A.M. (1977), 'Family Planning and the Emergency: An Unanticipated Consequence', *Economic and Political Weekly*.

Basu, A.M. (1995), 'The "Politicization" of Fertility to Meet Non-Demographic Objectives', paper presented to the conference on Population and Common Security, Centre for History and Economics, King's College, University of Cambridge.

Benefo, K. (1991), 'The Determinants of the Duration of Breastfeeding in West Africa: A Multi-Level Analysis', Paper presented at the Annual Meeting of the American Sociological Association, Cincinnati, Ohio.

Bertrand, J.T., K. Hardee, R.J. Magnani and M.A. Angle (1995), 'Access, Quality of Care and Medical Barriers in Family Planning Programmes', International family Planning Perspectives.

Bongaarts, J. and J. Bruce (1995), 'The Causes of Unmet Need for Contraception and the Social Content of Services', Studies in Family Planning.

Bose, A. (1991), Demographic Diversity of India, Delhi, B.R. Publishing Corporation.

Chatterjee, P.K. (1979), 'Attitudes to Additional Children; A Study of Motivating Factors', Journal of Family Welfare.

Dardir, A.M. and W. Ahmed (1981), 'Islam and Birth Planning: An Interview with the Grand Mufti of Egypt', Population Sciences.

Engineer, A.A. (1994), 'Status of Muslim Women', Economic and Political Weekly.

Ghosal, A.K. (1981), 'Fertility Differential between Two Major Communities in West Bengal: An Appraisal', Calcutta, Indian Statistical Institute, DRU Publication No. 30.

Government of India (1975), Polygynous Marriages in India; A Survey, Census of India 1971, Series 1, India, Miscellaneous Studies, Monograph Number 4.

Government of India (1992), Annual Yearbook 1990-91, New Delhi, Ministry of Health and Family Welfare.

Government of India (1995), Religion, Census of India 1991, Paper 1 of 1995.

Goyal, R.P. (1990), 'Differential Fertility by Religion in India', Delhi, Institute of Economic Growth, mimeo.

Guend, A. (1993), 'Political Discourse, Religious Discourse and the Fertility Transition in Algeria', Proceedings of the IUSSP International Population Conference, Montreal.

Hern, W.M. (1992), 'Polygyny and Fertility among the Shipibo of the Peruvian Amazon', Population Studies.

Hodgson, D. (1991), 'The Ideological Origins of the Population Association of America', Population and Development Review.

International Institute for Population Studies (1994-1995), National Family Health Survey (various issues), Bombay, IIPS.

Jacobson, J. (1994), Family, Gender and Population Policy: Views from the Middle East, New York, The Population Council.

Jones, K.W. (1984), 'Religious Identity and the Indian Census', in N.G.Barrier (ed), Census in British India: New Perspectives, Delhi, Manohar Publications.

Khan, M.E. (1978), 'Determinants of Muslim Fertility in an Urban Setting', Health and Population: Perspectives and Issues.

Khan, M.E. (1979), Family Planning Among Muslims in India: A Study of Reproductive Behaviour of Muslims in an Urban Setting, New Delhi, Manohar.

Lesthaeghe, R. and F. Eelens (1989), 'The Components of Sub-Saharan Reproductive Regimes and Their Social and Cultural Determinants: The Empirical Evidence, in R. Lesthaeghe (ed), Reproduction and Social Organization in Sub-Saharan Africa, Berkeley, University of California Press.

Musallam, B.F. (1983), Sex and Society in Islam: Birth Control Before the Nineteenth Century, New York, Cambridge University Press.

Obermeyer, C.M. (1994), 'Reproductive Choice in Islam: Gender and State in Tunisia', Studies in Family Planning.

Omran, A.R. and F. Roudi (1993), 'The Middle East Population Puzzle', Population Bulletin.

Operations Research Group (1990), Family Planning Practices in India: Third All India Survey, Baroda, ORG.

Page, H.J. and R. J. Lesthaeghe (1988), 'The Proximate Determinants of Fertility in Tropical Africa', *Fertility Determinants Research Notes*.

Pakrasi, K. and A. Halder (1981), 'Fertility in Contemporary Calcutta: A Biosocial Profile', *Genus*.

Pebley, A.R. and W. Mbugua (1989), 'Polygyny and Fertility in Sub-Saharan Africa', in R.J. Lesthaeghe (ed), *Reproduction and Social Organization in Sub-Saharan Africa*, Berkeley, University of California Press.

Pebley, A.R., W. Mbugua and N. Goldman (1988), 'Polygyny and Fertility in Sub-Saharan Africa', *Fertility Determinants Research Notes*.

Reddy, M.M. (1981), 'Fertility and Family Planning Behaviour Among Muslims: A Study in a Village in Andhra Pradesh', *Health and Population: Perspectives and Issues*.

Sachedina, Z. (1990), 'Islam, Procreation and the Law', *International Family Planning Perspectives*.

Shaikh, K., K.M. Aziz and A.I. Chowdhury (1987), 'Differentials in Fertility Between Polygynous and Monogamous Marriages in Rural Bangladesh', *Journal of Biosocial Science*.

Sharif, A.S. (1993), 'Some Socioeconomic and Demographic Aspects of Population According to Religion in India', Bombay, Centre for the Study of Secularism.

Srivastava, H.C. (1979), 'A Study of Fertility Differentials Among Hindu and Muslim Women in Bhiwandi', in K. Srinivasan, S. Mukherji, R.B. Gupta (eds), *Dynamics of Population and Family Welfare in India*, Bombay, Himalaya Publishing House.

Visaria, P. (1974), 'Religious Differentials in Fertility', in A.Bose, A.Mitra, P.B. Desai and J.N.Sharma (eds), *Population in India's Development*, 1947-2000, Bombay, Vikas Publishing House.

Weiner, M. (1993), 'Rejected Peoples and Unwanted Migrants in South Asia', *Economic and Political Weekly*.

The Spatialization of Violence: Case Study of a 'Communal Riot'

MOST STUDIES of ethnic or communal riots use a framework of causes and consequences, in which the riots are either a result of socio-economic deprivation or are symbolic statements of an ideological nature. Despite the disagreement on the particular causes of violence, processual models of collective violence deployed in these studies are identical. Allen Feldman (1991) describes this schema in the following terms: 'This is a psychogenetic schema that begins in grievance (material or ideational), moves to expression, and culminates in violence in the absence of redress. In turn their common approach advances a given diagnostic agenda; aberrant cause, pathological symptom (violence), potential cure (elimination of cause). These theorists share in common with the popular ideologies they analyse, the narrative model of linear history'.

Although one may cite many contexts in which violence is viewed as an expression of social order or as an instrument for the restoration of order (e.g. the institution of feud in segmentary societies or in the notion of legitimate violence used by the state to protect its citizens), the archetypical case of the riot brings up visions of the complete collapse of social order. The phenomena of crowds as the human collectivity that is the agent or instrument

[1] I am grateful to Arthur Kleinman and Kaushik Basu for their thoughtful comments. The relief efforts in Sultanpuri were supported by the Indian Express Relief Committee and are gratefully acknowlwedged. My gratitude to my colleagues and students who helped in the organization of the relief work goes beyond words.

of riots has fascinated social historians, social psychologists and social anthropologists. At least three different views of the crowd have emerged in the recent literature.

The first view is that crowds act in a rational way to right a moral wrong that they see has occurred in their local moral worlds; they work within a limited repertoire of cultural symbols and can innovate only on the margins of this repertoire. The elegant analyses of the food riots or tax riots in sixteenth and seventeenth century England and France by Thompson (1971) and Tilly (1986) respectively, are the finest examples of this genre of writing.

The second view of crowds sees them as instrumentalities of social action, but insists that we must understand the characteristics of the historical *event* within which crowd action occurs in order to comprehend its modality. This is particularly important when the historical event under consideration transforms the existing structure, initiating a new mode of social action that was not part of that situation. Furet's (1981) critique of the explanatory structures within which popular urban uprisings were understood by historians of the French Revolution makes this point in a telling manner. 'One could also explain the popular urban uprisings of June-July by the economic crisis, the price of bread, unemployment, the commercial treaty between England and France, and so forth; but that type of explanation does not account for the transition from the grain or tax riot – a relatively classic occurrence in towns under the Ancien Regime – to the revolutionary *journee*, governed by an altogether different dynamic' (Furet 1981 : 22). One important consequence that follows from Furet's classic analysis of the historiography of the French Revolution is the need to pay attention to the specificities of a historical or a sociological event before we can understand the meaning of the actions of crowds within that context. A recourse to general theories of crowd behaviour would be extremely misleading as a mode of analysis.

Yet a third view sees crowd behaviour in terms of irrational outbursts which happen when the social order is pried open and there is an absence of authority to regulate social hostilities which come to the surface. The examples of this kind of crowd behaviour are cited from race riots, communal riots and ethnic riots after the work of Le Bon (1952). But recourse to this mode of interpretation is evoked in other contexts also, for instance by Engels (1870) in explaining the Great Terror of 1794. He writes that 'to a large extent the terror was nothing more than useless cruelty, perpetrated by frightened people who were trying to reassure themselves by it' (quoted in Furet 1981 : 128).

One important contribution of the French historians to our understanding of the historical modality of the French Revolution is to point out that there was not one but several revolutions. The interests and ideas of the peasantry and the urban masses as to what the meaning of the different events including the Jacobin terror were, differed greatly. It is only later historiography which bestows a unity on these events. In a similar way I would contend that the behaviour of a crowd cannot be understood in terms of homogeneous categories, for in many cases crowds do not have a common purpose or even a common understanding of the event. Analysis of crowd behaviour in terms of a singularity of purpose and understanding almost bestows them with a common metaphysical essence.

In this paper I hope to show that a riot takes shape in a concrete local context and that there are many heterogeneous categories of social action and meaning attached to it. My analysis is based upon the description of the violence against Sikhs in Delhi following the assassination of Mrs. Indira Gandhi, the then Prime Minister of India, by two of her security guards who were Sikhs.[2] Instead of giving a general description, my strategy is to provide a deep focus on events in a microspace – viz. in a few wards (locally referred to as blocks) in a resettlement colony in Delhi. My analysis shows that the social disorder brought forth by a rioting crowd provides a window on normality since it is anchored upon processes of normality in everyday life in the resettlement colonies.

A voluminous literature has been produced on these riots and I cannot hope to add anything new to the general observations.[3]

---

[2]According to some accounts, their action was to avenge the desecration of the Darbar Sahib, the holy gurudwara in Amritsar, during the military operations conducted by the Army in July 1984 (Operation Blue Star). See, for instance, Kapur (1987) and Das (1995).

[3]See Chakravarty and Haksar (1987), Das (1990), Kishwar (1985), Kothari and Sethi (1985), and Srinivasan (1990). See also the report by PUCL-PUDR (1984), Report of the Citizen's Commission (1985), *Report to the Nation*, Citizens for Democracy (1985).

There are, however, two distinct accounts of the event and the riots that followed through which agency of the crowds was constructed. The first account invested crowds with a quality of madness and implicitly assumed that the destruction for those three days was authored by this madness. This was the predominant view of the officials responsible for the maintenance of public order. They frequently evoked categories such as 'antisocial elements' to explain the violence against the Sikhs, as if it was somehow 'natural' for people classified thus to engage in the most gory acts of killing and looting.

A second account that challenged the first, saw the crowds as the instrument of the machinations of the Congress leaders who used antisocial elements, dacoits, and even the Pradhans of other castes to teach the Sikh community a lesson as a relatiation against their aggression towards the leader of the nation.

Despite the differences in the two accounts – one explaining the action of the crowds as a form of madness and the second explaining it in terms of their manipulation by leaders of the Congress Party – neither of the two was able to ask from where these 'antisocial elements', 'dacoits', 'bloodthirsty mobs', or 'Pradhans' of lower castes emerged? What was the connection between the everyday life of the colonies from which these mobs came and the brutal violence witnessed during the riots? Were they already in alliance with local Congress leaders or was this an opportunity to create these alliances? If the crowds were acting rationally, why did they kill in such a brutal fashion? Does a crowd depend upon previous networks of relationships? Or does it simply emerge as part of the disorder and then disappear into nothingness?

It is to seek at least fragmentary answers to these questions that I turn to a microscopic analysis of events in a resettlement colony. The analysis can offer only tentative generalizations – indeed, it is my contention that the shape of a riot has to be investigated in every local context before we venture into making any strong propositions about collective violence (see also Roy 1995).[4] I

---

[4]This does not mean that collective violence cannot be prevented. Indeed, effective action to prevent a disaster does not have to wait for full information. In the case of the 1984 riots, large scale violence against Sikhs was prevented in West Bengal by strict enforcement of curfew.

hope such a description will add to our understanding of the anchorage between local and national events in the case of collective violence.

The Event in the Official Narrative

On 31 October 1984, Mrs. Indira Gandhi was shot by her security guards and was rushed to the All India Institute of Medical Sciences (hereafter AIIMS).[5] Although rumours of her death started immediately, it was only at 2 p.m. that the Spot News of different newspapers announced her death. Meanwhile a large crowd had gathered outside AIIMS. The first incident of violence started at about 4 p.m. outside the institute. Different accounts have been given of these incidents. Some described the violence as a spontaneous reaction of an enraged crowd. Others present, including the veteran journalist Dev Dutt, stated that they saw a crowd of thirty or forty young men slowly separate themselves from the people and then begin to shout slogans, disrupt traffic, and attack the Sikhs who were gathered outside AIIMS. The death of Mrs. Gandhi was announced by the All India Radio at 6 p.m. At the same time it was announced that Rajiv Gandhi had been sworn as the Prime Minister.

On the following day (1st of November), the newspapers reported that following the death of Mrs. Gandhi, widespread violence had taken place. Large number of scooters, cars and trucks owned or driven by Sikhs were burnt while their occupants were badly beaten up. Shops were burnt in many parts of Delhi including Karol Bagh, Connaught Place, South Extension, Sabzi Mandi and Azad Market. The persons engaged in these acts were described in such terms as 'irate public venting its venom', 'youth wielding lathis, iron rods, and other weapons attacking Sikhs'. It was said that the police had been heavily outnumbered and were powerless to cope with the situation. The police denied any casualties but under mounting criticism of inaction, an indefinite curfew was announced at 6 p.m.

---

[5]The following account is based upon the newspaper reports of four national dailies – *The Times of India*, *Indian Express*, *The Hindustan Times*, and *The Statesman*.

Mrs. Gandhi's body was moved to Teen Murti House, which had been the official residence of Jawaharlal Nehru, her late father and the first Prime Minister of India, where it was laid in state so that mourners could pay their homage to her. The newspapers described lakhs as having gathered there to do so. Meanwhile it was assumed by most people that the acts of violence being witnessed were due to 'mob frenzy'. Rajiv Gandhi's speech on taking over as Prime Minister confirmed this interpretation when he stated that 'the foremost need now is to maintain our balance. We should not let our emotions get the better of us because passions would shroud our judgement'. Several editorials and appeals issued by prominent citizens appealed to people to stop this madness and to rise above communal frenzy.

Headlines on 2nd November announced that Delhi burnt as mobs ruled the streets. It was reported that several trains coming from outside Delhi had been attacked and Sikh passengers had been dragged out and beaten or killed.[6] Rioting was reported from areas in Central Delhi and South Delhi while a passing mention was made of trans-Yamuna colonies. The Prime Minister was reported to have sternly told his officials to check the violence at all costs. As many as 300 persons were said to have been brought to Lohia hospital and 14 were admitted in AIIMS. Crack troops were asked to take position.

Despite the assurances that the violence would be controlled, ghastly murders committed in block 32 of Trilokpuri, a trans-Yamuna area, came to light the next day. The newspapers reported that on 2nd November, a crowd had surrounded block 32 and killed 100 persons by burning them alive. The local police were informed of the carnage, even while it was being perpetrated, by several people in the area and by some journalists but no attempt was made by the police to control the violence. Later investigations showed that two journalists had come to the area when they had received information of violence being committed and had tried to enter block 32, but were turned away by hostile crowds. They had

---

[6]I cannot examine the role of rumours in this paper but it is worth noting that the images of trains from Punjab coming with bodies of dead Hindus evoked all the horrendous stories of the riots in Punjab during the partition of India and for a while managed to confuse the distinctions between aggressors and victims.

personally reported their fears that gruesome violence was taking place in the block to one senior police official with an urgent request to take action but he had clearly not taken any steps to prevent or control it. Later (on 5th November) one of these journalists, Rahul Kuldip Bedi, filed a criminal complaint against these officials for dereliction of duty. On the public outrage following these events, lower police officials – viz. Inspector Surbir Singh and Duty Officer Justi Ram of Kalyanpuri Police Station were arrested. Although army jeeps went around the colony on that very day, they did not have information about the precise locations in which the worst violence was taking place. The description of the crowds in the newspapers continued to deploy the same language, casting them as 'street urchins', 'antisocial elements', 'thugs' and 'lumpen elements'. Alternately they were described as 'irate mobs' or 'blood thirsty mobs of youth who came in waves'. While the carnage at Trilokpuri finally brought home the extent of the brutality and the terror, it is clear that many peripheral areas in which violence was taking place remained hidden from view. Mangolpuri, a colony adjoining Sultanpuri, was mentioned in the newspapers for the first time on 4th November. I believe a report prepared by four university professors (including myself) published in the *Indian Express* on 11 November gave the first indication that violence had continued in peripheral places, like Sultanpuri, till the third and that there was a strong element of organization and of involvement of prominent Congress politicians in the riots. Subsequently enquiries by journalists and civil rights activists provided decisive information on these issues.

Mrs. Gandhi's body was cremated on the 4th of November. On the same day the Police Commissioner of Delhi, Mr. Tandon, made the statement that only 40 deaths had occurred in Delhi but admitted that the situation in peripheral areas was bad. The same day four truckloads of corpses were recovered in block 32. The Lt. Governor of Delhi, Mr. Gavai, who had refused to admit the seriousness of the situation, was sacked and the then Home Secretary, Mr. Wali, took over as Lt. Governor.

On 5th November, Mr. Wali gave a press conference in which he stated that 450 deaths had occurred and 20,000 people had been given shelter in relief camps. He said that five relief camps had been established and that with the arrest of 1809 antisocial elements the situation was expected to fast return to normal. He gave a clean chit to the Delhi Police saying that they had done their job excellently to curb the violence. He attributed the violence to antisocial elements and ruled out the possibility that any residents of the riot-torn areas had been involved.

Relief efforts had meanwhile started primarily with the help of voluntary organizations. Many Sikhs had taken shelter in gurudwaras. On 4th November relief camps were set up in an *ad hoc* manner by concerned citizens and organizations in public buildings like schools and colleges. These were run primarily by voluntary effort. Several prominent citizens of Delhi, including ex-bureaucrats and servicemen, retired judges, teachers, and some politicians were putting pressure on the home ministry to bring out the army – though they uniformly reported lack of serious response. Meanwhile the number of people given shelter in these camps rose to 50,000. There were 28 relief centres which were set up by 5th November and conditions were understandably chaotic. Only on this day did the administration recognize 10 of these camps and from the 6th, bureaucrats of the rank of joint secretary were put in charge of the camps. The lack of interest on the part of the administration to provide relief to the affected population was commented upon by the Citizen's Commission set up by prominent citizens of Delhi in January to enquire into the riots. Its report contained a stricture: 'In the event, it was left almost entirely to non-official agencies to provide cooked food, medical relief, clothing, shelter and most importantly, psychological reassurance to the ever increasing number of victims.'

It would be clear from this description that the initial understanding of the violence as it appeared in media reports, constructed agency of the crowds in a particular manner, depicting them as irate, mad, bloodthirsty, and composed primarily of antisocial elements. This shows the power of the model which depicts crowds in terms of madness and its metaphors. Initially it was assumed that crazed by grief, people had lost control but this description was soon replaced by the notion that it was street urchins, thugs, and antisocial elements who had gone about looting property and killing people. It was assumed that the police force was outnumbered, explaining their inability to restore order. I shall treat this particular account as the official narrative of the riot. As the description culled from the newspapers makes it clear, representatives of all major political parties as well as concerned officials reiterated its essential elements which constructed agency in terms of madness. Settling for this particular representation of the crowds would have exonerated the authorities from fixing responsibility since madness is said to be its own explanation.

It was only when detailed investigations began by voluntary organizations that a different story began to emerge which challenged this view of the violence.

The Second Narrative

In direct contrast to the account given above, a second story emerged through the investigative labours of voluntary groups which proposed an explanation of the violence entirely in terms of the rational deployment of crowds in a conspiracy by the state to eliminate the Sikhs. The strongest formulation of this was found in a report by Citizens for Democracy (Rao, Ghosh and Pancholi: 1985). The authors of this report stated: 'We have shown in this report that several meetings were held all over Delhi – Central, Outer, and trans-Yamuna areas in the late hours of 31 October to give final touches, as it were, to the plan already prepared with meticulous care, with an eye to every minute detail that nothing was left out to successfully exterminate the Sikhs' (p.x). As evidence, they presented the following facts.

After interviewing hundreds of victims they had found that 'not a single Sikh was killed on 31st October'. Second, there was a claim that on the 31st night, meetings of Congress functionaries were held in different parts of Delhi in which every act was planned in meticulous detail. The authors inferred that this is when it was decided that attacks on the Sikhs would be launched simultaneously between 9 a.m. and 11 a.m. on 1st morning everywhere. The attack, they state, was in four phases. These were: Gurudwaras were first attacked. Then Sikh houses were looted and set ablaze. Next men were humiliated by cutting off their hair and shaving off their beard and then killed. Finally

165

women were molested and raped and some were killed. The purpose of this was to win the elections by getting sympathy votes from the Hindus.

Other reports were more measured in their claims, but all of them found evidence of some previous organization and the involvement of local leaders of several lower castes and some Congress (I) leaders. The police were invariably found to be partisan or passive.

The Local Context

First let me describe the context in which the data presented here was collected. From the second week of November 1984 to July 1985, I was engaged in the task of rehabilitation of riot victims in Sultanpuri, a resettlement colony in West Delhi. In order to describe the initial encounter with the survivors, I would like to loop back to what I wrote soon after the event.

'We went into the block (i.e. A/4) for the first time after four days of riots. We had met some of the women of this block in the crowded conditions of the relief camp where we learnt that many of the women were still within the colony. On our first visit we were taken around, primarily by a self-styled social worker who was assigned by the rioters to keep them informed about events in the colony. We had been able to shake this man off on some pretext or the other and had then been taken around by Vakil Singh who had lost two sons in the carnage. We saw blood splattered on the walls, bullet holes, heaps of ashes in which one could still find bits of hair or skull and bone. But what we encountered in the women was mainly fear. Their men had been killed before their eyes. Their children had been spared but they had been warned of dire consequences if they spoke about the murders. A sullen resistance was beginning to take shape in the women. They felt surrounded by the murderers, who had established a "camp" in the colony and were ostensibly doing "relief work" to impress the press and the social organizations that had come to discover the carnage' (Das 1990 : 363).

In such a context the task of rehabilitation depended upon the degree of correct information about who were the affected people and what were their immediate and long term needs. In order to collect reliable information on the needs of the victims so that relief would not be siphoned off to the unaffected populations and to identify cases requiring emergency attention, it became necessary for my students and me to conduct a survey of the affected population in the area. Our team surveyed affected households in 13 blocks consisting of 523 households. Other affected blocks (including C/3 and C/4) were helped by several other voluntary organizations who were working in the area. The blocks surveyed by us were – A/2; A/3; A/4; B/2; B/3; B/5; D/2; D/4; D/6; E/3; F/3; F/4; F/7. Each block was spread over several adjoining streets. Since only the Sikh households could be surveyed,[7] I do not have information about the total number of households in these blocks, but the largest concentrations of Sikhs of different castes were in blocks A/4, B/2, D/2, D/6, F/2 and F/4. There were several jhuggis in F/7 in which Sikhs resided. However, the point to remember is that the Sikhs were not a homogeneous group – they differed by caste, sectarian allegiance, place of origin, and these differences could be mapped on the spatial organization of the resettlement colony. The first survey of these households was conducted between 18th and 28th of November. A second survey became necessary in January 1985 to assess the nature and amount of relief that had reached the victims and to identify individual cases which may have not received any help at all. Subsequently some smaller surveys were conducted to assess very specific needs.

It must be remembered that the surveys were conducted not for any disinterested social science enquiry but because we were engaged in the urgent task of collecting information which we hoped would help to identify the guilty and which would help us organize the relief work in a systematic way. Till late in the night of 3rd November, the Lt. Governor of Delhi had categorically stated to teams of volunteers that there were not more than four widows as a result of riots in the city of Delhi. The army was called out

---

[7]This was both because we urgently needed information on Sikh households and because there was both hostility to and fear of voluntary groups collecting data on the carnage. Our movements were restricted to certain parts of the colony in order to minimize danger to the students who formed a major part of the survey teams.

in the city on the 2nd of November but was not visible in the affected colonies till the evening of the 4th whereas complete devastation and destruction had stalked the streets of resettlement colonies in the west and east of Delhi.

So it was that when we were conducting our first survey there was very little material help and we could not assure the victims that apart from the daily struggle of providing them food and making sure that they would not be attacked again, we could promise anything. Ultimately, these surveys helped enormously in distributing relief gathered with the help of voluntary organizations (especially the Indian Express Relief Committee) and for identification of widows or other heirs of the dead who were finally granted compensation of Rs. 10,000 for each dead person by the central government. All this is by way of explaining that while I have written on the survivor experience, I had not been able to look at the surveys from any other point of view. Now, ten years later, it seems that the dry record of who was killed in each family, at what time did the killers come, what was the mode of killing, who were the people in the crowd, who were the other relatives of the survivors who could be contacted, what goods were looted by the rioters – all these lend themselves to an analysis of the violence in terms of an ethnography of surfaces that I shall later propose.

A Sketch of the Affected Wards

As stated earlier there was sporadic violence in the streets on 31st October but from all available evidence this was anonymous violence. In Sultanpuri one family was killed on that night (the importance of this event will appear later) but the maximum number of people killed in an organized manner was on the 1st and 2nd November with some sporadic killing on 3rd November. In one of the blocks, which was a cluster of jhuggis, there was mass killing on the 3rd evening.

The following would give an idea of the nature of the community inhabiting each of these blocks and the kind of violence that they were subjected to.

Block A/2: There were five households of Siglikar Sikhs on the edge of one street and one mud structure on the corner. The people described their work as that of pheri, that is, supply of small iron and metal clippings for construction work and repairing iron tools. They were migrants from Alwar and nearby villages but did not have other relatives staying in Delhi. Three men were killed and some household goods were looted. One person who was reported lost was found later. The rest of this ward was inhabited by members of a scheduled caste. Sometimes they were referred to as 'Chamars' from U.P. and at other times as 'Bhangis'.* Some of them told me that they had migrated from Baraut and Baghpat near Meerut.

Block A/3: There were only three households of Siglikar Sikhs. The houses were mud structures with asbestos roofs. No killing or looting was reported from these households. The block had a mixed membership consisting of some Muslim familes, some low caste families and some migrants from Nepal.

Block A/4: There were 190 households which we could survey, of which 125 were of Siglikar Sikhs from Ajmer and neighbouring villages. Twenty more households were of Sikhs from other parts who resided as tenants in the houses of the Siglikar Sikhs. Each house was on a 25 sq. yd. plot. The Siglikar households were on two adjoining streets in A/4. The total number of houses was 350, and in addition there were plots marked up to 500. Our work was confined to the two streets in which the Siglikar Sikhs lived. The houses of the Siglikars were pucca structures with a second floor that had been added. All the Siglikar families in this block constituted a single kinship network with the structure of a bilateral kindred. There were other relatives of these families living in blocks D/2 and D/6, and in some cases in Mangolpuri and Trilokpuri. Of all the surveyed households the highest concentration of households with men working in countries in West Asia was from A/4. There were 42 men who had been or were currently in one of these countries. The highest number of killings were recorded from A/4. Here, 77 men and 2 women were killed by being either burnt alive, or beaten and burnt and in one case shot. Everything was looted and most households reported loss of gold and silver ranging from 2 tolas to 10 tolas, large amounts of cash, imported clothes, watches and electronic goods. The houses were all burnt, windows and doors were systematically broken.

* Specific caste terms were used in the locality and these have been followed for the purpose of this study. Similarly the caste hierarchy is given as it applied there.

B/2, B/3: We surveyed only 40 houses in this block since it seemed completely unaffected. The inhabitants were a caste of bangle makers and bangle sellers. The houses were mud structures with very little signs of affluence. The killers did not come into this block – not a single death was reported.

D/2, D/6: The members residing in the streets of D block were part of the kinship network of the Siglikar Sikhs in block A/4. This block also showed affluence in the form of *pucca* houses, double storeyed structures and household *karkhanas* (workshops). One death was reported of a person who ran a *jhatka* meat shop in the area. There were no reports of arson and looting from this block although some residents tried to register cases of looting when the relief process started.

E/3: This block had scattered Sikh households from the Lohar caste who were migrants from Lahore and came to Delhi in 1947. There were three households of auto-rickshaw drivers. No deaths were reported from this block. On the edge of an adjoining street, there was a single household of a granthi, who was caught from the nearby fields and burnt. His wife was from Mathura and they had no kinship connections in the colony at all.

F/2, F/4: These were two adjoining streets which again showed a certain cohesiveness since the households were all from the Lohar castes migrated from Lahore. Only five households reported male members to be working as masons in the Gulf. Our records showed a total of 120 households in these two blocks with some low caste Hindu families living as tenants in F/2. In all 12 deaths were reported from these two blocks but unlike the A/4 block, the streets and houses did not have the same visible signs of arson and destruction.

F/7: The Sikhs living here were living in *jhuggis*. Unlike the blocks in which houses had *pucca* structures, here the men worked as daily labourers in construction work and the women were employed as part-time workers in the households of various adjoining colonies. Some of the *jhuggis* had eunuchs who lived with either a single male, or shared the household with his family. There were four deaths reported from Sikh households in the *jhuggis*. The caste background could not be ascertained in these cases. Two persons who were killed were auto-rickshaw drivers

VEENA DAS

and had been caught in the morning of November 2 when they had gone to defecate in the fields. Their scooters had been burnt. Two others had been dragged out from the *jhuggis* in which they were hiding and burnt. No looting was reported from here but then there was nothing to loot in the *jhuggis*.

P/1: Although our initial survey did not include the P/1 *jhuggis* which were on the other end of the colony from A/4, subsequently we did work among the survivors here. In the absence of the survey, exact numbers of death could not be ascertained but at least 20 households reported death of the male members on the 3rd of November. The P/1 *jhuggis* were of a mixed composition. The area had more than 200 *jhuggis* and included a larger number of Muslims than any other block. Perhaps the Muslim households would have numbered somewhere near 40 or 50. The inhabitants of the *jhuggi jhopdi* colony in Mangolpuri along the sewage canal which divided the two colonies were subjected to similar violence. According to the PUCL-PUDR report (see Footnote No. 2) the deaths occurred on 1st November here and the bodies were dumped in the sewage canal. Later the canal was dredged during a departmental inquiry initiated by the Police Commissioner, Mr. Ved Marwah who had replaced the earlier Commissioner, Mr. Tandon. The information on how many bodies were recovered was not made public. The following table summarizes the information given above.

Table 1

Block	Sikh Households	Persons Killed
A/2	5	3
A/3	3	0
A/4	145	79
B(1, 3)	40	0
D(2, 6)	180	0
E/3	30	1
F(2, 4)	120	12
F/7	uncounted	4
P/1	uncounted	20
Total	at least 523	119

171

Localized Narratives

It would be evident from the brief description of the blocks and the differentiated picture of the violence, that the general theories of riots and crowd behaviour would be unable to account for this differentiated picture. If crowds are like rational agents and are acting here to right a moral wrong, then how did the Siglikar households in A/4 become the primary target of their attack? Suppose it were true for the moment that Hindu groups reacted with anger and acted to 'punish' the Sikhs who were held to be collectively responsible for the assassination of Mrs. Gandhi, then how did they differentiate between the bangle maker caste of B block and the particular kinship network of the Siglikars that resided in A/4? Conversely, if the riots were simply an expression of a blind rage in which all normal taboos had been suspended, how did the crowds act to differentiate the persons against whom violence was unleashed? If it is sufficient to explain the riots as 'state sponsored' or a result of a well planned Congress conspiracy, as many activist groups and scholars argued, then how do we account for the particularity of the choices that seem to have been made? Or were the blocks attacked and the people killed chosen completely randomly? Finally if we look towards institutionalized ideologies, such as communalism, we find that local political action cannot be derived from this ideology as one derives practice from theory. Instead, institutionalized ideology and local political action seem to form two discontinuous significative systems. The question is whether placing the body rather than a reified consciousness of the political subject would help locate the discontinuities between these two systems and provide points of articulation between them.

As I seek to fill out the narrative further, there are four propositions I take from Feldman (1991), which will sometimes form the frame within which the description will move and sometimes the theoretical content that itself needs revision in the face of these descriptions. It is as if the frame which held the depiction of a scene might itself be changed through pressure from those inside the frame. The perpetrators and the victims of this violence are therefore not only objects of analysis – they also reveal

172

the potency to change the framing thoughts of those who seek to understand collective violence in a society.

The four propositions that I take from Feldman (1991) are the following:

a) collective violence is not an expression of structural features such as class conflict but is rather to be found in the fractions of 'working class' locked in conflict with each other, and with the state;

b) no sphere of social practice can totalize society – violence presents society as an entity to be 'made';

c) political agency is the product of multiple subject positions – it is not given but achieved on the basis of practices that alter the subject;

d) the very act of violence invests the body with agency – not only the body of the perpetrator of violence but also that of the victim and the survivor. The body, altered by violence, re-enacts other bodies and other political discourses.

The Riots in Sultanpuri

Although news of Mrs. Gandhi's death and the sporadic violence in central and south Delhi became known in Sultanpuri immediately due to television sets and information carried by those who work in that part of the city, the Sikh families in Sultanpuri did not fear any reprisal for the assassination. As several of them told me, what did we have to do with the assassination? But there was one local event that worried some.

Some days previous to this event, a fight had broken out between the Pradhan of the Siglikars in the A/4 community and the Pradhan of the Chamar community in the A/2 block. These two persons had often been in quarrels. Each had ambitions to displace the other as the major local link connecting political activities in the locality to that of a powerful leader of the Congress Party there. Let us call this leader X. There were different kinds of advantages to be had from this patronage. First, the legal status of the plots allotted to people in this locality was never clear.

They had been *jhuggi* dwellers who had occupied land near the embankment of the river Yamuna till 1977 when the beautification drive of Sanjay Gandhi during the Emergency led to their forcible relocation in this area. As many of them told us, their *jhuggis* were destroyed by the demolition squads and they were bodily shifted to this place which was nothing but open ground then. 'We had nothing but the sky above our heads. We were given Rs. 50 each and were told that these plots of land had been allotted to us. Nearby were the villagers whose common lands had been forcibly acquired and they were hostile. It was by sheer hard work that we built *pucca* houses here.' X, who had arisen due to the patronage of Sanjay Gandhi during the Emergency, was seen by them as a patron and they believed that it was on his mercy that their entitlement to the plots of land depended. Although they said that they had been given legal documents proving allotment, they were not able to produce these. In the case of the households in A/4, the arson and looting did not leave anything in the house intact, but even in other blocks, legal documents were not available with the poeple. I suspect that a lot of encroachment had taken place.

Over the past seven years this community had become affluent partly because of the spurt in the construction industry in Delhi and partly because opportunities had opened up for semi-skilled labour in West Asia. The patronage of X was important, though, for them to get employment contracts, visas, etc. for migration to the region for which they apparently had to pay substantial sums of money. The results of this affluence gained in the Gulf were visible in the form of consumption items for 'display'. The women had clothes imported from these countries. Every house had a television; some had tape recorders and many kept gold and silver, smuggled from these countries in substantial amounts. The community had also gathered in strength by inviting relatives from Alwar and adjoining villages to Delhi – getting them jobs, occupying land and making unauthorized constructions. In contrast to the visible affluence of the residents of these two streets in A/4, the street where the Chamars lived had only some mud walls to mark boundaries of the individual plots and almost no consumption items displayed in the manner of the Siglikar houses. Various kinds of conflicts had surfaced between the inhabitants of these two streets in the last two years in which the Pradhans of the two communities played an important role.

When I asked people what the employment of the Pradhan of the A/2 block was, they said, '*Vaise to uski Corporation mein naukri hai par vo goonde palta hai*', which would roughly mean that though he had a job in the Municipal Corporation his main job was to keep hoodlums and secure their services. People said that his power came from the fact that he could provide the manpower for any activity – for a murder, for theft, for breaking strikes, intimidating people. He was an important source for keeping the colony in control for the Congress leader and for collecting crowds for political demonstrations or rallies. Although his control over violence was acknowledged by all, he was not by any means the most influential person in the locality. He was in turn controlled by certain Jat leaders who were from the nearby village, by two Muslim big men, and by a Bania trader in the locality. In turn this network was linked to X, who was the major user of their services. The SHO of the local *thana* also owed allegiance to X.

In the last two years fights had erupted because the community of Siglikars had occupied some land in the park on the entrance of A/2 and A/4 and built a gurudwara there. The Pradhan of A/2 felt this to be a direct challenge to his power since control over all persons in that locality and command over common resources were markers of the power of X and his lieutenant and the A/2 Pradhan's own power was derived from his connections with them. One important way that power of a local big man was articulated here was in the control that he exercised over the common spaces and resources – parks, streets, water pumps – to which others were assumed to have access due to his patronage. This power may be translated into money but that was not necessarily so. For the Pradhan it was sufficient that people acknowledged his 'territory'. This was what the affluent A/4 residents seemed to be challenging. Other squabbles had broken out, the Siglikars said, because their affluence was offensive to the Chamars (*hum se jalte the*). Finally some women among the Siglikars flaunted their higher caste status by taunting the Chamar women that they had traditionally survived by eating the leftovers of others.

All these factors came to be articulated in the 'speech' of the perpetrators as the following incident will show.

When we went into this locality first on 5th November, we were sitting in a *dhaba* and having tea when a group of young men strutted in aggressively. They were in fits of laughter recalling the three previous days of the carnivalesque violence. Snatches of conversation that I overheard were: 'So I said, what happened to your swagger – do you feel light in the head?' Later we learnt that they were referring to the fact that men who were spared had to agree to have their hair shorn publicly to the accompanying jeers of a crowd. 'And how the women had to grovel (lit. *gidgidana pada*) – where was all that arrogance (lit. *ainth*) of foreign made clothes?' Later we shall see how the commodities that seemed to have defined the bodies of the Siglikar women and were the cause of pride for their men, 'spoke' through other bodies. This and other such evidence we gathered pointed to the regular sources of tension between the two streets. But as many families in this and other blocks told us, these were tensions and occasional fights, which had led to the maximum pitch of *pathrav* – fighting by pelting stones on each other. While decisive violence to curb individual defiance had been exercised earlier, such brutal violence had not been seen at the collective level before.

On 31 October, fights began to erupt between the Siglikars of A/4 and the Chamars of A/2 blocks. There was some stone throwing and exchange of abuses. According to many residents, both Sikhs and others, the situation would not have deteriorated so much if the two Pradhans had not been completely drunk. The rumours that some Sikhs had celebrated the assassination of Mrs. Gandhi had filtered in. The A/2 Pradhan had begun shouting that the Sikhs must apologize and the Pradhan from A/4 had laughed and taunted him that he was a person of no worth (lit. *do kauri ka admi* – a penny worth person). Some elders had tried to restrain the Pradhan from exchanging insults and abuses with the A/2 residents. But he told them that they had no reason to fear. Instead of restraining himself, he had begun to taunt the other group with such remarks as '*Arre tum logon ke hath mein kabhi bandook ayee hai – pakadna bhi ata hai bandook ko*' i.e.

176

has a gun ever reached you people – would you even know how to hold one?). This was in response to jeers from the other side that the guards of Mrs. Gandhi had been cowards – killing a defenceless woman. It appears that there was a lull in the fights in the evening. But the entire locality – including the other blocks – was now alive with rumours that Sikhs were being killed in the city. Some people wanted to negotiate but the Pradhan was adamant that no one had the guts to touch them. According to many people, they heard later that there were negotiations and plans between the Pradhan of the Chamar colony, two local Muslims, the ration shop owner, and X. According to them, X's car was seen that night in the vicinity several times. On 31st night when people were in their homes, a crowd came at about 10 p.m., led by the Pradhan of A/2. They were accompanied by the local SHO and some police constables. People in the A/4 block said it was not a large crowd – probably only 30 to 40 persons – most of them neighbours whom they recognized, some Jats from nearby villages such as Sultanpur and Pooth, and some persons whom they had earlier seen but could not identify. They were firm that although they had told several journalists (*akhbar wale*) that they were attacked by outsiders, this was only because they were too scared to name their neighbours.

The crowd came and stood outside the house of the A/4 Pradhan and challenged him to come out.[8] The Pradhan owned a revolver (the term used was *bandook*) and came out with it. He was ordered by the SHO to go and leave the revolver in the house. Some others hearing the noise gathered near. All the Siglikars were told that they should go into their houses – otherwise they would be hauled off to the police station. Frightened and somewhat confused, they went back in.

When the Pradhan came out without his gun, accompanied by his two sons, the crowd started hurling abuses at him. I am not

---

[8] This description is based primarily on the accounts given by the survivors in A/4 but many others in the adjoining blocks who were at a distance from the events gave similar accounts. There were others, such as the supporters of the Pradhan from A/2 or simply those who feared they might be named as the culprits, who denied these accounts completely.

very clear as to what was said at this time but it seems the abuses and insults were a mixture of fragments from different kinds of discourses. There was the continuing anger at the Siglikars having made good and the admonishment that now they could pay the price for having been so arrogant about their wealth. But other abuses were also hurled. One frequent challenge (*lalkar*) was '*khun ka badla khun*' and '*tumne hamari ma ko mara hai*' – blood must be avenged with blood and you have killed our mother. These slogans had been occasionally shouted by the crowds that had gathered outside the hospital and were to gain in intensity for the next few days till the funeral. It appears that at the moment of violence, a certain 'nationalist' discourse, picked up from the images on television, began to speak through the body. The Pradhan was badly beaten, the crowd asking him repeatedly to seek forgiveness, to apologize. Apologize for what, he had asked repeatedly. For having abrogated privileges beyond the status of the Siglikars, for having killed 'our mother'. The more he tried to fight, the more he was beaten with *lathis*. His sons tried to come to his help and were beaten. Finally the leaders assisted by the constables poured kerosene over his beaten and bruised body and set fire to him. The same fate was handed to his two sons. His wife who was inside hiding could not contain herself when she heard her sons calling out to her. She was threatened but she insisted on coming to her sons and was similarly killed. All the while the bodies were burning, and the dying persons were calling out for water, the SHO was shouting that if anyone dared to come out and interfered with the law (*kanoon ke khilaf kisi ne hath uthaya*) he would be shot dead. The crowd dispersed – no one could tell us when – but the SHO announced that all the Siglikars were to stay within their houses if life was dear to them. People said, at first, they were stunned. Was this a legal operation? The SHO had evoked the authority of the law. Suppose the crowd came back the next day? Should they try to escape in the cover of darkness? But escape where? When some people tried to sneak out to the neighbouring houses to consult (and here we have to remember that many of the neighbours were close kin), they discovered that a watch was being kept from the terraces of two houses and they were warned that if they did not return immediately, they would be shot dead. From the voices and from their personal knowledge of past histories, they all identified the two voices as one belonging to a local Muslim and one to a Jat from the Pooth village. Nevertheless some persons did try to sneak out. From the records I have, there is definitive evidence that early morning at about 4 a.m., three young men sneaked out dressed as women. They were initially reported missing but found their way back in a fortnight's time. They told me that they had hidden in some relatives' houses in D/2 and D/6 blocks.

The crowd returned at 7 a.m. the next morning and then started a carnage of pulling men out from the houses, dousing them with kerosene – which was being continuously supplied from the ration shop – and burning them. Most of the 76 men who died in this block, died of lathi blows, followed by dousing with kerosene and being burnt alive. One man was thrown down from the first floor. The men who escaped were the tenants in this block, although their houses were also looted. The crowd went around setting fire to every house, breaking doors and windows, looting and carrying away cash, gold, silver, electronic equipment, stainless steel vessels, and whatever they could lay their hands on. This carnage went on for two days. On the 1st of November, the crowds came at 7 a.m. and then again at 11 a.m., at 3 p.m. and at 7 p.m. They were accompanied by the SHO and some constables. On the second day, they were accompanied by more men including a dreaded henchman of X, and the assistant of a local don well known for his underworld activities. Apparently these two men made the killings more technical by using what people called a 'white kind of chemical' which burnt very quickly. In between, watch was kept by two gun-wielding men from the terraces of adjoining blocks as well as two constables who were posted on 'duty' at the entrance and the exit of the block. At least two men who tried to escape when they thought there was a lull in the intensity of the killings were shot dead. The marks left by the bullets, the blood splattered on the walls, and the heaps of ashes and the burnt out houses that we found when we went to the block on the 5th of November bore evidence to the truth of these horrific accounts.

After the first night it seems that leadership of the crowd shifted to hands other than the Pradhan of A/2, who now had to undertake the job of removing and disposing the bodies. X is said to have arranged for tempos in which half-burnt bodies were dumped and carted under cover of darkness to the cremation grounds near the Yamuna. Subsequently I was given the clue that two prominent persons from the Dom and Panda community who lived near the cremation ghats arranged to have the bodies mass cremated.

I have been able to trace one of these two men but would like to reserve the story of his subsequent rise for another occasion. On the 3rd morning three terrified Sikhs who had houses in A/2 tried to escape, were caught and beaten to death. On the 4th morning when the army moved in there were no bodies to be found – but the evidence described earlier of broken houses, bullet marks, burnt doors, small heaps of ashes, as well as the devastated human survivors was very much there.

As news of the carnage in A/4 began to spread in the other blocks of the colony, several blocks acted in different kinds of ways to protect themselves. In Block A/3, all families attested to the fact that they were helped by their Hindu neighbours to hide. One man and his wife were hidden in a nearby mosque by a Muslim neighbour. In Block B, the bangle sellers did not apprehend any danger to themselves. They were assured by their neighbours that what was happening in A/4 was a tale of vengeance between the Chamars and the Siglikar Sikhs. Though frightened, they said they thought they were too poor for the crowds to be attracted by the prospect of looting them.

The cases of D/2 and D/6 were entirely different. The inhabitants of D/2 were part of the same kinship network as A/4. They were also affluent with *pucca* structures and many of the goods that had aroused envy against the Siglikar Sikhs of A/4. As news of the carnage in A/4 began to come in, and especially the complicity of the police in the carnage, their leaders decided that they could not expect any help from anyone. So they collected together all the able-bodied men, collected whatever weapons they could lay their hands on and worked through the night to erect barricades at the entrance and the exit of the block. The few Hindu households that were there in this block cooperated with them completely and acted as spies to bring news of what was happening in the other blocks. We had asked people in A/4 if anyone had come to their help during the carnage and the invariable answer recorded in our survey is that neighbours did not help for they were themselves the killers. Their relatives in D block were aware that they had left their kin such as married daughters or close cousins to the mercy of the killers. But as the D block residents explained, 'What could we do? We did not have the weapons to fight with the police. But we were determined that we were not going to go like the sacrificial goat (*bali ka bakra*), we would fight and injure them if they came near us.' It seems the crowd did come several times that side but apparently decided not to fight with the people in this block. The lone death was of a meat shop owner who was caught unawares when he had gone out to defecate.

In blocks F/2 and F/4, there were similar deaths of people who were caught outside their houses. There were two cases of scooter drivers who were outside the colony and were caught and killed by anonymous crowds. Two others were caught in the fields while some members of a crowd were returning on the night of 2 November. They had gone out to defecate. The bodies of the two scooter drivers were never found but some people reported that they had been killed quite near the colony.

In F/7 *jhuggis* the story was different. Here the police had been locked in an earlier conflict with the *jhuggi* dwellers when a person (a balloon seller by the name of Wilson) arrested on suspicion of theft had been taken to the police station and had died under torture. A group of Jesuit social workers had filed a criminal complaint against the SHO with support from the *jhuggi* dwellers. Two Sikhs who had been active in their support to the social worker had been dragged out and burnt by the police constable and some persons accompanying him.[9]

There were major killings in C block which we could not investigate. As I said earlier, we did get involved with the

---

[9]There was also one case of a Sikh police constable from the area who was burnt to death, but we could not trace the family.

rehabilitation of the *jhuggi* dwellers in P/1, but we had not initially surveyed the households. P/1 was a cluster of *jhuggis* at the edge of the colony with a park and a broad street dividing the *pucca* dwellings of P block from the *jhuggis*. At a little distance from the other side was a sewage canal which divided Sultanpuri from a *jhuggi jhopdi* colony in Mangolpuri. The *jhuggi* dwellers of P/1, both Hindus and Muslims, had assured the Sikhs living with them that they would be protected at all costs. On the 1st and 2nd of November, when aggressive crowds, sometimes accompanied by policemen, had roamed around in the colony, the Sikhs in this block had hid in their neighbours' *jhuggis*. On the 3rd night a police jeep had gone around announcing a curfew and threatening the *jhuggi* dwellers that if they continued to keep the Sikhs hidden, their whole cluster would be set on fire as it was illegal to hide the Sikhs. Frightened by these threats to their neighbours and feeling themselves under a moral obligation not to endanger their lives, the Sikhs decided to run towards the sewage canal which divided the colony from Mangolpuri. Some hoped to hide in the fields but the police followed them and shot at them. It was later stated by the SHO that these were trouble makers who had tried to defy the curfew. While precise estimates are not possible, at least 20 persons died in this carnage.

There were also sporadic killings. For example, one man from a *pucca* house in P block, a scooter driver, had hidden in an abandoned house along with his three sons. A crowd, among whom the widow and his daughters had recognized some of the immediate neighbours, had doused the house with kerosene and burnt it, after challenging him to come out. There was no history or pattern of previous quarrels that we could discover. This and similar deaths which did not fall in any clear pattern happened towards the end – i.e., the 3rd November. The only interpretation I can put on it is that a lot of individual enmities got woven into the event so that a break of normal constraint pried open the closed social situation and allowed new possibilities to occur. In such a context, different kinds of hostilities were translated into violence as long-standing problems were sought to be resolved with one stroke. I was given three other cases of this kind of settling of individual scores.[10]

Is There a Pattern?

If we now try to put some of the elements of this narrative together, we find the following pattern.

The killings started on the night of 31st October in the colony and were initially grafted on to the previous fights between the respective Pradhans of A/2 and A/4 blocks. Sporadic killings also happened that day on the edge of the colony and some people who were in the other parts of the city sustained beatings. Watch was already being kept on the 31st night on this block by armed men. On the 1st and 2nd of November the violence became intense. Mobs of different sizes went around various parts of the colony. The leadership seems to have come from the lieutenants of X, the local big men, and some Jats and Gujjars from nearby villages, especially from Pooth and Sultanpur. People who had previous enmities often joined in or gave information about the hiding places of the Sikhs. Sometimes curious neighbours joined in but often remained on the periphery of the crowd. At least two teachers of the local school went around with the crowd, according to information given by children that was not solicited by us but accidentally offered when we were trying to discover why the

---

[10] I cannot describe these cases in any detail here. Let me give a quick example of this kind of event. I was repeatedly begged by a woman to go and visit her in the *jhuggi* where her brother lived and which was in an extremely crowded settlement near a drain, about two miles away from her conjugal home. This woman's husband had been reported missing. For a long time I was hesitant to go there because she insisted that I had to come alone and I was scared that this might be a trick to ambush me and hurt or even kill me. But one day I simply gave way and went to this *jhuggi* where she told me that her husband was not killed or missing but was in hiding. She said that she had a clandestine relationship with another man and they had many quarrels over this. Seeing that so many Sikhs were being killed during the riots her husband had probably taken the opportunity to kill her lover and had then run away to avoid suspicion. She was scared to report this to the police because then her lover's family would be unable to claim compensation and would turn against her and her husband's family would also 'finish her off'. She wanted my advice – I could not give any.

children were so terrified of school. In each case the police were present and in fact tried to put this across as a legal operation. It is important to remember, however, that this was not a result of a policy decision in which police officials were enacting what they were required to enact by law as in Nazi pogroms against the Jews, but was evidence of the corruption of legal norms and values as they operate at the level of political parties, bureaucracies and local societies. The implications of this for understanding the nature of the state in India are profound but not adequately theorized.

Due to a variety of local factors, killing was more random in blocks other than A/4, and those who were killed were usually found unawares. Two cases in F/7 *jhuggis* were an exception since the police were already locked in a conflict with people here over a case of illegal detention and torture. In P/1 *jhuggis*, the killing was primarily a police operation with little support from the neighbours.

In the light of these descriptions, let us return to the propositions on collective violence that I mentioned earlier. The first two propositions were about the nature of collective violence. First, riots are not an evidence of a class conflict or a straight-forward caste conflict. It is fractions of the working class which are in conflict with each other and with the state. Second, that collective violence represents society as in the process, *in the making*, rather than as a finished product.

Seen from the perspective of the local society, the violence of those three days clearly brought home the nature of conflicts between the 'fractions' of the working class which is rooted both in the structure of production and in the articulation of consumption. Thus we have to understand the place of these fractions in local society. I propose to do this by explaining the functioning of the economy in everyday life in the colony.

With the exception of the persons residing in the Chamar colony, among whom each household had at least one member working as a *safai karamchari* (the official designation for scavengers) in the Municipal Corporation, and the male members of the Siglikars who found opportunities to get employment contracts in the Gulf, all other households were engaged in what is called the informal economy. Even in the case of the Chamar colony, the income from jobs in the municipal corporation was not sufficient and there were various kinds of jobs, including household manufacture, petty trading, and pig rearing, that members were engaged in.

The following table gives the occupational distribution of 432 males in the Sikh households.

Table 2
Occupational Distribution of Males in Sikh Households

Occupation	Number	Percentage
Blacksmith	302	69.9
Carpenter	12	2.7
Shop owner	12	2.7
Construction work	14	3.2
Hawker	11	2.5
Scooter Driver	7	1.6
Rickshaw Puller	4	0.9
Unskilled labour	9	2.0
Bangle maker/seller	32	7.4
Tailor	13	3.0
Registered Medical Practitioner[11]	2	0.4
Other	14	—
Total	432	

As we see from the above table, only nine (eight salaried employees and one driver) out of the 432 males were employed in the formal structure. This distribution is hardly surprising given that several studies have postulated that 40 to 50% of all income earners in the country are in the informal sector (see Breman 1994). To this we should add that the links between the formal and the

---

[11]This occupational category refers to licensed persons engaged in therapeutic practice who do not have a formal medical degree but are licensed by the state to practice medicine.

informal sector, at least for people living in areas like Sultanpuri, are varied and complex. I shall comment on two aspects of these links which have a direct bearing on the violence.

In a recent study, Breman (1994) has described the processes of recruitment and access to work in the informal sector where, he says, work is sought primarily by means of personal contacts. Describing these processes for unskilled labour, he shows the improvised existence that labourers are compelled to live and how they have to maintain a large network of contacts to obtain work. In contrast, there are formal bureaucratic rules which govern entry into the formal sector but, as Breman says, the situation of shortage in respect of jobs necessitates the use of influence along personal channels. He cites how influence may be used, positions may be bought, and how posts in the government may be more or less at the disposal of local politicians. As for small-scale enterprises, new personnel are recruited primarily from among the families or friends of present personnel. In Sultanpuri, these practices were mapped on the kinship and locality networks on the one hand and the structure of local power relations on the other. Clearly the fact that among the Siglikar Sikhs and the Lohars from Lahore, 302 out of a total of the 390 men belonging to this caste were engaged in their traditional caste occupation, tends to show the continuities between caste and occupation for the artisan castes (32 bangle makers as well as ten other persons did not belong to this caste). We must remember here that a growing construction industry in Delhi and the employment opportunities in the Gulf countries may account for the fact that the men did not find any need to search for other kind of employment. Within the caste, however, differences were apparent in the fact that men could be employed in the lucrative work of truck body building, or masonry but they could also be engaged in the less lucrative positions of forging metal clippings for buildings in the small *bhattis* outside their houses. Breman mentions the importance of 'fencing' in the informal structure – i.e. creating boundaries to block the entry of other competitors. In this case fencing operated to limit the opportunities of the kinship network versus another.

Take the instance of A/4 – the affluent households of the Siglikar Sikhs had managed to get their own close kinsmen from

Alwar and the surrounding villages and incorporated them in their network of local manufacture and trade. Similarly though the members of the Chamar households of A/2 were employed in the formal sector, their own kinship network flourished because of the importance of their Pradhan in securing jobs. It should be noticed that power operates here not only along caste lines but in order to distinguish one network of kinship from another. Fencing operated in relations to the formal structure also and was evident in the colony through the institution of local big men. Thus the women in A/4 said that no one could secure a job contract in the Gulf till X was paid a certain amount – the amount quoted was Rs. 15,000 to get the job contract and Rs. 10,000 to get the passport, visa etc. Thus the fencing operated in two ways. First, you needed the capital for the *dalali* (i.e., fee for middlemen), a position monopolized by X and his men. This meant that only those who had already made sufficient money could sponsor the others. Second, those who dared to defy the local networks of power had to face the risk of violence from X and his local lieutenants. Frequent fights had broken out earlier between the different networks of kinship which segmented the caste groups as well as between others who had the requisite skills, such as the Lahori Lohars in F/2 and F/4. Finally the fight between the A/2 Pradhan and the A/4 Pradhan had been the most persistent since the Pradhan of A/2 suspected that his influence would be on the decline and also because one other factional leader in the Congress Party was trying to make inroads into the colony by recruiting support for himself.

The second way in which the formal and informal sector were linked was through the system of bribes and offering of personal allegiance to local Big Men and the police. Every household in A/ 4 had constructed a second storey or expanded the building in unauthorized ways. In order to prevent demolitions the local policeman and the local politician had to be given protection money. I was told that if the demolition squads of the Delhi Development Authority threatened them with demolitions, it was the responsibility of X to protect them. This he could do by either influencing the police or getting crowds to gather at the site who would prevent the staff from proceeding. X himself had acquired several illegal

properties in this way and had built a palatial building in a nearby
middle class locality. His rise in material terms since the
Emergency had been quite spectacular. No one in the colony thought
that his wealth was acquired through legal means. People told us
that even if cases were registered against him the police would be
unable to arrest him because of his strong local support earned
through the local networks of patronage. This was proved to be
correct by subsequent events.

Other forms of illegalities were evident. Most men in the colony
had two ration cards on two different names. Indeed one of our
tasks when we had to help them to fill claims for death
compensation or compensation for injury was to sort out the 'legal'
name from the other names they had used to secure different
resources for themselves. Those who were engaged in petty trade,
those who were hawkers, as well as rickshaw pullers and auto
rickshaw (scooter) drivers, had to pay a regular amount of
protection money to the big men who would protect them from
any police action. People hinted at a flourishing narcotics trade –
evidence of that was clear in the way in which one could pick up
nashe ki goli (drugs of unknown composition) for as little as Rs.
15. I could not investigate this with any precision for reasons of
safety. I hope the point is sufficiently clear though, that the fencing
mechanisms and the regulation of entry into most sectors of the
informal economy were a product of several factors – caste and
kinship networks, defined spheres of influence by politicians and
local Big Men,[12] and the constant threat of violence to regulate
behaviour.

The informal sector does not consist only of those who live
on the disaster threshold. Enormous differences of wealth may be
found in the resettlement colonies – there were households which
reported that anything up to 10 *tolas* of gold and cash amounting
to twenty thousand was looted from their houses. Yet one must
not imagine that they lived a secure life. Much of the wealth of
this kinship network had come as remittances from West Asia.

---

[12]The concept of Big Men is adapted from Godelier (1986) and is distinguished
from Great Men to signal that the former grow in influence and power by using
new opportunities while the latter achieve their position by excelling in skills
that go with their traditional positions. See also Godelier and Strathern (1991).

Sometimes a woman left behind by her husband who had migrated for work would receive regular remittances. At other times nothing would be heard for months. If a man set up house with another woman, then the wife's source of survival would dry up. Such women normally set house with other men from within the *biradari* or entered into secret liaisons with men of other castes. I wish we had investigated the impact of these marriages or liaisons on the survival of the children, but for a set of very difficult reasons this could not be pursued. I can, however, state the contrast this situation offers to that of poor women from a small town in Brazil, described by Nancy Scheper-Hughes (1992) in her monumental study of hunger.

In this study Scheper-Hughes describes how poor women in this small town frequently entered into new liaisons with men who became a source of gifts, especially of food, for the impoverished women. But it is not only the search for material gifts that drove women to form these liaisons. They were also experienced as acts of sexual autonomy. Scheper-Hughes quotes from statements made to Fatima Quintas by poor women living in the urban shanty town in Recife.

One woman told Fatima, 'Sure I'm hungry. Almost every day my house is without food. My compensation is screwing. You ask me if I take pleasure in sex? Of course I do. How else am I going to know if I'm alive if I don't screw?' (p. 165).

From the descriptions given by Scheper-Hughes herself, it appears that women often name these relations in terms of 'love' or sexual attraction, whereas they *experienced* them equally as relations of hate and abuse. One woman articulates this with great clarity.

'At first Nelson was good to me. Every Saturday he would climb the Alto to visit, and he always brought a basket of groceries for the week. He never once came empty-handed . . . But after I got pregnant, everything changed. Nelson began to abuse me . . . I was actually glad that my first born died right away. Things got better for a little bit, and then I was pregnant again . . . But finally I began to see that Nelson was abusing me for the fun of it. It was a kind of sport. He wanted to keep me pregnant just so he could threaten to leave me again and again' (p. 349).

The woman seemed to be saying, he could make me pregnant but he could not make me mourn for his child. Whereas Scheper-Hughes is able to show that such sentiments as maternal love depend on the materiality of the conditions in which women live and construct their sexuality, it seems to me that comparisons across cultures are absolutely essential for our understanding of how poverty, precariousness of women's existence, and the relations between the sexes, interact to give shape to such sentiments as maternal love. The complexity of cross-cultural comparison can be seen from the fact that in the oppressive context of South African society where manipulation of sexual and reproductive capacities has been described as a major part of the 'survival kit' of women (see Ramphele 1993), they do not seem to invest the self in sexuality in the same way as appears from the descriptions of poor women in Scheper-Hughes' account.

In Sultanpuri women did not talk of the new liaisons they formed *as acts of sexual autonomy* but rather as the evidence of the power that the *biradari* had over them. This is, of course, easily attributed to the fact that it was not by choice but by compulsion that they married other men of the *biradari*; but they also saw it as a means of protecting their children in whom the members of the *biradari* had an equal stake. One often found a woman beating a child (when I am angry with the world, I beat up my child) but I did not ever encounter a woman who was angry with her child because the father had abandoned her or abused her. Even in the period of grave crisis as that witnessed during the riots, women did everything in their power to save their children from the violence of the riots. When we went into the colony, we found five women who had given birth either while the violence was going on or right after it, and in each case the community of women had treated the question of the survival of the newborns as the most urgent task for the whole community. The cultural context of poverty as the site in which the construction of sexuality and maternal love are shaped clearly offers many variations.

The precariousness of the informal economy in which men participated and the dangers of political violence were thus mediated by the marriage practices for the women. A survey of 220 women, between the ages of 15 and 70, showed the following distribution.[13]

Table 3
Age and Marital Status of Women

Age	Never Married	Married	Separated	Widowed
15 - 30	36	82	1	0
30 - 45	0	63	1	2
45 - 60	0	20	0	1
60 -	0	7	0	7
Total 220	36	172	2	10

All the women under the category of 'never married' were below the age of 18, the maximum (22) cluster around the age of 15. It would be clear from this that the norm of marriage is universal for women. Second, the small number of separated or widowed women in the sample may be attributed to the high rate of levirate or leviratic remarriage which not only prescribes high rates of remarriage but also does not permit much time to lapse between the death of or desertion by a husband and the remarriage of the woman. Third, the small number of women in the age group of 45 and above and the near disappearance of women above the age of 60 is due to a combination of two factors – the low levels of life expectancy and the tendency of older persons to return to their villages of origin, since this community migrated to Delhi only twenty years ago. Although the practice of leviratic marriage may sometimes be experienced as traumatizing for women, as I have described elsewhere (Das 1990), it does assure that women are not left to fend for themselves and their young children. This does not protect them from the everyday violence

---

[13]I have ignored the deaths that occurred in the three days of the riots, taking the marital status on the day before the occurrence of the riots. This was necessary to obtain the normal distribution of marriages in the sample.

or from experiencing violence from the local Big Men, but it does mean that the men of the *biradari* form a kind of collective insurance against widowhood and devastation for women.

Perhaps one incident that was related to me, may make clear the nature of the precarious existence that women who lacked this *biradari* structure were compelled to lead.

One day as I was coming out of a dhaba after a cup of tea, I was stopped by a woman I did not recognize. It turned out that she was from a block nearby, belonged to a higher Hindu caste, and made her living by stitching school uniforms. She said rather aggressively to me, 'What is the big thing about these riots – *dange*? Why are you so concerned with these? It happens all the time.' Then she pointed to the ground and said, 'This spot here – this is where they killed my husband four years ago. He was a simple man. We had just bought vegetables one day and we were walking back when we saw one of these men – the ones who are the lords here – beating up his kept woman (*rakhail*). Without realizing what he was doing my husband said: Why are you beating her so mercilessly – leave the *jat* (caste, but here species) of woman alone, don't raise your hand on her. The man turned on my husband and said: What is she to you? Is she your sister? Is she your daughter? No. So the slut (*randi*) is having an affair with you? I will teach you how to interfere.

'He started to beat up my husband. My husband shouted – run and get some help. I ran towards our block but by the time I got back his dead body was lying on the ground. The police came. No one admitted to having seen anything. I made my peace. Do I want the same thing to happen to my sons?'

On the other end of the spectrum from those who had achieved a temporary affluence were people living in the *jhuggis* – daily wage labour, balloon sellers, eunuchs, petty thieves – whose lives were even more precarious in economic and political terms. The presence of politicians, big men, and the local police dominated the lives of people. Territories were jealously guarded and violence was ever present in the form of local lords exercising different kinds of control for access to the resources of survival. The use of water pumps for the *jhuggi* dwellers had to be paid for; right to the use of pavements for selling one's wares or setting up *bhattis*

192

where women could forge metal clippings or glass could be shaped into bangles, all this was subject to the control of the Big Men. As in the case of Wilson (the balloon seller) the police seemed to have the power to arrest you for any theft reported anywhere in the city and claim that loot had been discovered from your *jhuggi*. Death in police custody was greatly feared.

It is within this context that one must seek an understanding of how the violence of the riots became an opportunity to remake local society. In the fights between A/2 and A/4 blocks, the stakes were equally loaded. The newly acquired wealth of the Siglikar Sikhs had become a danger to the existing balance of power. While a different set of considerations at the level of the home ministry, the office of the Police Commissioner and the office of the Lt. Governor must explain how it came to be that despite public pronouncements about the deployment of the army and strict orders to shoot at sight, the carnage continued for three days, it is only through the understanding of local factors that we come to see that this became an opportunity to rearrange relations of power at the local level. The Siglikar Sikhs of A/4 lost decisively, but the gains of the A/2 faction or of the local politician were not as decisive as it appeared at first sight. This was partly due to the fact that the local context, earlier hidden from view, became visible to the general public, through the intervention of several voluntary organizations and the exposures in the media. In addition, the government had to respond to pressures to act in the interest of establishing its own legitimacy. Thus the loot could not be retained by the looters and the local leaders had to spend some time in gaol. Further, through a combination of several factors, most of the affected people were re-allocated houses in Tilak Vihar along with the riot victims of the colonies from the trans-Yamuna area such as Trilokpuri. This could not have been anticipated by the perpetrators of the violence. The residents of D/2, who were close in affluence and power to the A/4 residents and had escaped the violence thanks to the choices they were able to make at the crucial time, were not entitled to allotment of houses in any new area. They continued to live in Sultanpuri but they had understood the perils of challenging the local lords. They settled for the peace of the defeated. The local society returned to its own level of 'normal' violence indexed in such scattered facts as that the maximum number of rapes in Delhi reported in the newspapers in the last ten years have been from Sultanpuri. Meanwhile a new set of relations between the different sections that had been shifted were being forged in Tilak Vihar but new kinds of political agencies had also emerged. In short, there was a recirculation of people in different spaces in the city and in the colonies in which violence had occurred.

The Question of Political Agency

It is the fundamental premise of Feldman's (1992) argument that agency is not given but achieved. It has no fixed ground, for it is not the author but the product of doing (cf. Nietzsche). However, it is a factored product – since there are multiple subject positions which go to make political agency.[14] In any understanding of violence the body emerges as the new political subject even as action moves from one transactional space to another – from discourse to somatic practice. It is not only the body of the perpetrator but also that of the victim which, altered by violence, reenacts other bodies and is appropriated by different kinds of political interests as their symbolic possession.

In the context of the violence described here, what were the subject positions enacted by the perpetrators in the riots? There is more than one register in what was said and what was heard in the very act of killing. As we saw, the rioters were not a crowd gone 'mad' but were literally embodying local and national narratives in their somatic actions and in their speech. The local hostilities were evident in the jeers, daring the Sikhs to hold their heads high after they had been submitted to the violence as well as the humiliation of having their hair shaved. They were taunted

---

[14]While the theoretical propositions of Feldman (1992) are elegantly presented, the ethnographic experiment is relatively less successful in moulding of the different subject positions towards the creation of agency. I was particularly struck by the absence of female voices within the narrative accounts given by his male informants. I wonder whether this is a consequence of the male space (e.g. pubs) in which the ethnographer interacted with the men who related their stories to him.

for the manner in which their women would proudly embody the commodities brought from abroad – where is that arrogance now, the crowd had demanded. Thus one kind of discourse was that of the local fights, hostilities, and jealousy. But is the local structure and practice sufficient to provide an interpretation of the events? After all it was the killing of Mrs. Gandhi which seemed to have opened up a new kind of space in which such gory rituals of revenge could be enacted.

It is when we pay attention to the specificity of the quality of time which was brought into existence between the assassination of Mrs. Gandhi and her funeral, we see how a certain discourse of nationalism reckoned through genealogical connections, enacted itself in the speech of the perpetrators. The crowd at various stages of its operations was shouting *'khun ka badla khun'* – blood must be avenged with blood, and *'tumne hamari ma ko mara hai'* – you have killed our mother. Anderson (1983) has made the point that nation as an imagined community uses the discourse of genealogical connections; here we see how these genealogical connections translate themselves into the bodily practices of vengeance. The obligation to avenge the death of Mrs. Gandhi through the metaphor of kinship connections by this particular fraction of the working class must appear ironic for it is the people occupying the lowest rungs of power and economic security that seem to have been made to embody this discourse of vengeance and through it to metaphorically claim genealogical connections to the most powerful and inaccessible realms of Indian politics.[15]

If nationalism 'spoke' in this vein in the somatic practice of the perpetrators, so did notions of masculinity. I have described elsewhere the challenges that the crowd threw at men who were hiding. One particular case that occurred in the P block was of a man who was hiding in an abandoned house with his three children.

---

[15]The evocation of genealogical connections does not seem limited to this case. After the assassination of Rajiv Gandhi, one of the slogans shouted by a few of his supporters was *Bhabhi hum sharminda hain – bhaiya ke katil zinda hain.* Addressing the surviving widow as sister-in-law, it says, we are ashamed that the killers of our brother are still alive. Yet, firm action on the part of Mrs. Sonia Gandhi did not permit this slogan to become part of the repertoire of speech outside the limited circles in which it was first evoked.

The crowd repeatedly challenged him to come out and face them if 'he was a man'. When he failed to open the locked door, the crowd poured kerosene over the house and burnt it. Even his widow, sometimes mourning the death of her sons which was unbearable to her, would accuse him of having been a 'coward' ('If he had not been such a coward my children could have lived'). One of the most traumatizing experience the survivors had to live with was the memory of the 'cowardice'. The Siglikar men would repeatedly assure us that they were not cowards, they could take vengeance but were restrained by the police complicity with the rioters.

The manner in which the illegality of modern law, to use the felicitous phrase of Foucault, was inscribed on the local practices would have been evident from the preceding description. At the time of the killing, the police were able to 'order' people to leave their weapons in the house. The SHO made a threat in A/4 that anyone coming to the aid of the Pradhan would be guilty of stalling the processes of law. In P/1 *jhuggis*, the police first threatened the *jhuggi* dwellers with dire consequences if they gave shelter to the terror-stricken Sikhs. When the Sikhs tried to run away under the cover of darkness in order to save the neighbours who had given them shelter, they shot at them on the grounds that they had broken the curfew. Yet it is to the police that the victims had to turn to, in order to acquire the 'legal' status of victims. As the processes of relief and rehabilitation started, everyone was required to submit a copy of the FIR (First Information Report) they had registered to lay claims over any compensation. It was not only the governmental bureaucracy which required this, but also the gurudwaras that were offering Rs 200 p.m. for the women who had been widowed. So one of our tasks was to trace women who had not filed FIRs and to help them file these.

An examination of the FIRs that were filed shows how the official narrative of the riots penetrated the discourse of the victims. When someone went to the police station, at least in Mangolpuri and Sultanpuri, to register a criminal complaint, the framing sentences of the FIR were dictated by the policeman on duty. Hence the standard framing sentences were:

'*Dinank 31.10.84 ko Bharat sarkar ke pradhanmantri Shrimati Indira Gandhi ki unke do suraksha karamchariyon dwara nirmam*

*hatya karne ke karan Bharat ki rajdhani Dilli mein janta mein
bhare rosh hone ki vajah se kai sthanon per janta ne majma khilafe
kanoon banakar aagjani, lootmar va katle aam kiya. Vibhinn
gurudwaron Sikh gharon va unki dookanon ko loot liya.*

'On date 31.10.84, due to the fact that the Prime Minister of
India Mrs. Indira Gandhi was murdered cruelly by her two security
guards, the people in Delhi, the capital of the country, being enraged
engaged in illegal activities of arson, looting, and mass killing.
Several gurudwaras, Sikh families, and their shops were looted.'

It is only after this framing sentence that people were allowed
to register the facts about who was killed in their family and the
things that were looted. In the framing sentences above, the
discourse embodied the complicity of the police, the perpetrators,
and the henchmen of X. The victims were terrorized into believing
that any departure from this formulaic opening, which gave an
account of the events as they actually happened and named the
people who actually constituted the crowd, would bring severe
reprisals on them. After the involvement of the voluntary organizations, several victims were encouraged to register the correct
details in the FIR and they did so. Similarly many survivors came
forward to give evidence in the Police Enquiry Commission that
was constituted by the new Police Commissioner, Mr. Ved Marwah,
in order to initiate disciplinary action against police officials who
were found guilty on the basis of the criminal complaints. Clearly
we can see that although the same act – viz., registering of a
criminal complaint – is at issue, the representation of the agency
of the crowds shifts in these complaints from the subject position
of people maddened by grief and rage engaging in random violence
against the Sikh households and gurudwaras, to that of people
engaged in calculated acts of destruction against whom the rule of
law is sought to be evoked. In the former case the legal format is
necessary for victims to claim victim status and nothing more; in
the latter case to be a victim is to be able to attest and witness the
acts of criminals in order to bring punishment according to due
processes of law.

Finally there was a subterranean discourse upon which I
stumbled completely by accident. One evening, late in March, I
received a call from the area that the police picket in one block

was being removed and people of that block were apprehensive of their safety. Since it was late I called a male friend and we went together to check on the report. We were able to ascertain that the police picket was being removed and to later liaison with the Police Commissioner to have it restored. But while walking back we found many men in the street enacting a spectacle while they were in fits of laughter. These were the Siglikars whose kinsmen had been butchered a few months ago. The men appeared drunk and as we stood and watched, it seemed they were enacting scenes of death with snatches of dialogue from Hindi movies. The dialogue of the film *Sholay* with an angry Gabbar Singh looming over his fallen victim was being enacted. A child was standing on the periphery. He said casually that the men took drugs (*goli*) every day and that they were repeating what some of the killers had said. In one particularly gory enactment, they would surround a man and poke him with a *lathi* and say, come Sardarji dance – you must have seen many dances, show us how they dance in Muscat. I was too terrified to stay.[16] And I offer this fragment only to say that there was so much that was opaque in the enactment of agency. Why did the bodies of the survivors reenact the somatic and speech practices of the perpetrators? And what shall we make of the bodies of men becoming 'possessed', as the women claimed, by the fate of their dead kinsmen? And the further possession of the body by the script of a film? The carnivalesque sense of the occasion could lend itself to analysis in a Freudian frame in which a crowd of victims was enacting its identification with the aggressor; in cultural-historical terms one may see this as an attempt to invent the symbolic order which had been lost; and in social experiential terms it could be transforming bodily practice from the receptive side of the experience to the active side.

Roy (1995) has said about crowds that 'crowds offer an opportunity for common citizens to speak openly at the very

---

[16]I cannot provide any reflections here on my sense of terror in seeing the men I had worked with every day in the mornings taking on an aspect that made them quite unrecognizable to me. I was to repeatedly have that feeling of suddenly not knowing where I was. I know for sure that despite an year of close association with the people there, much of their lives and their relations remained opaque to me. I am in the process of writing on this aspect of fieldwork.

moment when their lives are most unsettled and their consciousness most in flux . . . in fact what crowd studies do is to listen to public statements made by people which are ordinarily privatized statements made in the language of collective action'. In the case of Sultanpuri, the different registers in which the crowds spoke, how bodies enacted the speech and somatic practice of other bodies, make Roy's understanding appear to be extremely sweetened and sanitized.

The Agency of Women

I cannot describe the question of how women constructed their agency in any detail here. I have discussed some of these issues elsewhere. Here I want to take only the dualistic construction of the female body – as representing the power of men through display of commodities on the one hand, and loss of their world through embodiment of pollution on the other.[17] This dualistic construction of the female body oscillating between culturally constructed ideas of beauty and dirt has deep cultural roots. I shall give only some indications of how these ideas were transformed in the context of the riots.

The women in A/4 bemoaned not only the loss of their husbands and sons, but also of all the things that had constituted their house. In the initial phase of my contact with them, this appeared very puzzling to me. A woman would juxtapose the description of how her husband was killed with a description of how she lost an imported sweater with pearls (costume pearls) embroidered on it. Then she would say how the women of the Chamar basti were flouting these things on their bodies. It was as if the circulation of the desired clothes also symbolized for them the circulation of male power. When pressure began to mount on the police to produce the looted goods, the houses of the Chamars were raided and they lost all the looted things. This loot was then claimed as 'recovered' in the pronouncements of the then Police Commissioner, Mr. Tandon. The circulation of commodities thus had a local circuit of exchange initially but they were ultimately

[17]For a thoughtful account of the ambiguity of the female body in political movements, see Ramphele (1995).

appropriated by the state in support of its plea for renewed legitimacy. The discourse on masculinity which figured in the speech of men, resonated also in the language of commodities, for men proved their masculinity by clothing their women and their houses with these objects of desire. Violence allowed this circulation to create new circuits of movement; however, the appropriation of these finally by the police (which was bitterly resented by the Chamars) was symbolic of the manner in which the constantly changing face of the state presents itself to the poor – now as the one which instigates and collaborates with them in regimes of lawlessness, and now as one which punishes them for the very acts that it had instigated. As one man from A/2 put it to me, '*Pahle to kaha, uthao uthao – jo marzi utthao inke gharon se, phir dabav pada upar se to hamin ko thane mein pitvaya*' – lit. first they said pick up whatever you want from their houses, then when the pressure mounted from above we were the ones to be beaten up at the police stations.[18]

This emphasis upon the appropriation of commodities and their display adds another dimension to our understanding of the conflict between the fractions of the working class. It brings out the central place of consumption in signalling the distinctions between these fractions. In his study of the category of taste, Bourdieu (1992) has been able to show how money capital and symbolic capital serve to distinguish between the fractions of the upper class in contemporary France. Yet in considering the working class, he bestows a certain homogeneity on their patterns of consumption. As Miller (1987) has noted, Bourdieu's view ultimately rests on the idea of working class as authentic humanity and on an aesthetization of labour.

Yet if we begin to pay attention to the fractions of the working class in the same way as Bourdieu has paid attention to the fractions of the upper class, we see that there is an affinity between the structures of production and the dispositions to consumption. The precariousness of work in the informal sector bears an affinity

---

[18]One is tempted to think here that when the state needed to prove its legitimacy, the bodies of the Chamars with their stolen goods were available – thus their bodies in their very materiality became available for the state to produce its legitimacy upon.

to the emphasis on display and the socially constructed emotion of 'envy' that marks relations in the resettlement colonies. At least some of the conflicts between these fractions of the working class may be seen in terms of the articulation between the underlife of the politics and the dependence on the informal economy and its impact, in turn, on the way in which desire comes to be invested in items of display rather than, say, health and education.

The opposite of the body as a bearer of commodities, symbolic of the power of 'their' men was the female body as a bearer of pollution. I have discussed elsewhere how the women from A/4 displayed death pollution in a spectacular fashion.[19] As long as their suffering was not acknowledged and addressed, they insisted on sitting outside their ruined houses, refusing to comb their hair, clean their bodies, or return to other signs of normality. Here the somatic practice drew deeply from the Hindu tradition of mourning and death pollution − deriving its power from such figures as Draupadi in the *Mahabharata* who refused to remove signs of pollution from her body till the dishonour done to her was avenged.[20] I am not claiming that this discourse was explicit − it functioned rather as an unconscious grammar, but fragments of it were evoked when the women insisted that the deaths of their men should not go unavenged. I remember one instance in which there were rumours that Mother Teresa would visit the colony. X came to A/4 personally, imploring the women to go back to their houses, to clean up the dirt and to return to some normality. They simply refused, saying he could himself sweep the remains of the disaster if that offended him. The passive display of pollution so terrible that it could not even be gazed at, made the female body into a political subject that forcibly gave birth to a counter-truth of the official truth about the riots.

In the event it was voluntary organizations, including some Sikh organizations which took up this counter-truth and the task of seeking justice for the women through modern courts of law.

---

[19]See Das (1990) for a description of the symbols of pollution that women adopted and their meaning.

[20]I am not saying that Draupadi was a model for imitation. I am, however, struck by the tenacity of the cultural symbol of pollution that women may use to gain 'voice' in an oppressive situation.

The failure of the law to respond to the demands for justice is another matter. It was important for the women that they saw the obligation to give evidence against the perpetrators despite grave personal risks as an obligation they had incurred because they had accepted compensating money for the dead ('*unke naam ke paise khaye hain to unke naam ki gawahi to denge*' – we have eaten the money on their name, we shall give evidence evoking their names).

The Residue

The question of political agency is not yet completed. Each local event gets reshaped into a new event by being incorporated into a different discourse. I do not have the space to define how the residues of the violence, the unavenged men, the justice which was promised but not secured, the availability of the body of the widow as a symbol for the conduct of different kinds of politics got articulated in the last ten years. I do want to state, however, that it is the stringing of such local narratives by which individual biographies become transformed into social texts. These, in turn, provide founding myths and root metaphors for violent movements to be sustained.

By way of a conclusion, one comes to the compelling idea that it is perhaps by addressing everyday injustices, routine miseries, and the kinds of violence that do not even make it to the newspapers that we may be best addressing problems of communal strife and the issues of national security.

References

Anderson, Benedict. 1983. *Imagined Communities: Reflections on the Origin and Spread of Nationalism*. London, Verso.

Bourdieu, P. 1984. *Distinction: A Social Critique of the Judgement of Taste*. London, Routledge and Kegan Paul.

Breman, Jan. 1994. *Wage Hunters and Gatherers*. Delhi, Oxford University Press,

Chakravarty, U. and N. Haksar. 1987. *The Delhi Riots: Three Days in the Life of a Nation*. New Delhi, Lancer International.

Das, Veena. 1990. 'Our work to cry: Your work to listen' in *Mirrors of Violence: Communities, Riots and Survivors in South Asia* (ed. Veena Das). Delhi, Oxford University Press.

Das, Veena. 1995. *Critical Events: An Anthropological Perspective on Contemporary India. Delhi, Oxford University Press.*

Engels, F. 1870. *Marx- Engels Correspondence,* 4 September 1870, *Wereke,* Vol. 33, p. 53 (quoted in Furet 1981).

Feldman, A. 1991. *Formations of Violence: The Narrative of the Body and Political Terror in Northern Ireland.* Chicago, University of Chicago Press.

Furet, F. 1981. *Interpreting the French Revolution.* London, Cambridge University Press.

Godelier, Maurice. 1986. *The Making of Great Men.* London, Cambridge University Press.

Godelier, M. and M. Strathern (ed.). 1991. *Big Men and Great Men: Personifications of Power in Malenesia.* London, Cambridge University Press.

Kapur, Rajiv A. 1987. *Sikh Separatism: The Politics of Faith.* Delhi, Vikas Publications.

Kishwar, Madhu. 1985. 'Gangster rule: The massacre of the Sikhs'. *Manushi,* Vol. 25.

Kothari, S. and Harsh Sethi. 1985. *Voices from a Scarred City.* Delhi, Lokayan.

Le Bon, G. 1952. *The Crowd.* London, Ernest Benn.

Miller, D. 1987. *Material Culture and Mass Consumption.* Oxford, Blackwell.

Nietzsche, F. 1956. *The Birth of Tragedy and the Genealogy of Morals.* Garden City N.Y., Doubleday.

Ramphele, M. 1993. *A Bed Called Home: Life in the Migrant Labour Hostels of Cape Town.* Cape Town, David Philip Publishers.

Ramphele, M. 1995. 'Political Widowhood in South Africa: The Embodiment of Ambiguity'. *Daedalus* (in press).

Reynolds, Pamela. 1989. *Childhood in the Crossroads.* Cape Town, David Philip Publishers.

Roy, Mary. 1995. *A Matter of Cows.* Berkeley, California University Press.

Scheper-Hughes, Nancy. 1992. *Death Without Weeping. Violence in Everyday Life in Brazil.* Berkeley, California University Press.

Srinivasan, Amrit. 1990. 'The survivor in the study of violence' in *Mirrors of Violence: Communities, Riots, and Survivors in South Asia* (ed. Veena Das). Delhi, Oxford University Press.

Thompson, E.P. 1971. 'The moral economy of the English crowd in the eighteenth century'. *Past and Present* , 76-136.

Tilly, Charles. 1986. *The Contentious Frech. Four Centuries of Political Struggle.* Cambridge, Harvard University Press.

Reports

1984 *Who are the Guilty? Report of a Joint Enquiry into the Causes and Impact of the Riots in Delhi from 31 October to 10 November.* Delhi, PUCL-PUDR.

1985 *Report of the Citizen's Commission: Delhi, 31 October to 4 November.*

1985 *Report to the Nation.* Delhi, Citizens for Democracy.

The Construction of a New Hindu Identity

Sudhir Kakar

> Great disorders lead to great devotions.
>
> — Emile Zola

Some fifteen years ago, when what is today called the Nehruvian project of a modernized secular India was still vigorous and fundamentalism a distant gleam in the eye of an occasional *imam* or *mahant*, I had tried to peer into the crystal ball of the future. In conclusion to *The Inner World*, I wrote that as modernization picks up pace, individuals will increasingly seek membership of groups with absolute value systems and with little tolerance for deviation from their norms. The quote: 'Whereas initially the appeal of these groups may be limited to sections of society who are most susceptible to the pressures of social change—for example, youth and urbanized classes—we can expect an ever-widening circle of participation as more and more people are sucked into the wake of modernization...In short, we can expect an increasing destruction of nascent, western-style individualism as more and more individuals seek to merge into collectivities that promise a shelter for the hurt, the conflicted and the shipwrecked.'[1]

If I again take up the theme of those large social formations through which many individuals in India seek a sense of their cultural identity (a term which I prefer to the more sociological 'ethnicity'), then it is not to derive a melancholy satisfaction from any perceived prescience but to offer some psychological observations on an issue which is normally seen as the domain of political scientists and social commentators. First, to get definitional matters out of the way, by cultural identity I mean a group's basic way of organizing experience through its myths, memories, symbols, rituals and ideals.[2] Socially produced and thus subject to historical change, cultural identity is not a static affair even while it makes a decisive contribution to the enhancement of an individual's sense of self-sameness and continuity in time and space. This definition is particularly apt for the *Hindutva* movement—characterized by some as Hindu fundamentalism—through which a large number of Hindus today seem to be seeking a sense of their cultural identity. Let us again remember that fundamental does not mean traditional. As in other parts of the non-Western world, revivalism or fundamentalism in India, Hindu or Muslim, is an attempt to reformulate the project of modernity. Like its counterparts elsewhere, the leadership of *Hindutva*, for instance, has never been traditional but decidedly modern, consisting of individuals who turned their backs on their Western education.[3] Keshav Baliram Hedgewar, the founder of the Rashtriya Swayamsevak Sangh, the RSS, the core institution and the driving force of Hindu revivalism, had his schooling in English and went on to study medicine in Calcutta. In his youth, he is reported to have felt that orthodox Hindu ritual was rather silly. His successor, Golwalkar, was the son of a civil servant, did his Master's degree in biology at Benares University and was a lecturer in zoology at the same institution before he joined the RSS.[4]

Shadows of Mourning

Haunting images of loss and helplessness among large groups of people underlie many literary and scholarly accounts of transnational historical changes. These images constitute the sombre mood with which scholars have often relfected upon the periods and processes of significant transformations in human history. When Max Weber paints the portrait of Western man in the wake of Enlightenment, we see a face aglow with the promised triumph of rationality in human affairs, yet also etched with deep shadows of mourning. From Weber's canvas, we see modern man peering out with hopeful though 'disenchanted' eyes at a future which offers vastly greater control over nature, society and man's own destiny. Yet the portrait also conveys a palpable grief for the lost spontaneity and immediacy which the social forms and symbols of the Judaeo-Christian religious tradition had built up and guaranteed.

Nearer to our own times, as we study the anthropological, psychological and, above all, fictional accounts of another transcultural historical process, the process of modernization in the non-Western world, we again encounter the ghost of depression seated at a banquet table laid out with the eagerly awaited dishes of economic development and the fruits of industrialization. Let me, then, first outline the social psychological processes which are a consequence of modernization and which I believe are the foundation on which the edifices of the new Hindu and Muslim as well as other cultural identities in India are being constructed. These processes are, of course, not particular to India but common to most of the non-Western world.

First, population movements which take place during the modernizing process involve the separation of families and the loss of familiar neighbourhoods and ecological niches. Psychologists report and novelists describe the feelings of bereavement and states of withdrawal among those mourning for old attachments and suspicious of creating new ones. These tendencies are not only harmful for individuals but also hinder the birth of new social structures and forms while they rob community life of much of its vitality and therefore its capacity for counteracting the sense of helplessness.[5]

With increasing globalization, the migrations are no longer confined by national boundaries. Globalization, too, encroaches upon traditional group solidarities and the established relationships between different groups, whether in Cochin or Moradabad. The shifting demands of global markets for particular kinds of goods and labour make for rapid and bewildering changes in the relative status of many groups in a particular society. Whereas some groups dramatically increase their earning power (and thus claims to a higher social status) through their access to international markets in goods, services and labour, others are as dramatically impoverished, with many forced to migrate from their traditional geographical and cultural niches.

The vast internal migrations also give rise to overcrowded living conditions in urban conglomerations, especially in the sprawling shanty towns and slums with their permanent air of transience. On the one hand, it is undeniable that urban slums, however awful they seem to middle class sensibilities, represent to the poor a hope of escaping from deadening economic deprivation and the relatively rigid, caste-based discrimination and inequities of rural society. On the other, there is the lack of cultural norms in dealing with relative strangers whose behavioral clues cannot be easily deciphered, so different from the ritualized predictability of interactions in the communities left behind in villages or small towns as they are, which compels the person to be constantly on guard. He is in a state of permanent psychic mobilization and heightened nervous arousal.

In addition, the rapid obsolescence of traditional roles and skills as modernization picks pace seriously dents the self-esteem — when it does not shatter it completely — of those who are confronted with simultaneous loss of earning power, social status and identity as particular kind of workers. For the affected and their families, especially children, there is a collapse of confidence in the stability of the established order and of the world. What looms instead is the spectre of a future which is not only opaque but represents an overwhelming threat to any sense of purpose.

The feelings of loss are not limited to the migration from geographical regions and cultural homes or to the disappearance of traditional work identities. It also extends to the loss of ancestral ideals and values. For instance, compared to what many believe was a traditionally healthy eroticism, modernity, with its popular cinema, television, fashions, the comingling of sexes in schools, colleges and at work, is sexually decadent. 'People have lost their *brahmacharya* (celibacy), their character is destroyed and everyone has become an addict of bad habits. If you cannot control your libido, you cannot be pure.'[6] Once the Enlightenment values of universal equality, liberty and fraternity, of the pre-eminence of reason and moral autonomy of the individual were formulated through the political revolutions in the non-Western world, they became a universal heritage, inevitably triumphant when in conflict with the norms and values of the local culture. In spite of the disillusionment of some post-modern Western intellectuals with the Enlightenment mentality, its values continue to constitute what has been generally regarded as the most dynamic and transformative ideology in human history, closing any option of going back to pre-modern conceptions.[7] Yet the Enlightenment has a dark side, too. The modernization project is riddled with its own inequities, repressions and unfraternal conflicts. There is thus bound to be a palpable grief for the values of a lost — and retrospectively idealized — world, when in the brave new one progress often turns out to be glaring inequality, rationality becomes selfishness and the pursuit of self-interest, and individualism comes to mean unbridled greed.

Secret Wounds

Whereas loss and helplessness constitute one stream of feelings accompanying the modernization process, another stream consists of feelings of humiliation and radically lowered self-worth. One source of humiliation lies in the homogenizing and hegemonizing impact of modernization and globalization, both of which are no respecters of cultural pluralities and diversities. The imperatives of economic development which see many local cultural values and attitudes as outmoded or plain irrelevant, are a source of humiliation to all those who have not embraced or identified with the modernization project in its totality.

For the masses, there are other occasions for blows to self-esteem, such as the increase in the complexity and incidence of bureaucratic structures, with their attendant dehumanization, which has been a corollary of development. The cumulative effect of daily blows to an individual's feelings of self worth, received in a succession of bureaucratic and other impersonal encounters, cannot be underestimated.

For the elites of the non-Western world, there is an additional humiliation in their greater consciousness of the defeat of their civilizations in the colonial encounter with the West. This defeat is not merely an abstraction or a historical memory but one which is confirmed by the peripheral role of their countries in the international economic and political order of the post-colonial world. Their consciousness of being second class citizens in the

SUDHIR KAKAR

global order is reinforced by their many encounters with the more self-confident Western colleagues in the various international fora. An example of the role played by loss and sensed humiliation is seen in the case of those Indians, economically an elite group, who have migrated to the United States and are frequently exposed to indifference or condescension towards their cultural tradition. When they have not abjured their cultural identity altogether in what I would consider as an 'identification with the aggressor', they have turned back to embrace their ethnic identity as Hindus, Muslims or Sikhs with a revivalist fervour which is far in excess of their counterparts in the home country. Of course, migration itself plays a significant role in the revival of ethnic identity. Global migrations, tourism and communications confront people in a society with a foreignness of others which is unprecedented in their experience. All over the world our encounters with strangers are on a larger scale, over longer periods of time, with the strangers possessing a higher degree of strangeness, than has ever been the case before. Observations such as 'They think like that', 'They believe this', 'Their customs are like that', inevitably lead to questions which may not have been self-consciously addressed before: 'What do we (however that 'we' is defined) think?', 'What do we believe?' 'What are our customs?' In bringing together of people in closer proximity, the processes of globalization paradoxically increase the self-consciousness which separates and differentiates.

The portraits of loss and helplessness may sometimes seem to be overdrawn. Human beings have a remarkable capacity for adaptation, for creating new communities when old ones must be abandoned, for planting new gardens of love around them where old ones have withered. Yet before fresh psychological and social structures can emerge, there is a period — permanent for some — of apathy, chronic discontent or rebellious rage at those who are held responsible for the loss of old social forms and ideals. Historical and social changes, working through the psychological mechanisms of loss and humiliation, thus lead to a widespread feeling of being a victim rather than an active agent of events which are buffeting the individual and his group. Millions of people become patients in a broad sense, even if temporarily, patienthood being essentially a condition of inactivation. After all, *patiens*, as Erik Erikson has pointed out, denotes a state of being exposed to superior forces from within and without which cannot be overcome without energetic and redeeming help.[8]

Cultural Identity and Cure

The required energy and redemption to restore *agens*, that inner state of being which sanctions initiative and encourages purposeful activity in the outer world, is most often sought through increasing, restoring or constructing a sense of cultural identity. Cultural groups are not only a shelter for those mourning lost attachments but also vehicles for redressing narcissistic injuries, for righting of what are perceived as contemporary or historical wrongs. The question why such 'primordial' group identities as Hindus and Muslims are generally preferred rather than identities based on class, profession or other criteria cannot be discussed here. Perhaps the latter lack an encompassing world view, are impoverished in their symbolic riches and devoid of that essential corpus of myths in which people have traditionally sought meaning, especially at a time when their world appears to have become meaningless.

A core attraction and vital therapeutic action of self-consciously belonging to a cultural community lies in its claim to the possession of a future which, in a state of *patiens*, is felt to be irretrievably lost. To outsiders, this future may appear to be a simplistic perspective on the world such as a promise of restoration of the perfect civil society of the ancestors, what the Hindus, for instance, call *Ramrajya*. It may be the reproduction on earth of a paradise envisaged only in sacred texts. It may be hedonistic enjoyment of more and more goods and services in a heaven presided over by a benign, supply side God. The promise is of a future which 'works'.

The cultural group, which brings the 'primordiality' related to shared myths, memories, values and symbols to the fore, thus assumes a vital healing function. One of its most important aspects is to replace feelings of loss with those of love. This insight into the ways groups work psychologically goes back to Freud who postulated Eros as the vital cohesive force in a group.[9] He believed that the ties of love among members of a group came into existence though their emotional bond with the leader. In more technical terms, members of a group put the same object, the leader, in place of their ego ideal and consequently identify with each other. This shared idealization gives rise to the love ties which are experienced in the feelings of fusion and merger. Experientially, it is a reordering and opening up of the inner world of the individual to include members of his group who, in turn, open up to include him in their psychological space, a mutual affirmation which lies at the heart of love. In cultural groups, the shared ego ideal may not be the figure of a single leader but many historical and mythical figures from the group's tradition, as also its ideals and values, and even the community's social and intellectual traditions.

We are all aware of the profound effect the group can have on the consolidation of a person's 'sense of identity' and in increasing the cohesiveness of his self. Even in individual psychotherapy, we often see that it is not unusual for patients in a state of self-fragmentation to achieve a firmer and more cohesive sense of the self upon joining an organized group. The Nazis are not the only group who turned quasi-derelict individuals into efficiently functioning ones by providing them the framework of a convincing world image and the use of new cultural symbols and group emblems such as shiny brown uniforms. As Ernest Wolf perceptively observes, 'It seems a social identity can support a crumbling self the way a scaffolding can support a crumbling building.'[10]

Psychology *versus* Politics?

Before I look at the construction of the new Hindu identity, I would like to address the objections to a psychological approach to the subject. There are many social scientists and political analysts who would locate the enhancement of ethnicity (cultural identity in my terms) in a particular group not in social psychological processes but in the competition between elites for political power and economic resources. In fact, this has been the dominant explanation for the occurrence of Hindu-Muslim riots and is best exemplified in the work of Asghar Ali Engineer.[11] This 'instrumentalist', as contrasted to the 'primordialist' view I advocate here, has been succinctly formulated by Paul Brass: 'In the process of transforming cultural forms, values and practices into political symbols, elites in competition with each other for control over the allegiance or territory of the ethnic group in question strive to enhance or break the solidarity of the group. Elites seeking to mobilize the ethnic group against its rivals or against the state strive to promote a congruence of a multiplicity of the group's symbols, to argue that members of the group are different not in one respect only but in many and that all its cultural elements are reinforcing'.[12]

Cultural identity, according to this view, is not a fixed or given dimension of communities but a variable one which takes form in the process of political mobilization by the elite, a mobilization which arises from the broader political and economic environment. Brass questions the import of the primary dimensions of ethnicity in the subjective lives of individuals. Most people, he says, never think about their language at all. Millions, both in traditional and modern societies, have migrated to other countries out of choice (or necessity). And though many may have an emotional attachment to their place of birth or ancestral religion, many others have chosen to assimilate to their new societies and have lost all connection to their origins.

Brass's case for the relative insignificance of primordiality appeas to be overstated. Cultural identity, like its individual counterpart, is an unconscious human acquirement which becomes consciously salient only when there is a perceived threat to its integrity. Identity, both individual and cultural, lives itself for the most part, unfettered and unworried by obsessive and excessive scrutiny. Everyday living incorporates a zone of indifference with regard to one's culture, including one's language, ethnic origin or religion. It is only when the zone of indifference is breached that the dimensions of ethnicity stand out in sharp relief and the individual becomes painfully or exhilaratingly aware of certain aspects of his cultural identity. The breaches in the zone of indifference, as happened in the aftermath of Ayodhya, are not only made by momentous external events such as actual or threatened persecution, war, riots and so on. Inner psychological changes in certain stages of the life cycle may also cause these fateful incursions. Thus, for instance, youth is regarded as a period of life when issues of personal identity become crucial, when the conscious and unconscious preoccupation with the question 'Who am I?' reaches its peak. Many migrants who have willingly chosen to thoroughly assimilate themselves into their new societies and appear to have lost all traces of their ethinic origins, are surprised to find that the issues of cultural identity have not disappeared. They have only skipped a generation as their sons and daughters, on verge of adulthood, become preoccupied with their cultural roots as part of their quest for a personal identity.

I do not mean to imply that the instrumentalist approach is without substance. It is also not a monopoly of professional social scientists but is shared by many people in other walks of life. In Indian towns and cities where there have been riots between Hindus and Muslims, I have normally found that 'men of goodwill' from both communities invariably attribute the riots to the machinations and manipulations of politicians pursuing political power or economic advantage rather than to any increase in primordial sentiments. The instrumentalist theory of ethnic mobilization thus becomes an 'instigator' theory of violent conflict among religious groups. In concentrating on the instigators it underplays or downright denies that there are 'instigatees' too whose participation is essential to transform animosity between religious groups into violence. The picture it holds up of evil politicians and innocent masses is certainly attractive since it permits us a disavowal of our own impulses toward violence and vicious ethnocentrism. We all have different zones of indifference beyond which our own ethnocentrism, in some form or the other, will become a salient part of our identity.

The appeal of the instrumentalist or instigator theory, however, is not only because it allows us a projection of the unacceptable parts of ourselves into 'bad' politicians. Its allure is also due to a particular historical legacy of the literary elite in all major civilizations. This legacy devalues non-rational processes — what psychoanalysts call 'fantasy' — which form the basis of the primordial approach. As has been pointed out by others in a different context, the culture of fantasy lacks all meaningful status in the realm of serious public discourse which comprises the discussion of ideas, not of shared fantasies.[13] Fantasy is regarded as primitive, primordial, before reason; it is unconscious as compared to conscious, mythic as compared to scientific, marked by the pleasures of connotation rather than the rigours of denotation. A sensitive, introspective discussion of socially shared fantasies (rather than ideas) as the moving force behind the ideals and ambitions of large groups and communities is generally not possible. Steeped in a long tradition of respect for the culture of ideas, and their own professional role in its production and propagation, the scholarly elite of a society are not easily receptive to the culture of fantasy.

I do not mean to say that the political and psychological, the instrumental and primordial approaches should be viewed in either/or terms. Both the approaches are complementary to each other. Whether it be the history of Hindu-Muslim relations or the analysis of the causes of the riots between the two communities (economic-political versus social-psychological), or the explanation for the basis of emerging religious group identities ('instrumental' interests versus 'primordial' attachments), the arguments are invariably couched in a dualistic either/or mode. This, of course, is a testimony to the strong hold of the Aristotelian and Cartesian ways of thinking on the minds of our modern scholars and other sections of the Western-educated intelligentsia. Like most shared habits, we do not recognize this kind of thing as a mere habit but take it for granted as an unquestioned verity, as the way things 'naturally' are. Complementary thinking does not mean that 'anything goes', in a vulgar post-modernist sense. It has its own definitional constraints and boundaries; for instance, the more incompatible (not outlandish) the explanations for a phenomenon, the more complementary they will be. Complementarity is the belonging together of various possibilities of experiencing the same object differently. The wave and particle theories of light in physics, the primary and secondary processes in psychoanalysis, *mythos* and *logos* as modes of knowledge, are a few of the many examples of complementarity. Forms of complementary knowledge belong together in so far as they pertain to the same object; they exclude each other in that they cannot occur simultaneously. Complementarity is the acceptance of different possiblities and not their splitting and the exclusion of some. To describe a phenomenon complementarily is to reveal its wholeness, to understand its different aspects.[14] None of these aspects is more true than others; each is irreplaceable. In brief, the logic underlying complementary thought is not of an either/or kind but of an 'as well as' variety. Thus without the psychological perspective to complement the political-economic one, we will have only a partial and so dangerously inadequate understanding of the reasons for the success of political formations based on religious mobilization.

Search for Hindu-ness

The instrumentalist approach to ethnic identity, however, makes an important contribution by pointing out that these identities are not fixed and immutable but more or less variable. The self-consciousness of being a Hindu today is not of the same order as at other times in India's history. What is today called 'Hinduism' has emerged through many encounters between dissenting sects professing diverse beliefs and with other, more self-conscious religions, such as Islam and Christianity.

Today, there is a new Hindu identity under construction in many parts of India, especially the northern and central states. It is a process which is undoubtedly propelled by the fact that this identity is also the basis of political mobilization by the main opposition party, the BJP. Created out of a pre-existing though ill-defined and amorphous 'Hinduism', the new identity bears only a faint family resemblance to its progenitors. Indeed, some scholars argue that such sharply differentiated cultural identities as Hindus and Muslims which we encounter today, with their heightened self-consciousness, the kind of commitment they command and the intensity with which these identities are pursued politically, are a creation of the British colonial period. They are not only a product of the colonial 'divide and rule' policies which led to the emergence of 'identity politics', but are also a consequence of the imposition of alien modes of thought on native Indian categories. The political scientist Don Miller remarks: 'By their education, legislation, administration, judicial codes and procedures and even by the apparently simple operation of 'objective' classification, the

215

census, the British unwittingly imposed dualistic "either-or" oppositions as the "natural" normative order of thought. In a multitude of ways, Indians learned that one is either this or that: that one cannot be both or neither or indifferent. The significance of identity thus became a new, paramount concern... an orthodoxy of being was gradually replacing a heterodoxy of beings.'[15]

Leaving the issue of pinpointing the time and place of birth of the new Hindu identity in the late 20th century to historians, an identity which its critics have decried as Hindu nationalism, Hindu militancy or Hindu fundamentalism, we can only observe that this identity selects many of its symbols, myths and images from a traditional stock. The cultural values and forms it endorses have a recognizable ancestry. In its strong links with the past, this Hindu identity is neither wholly new nor completely old. It is constructed, yet also revived; it is a combination of the made and the given. The social and political forces which are self-consciously active in its constructed revival, the *Sangh parivar*, have some truth on their side when they maintain that the elements of this new Hindu identity were always there; it is just that people did not see them before. The question whether those propagating the new Hindu identity are embarked on its construction or merely on its articulation for others does not have a simple answer. The answer depends upon whether the vantage point is of an outside observer or of the insider directly engaged in the process. In any event, the political countering of this Hindu identity will involve the offer of a different *Hindutva* with other images, symbols and myths of the Hindu ethos rather than any abstract concept of secularism which for most Hindus is empty of all psychological meaning.

The Virtuous Virago

To look more closely at the constructed revival of Hindu identity, I have chosen as my text a speech by Sadhvi Rithambra, one of the star speakers for the *Sangh parivar*, the prefix sadhvi being the female counterpart of sadhu. It is reported that Rithambra was a sixteen-year-old schoolgirl in Khanna, a village in the Punjab, when she had a strong spiritual experience while listening to a discourse by Swami Parmananda, one of the many 'saints' in the forefront of Hindu revivalism.[16] Rithambra abandoned her studies and home and joined Parmananda's ashram. Soon she began travelling with her guru to religious meetings in the Hindi heartland and after a while addressed a few herself. Her oratorical talents were noticed by the political leadership of the *Sangh parivar* and after being given some training in voice modulation she was well on her way to become the leading firebrand in the Hindu cause.

The speech I have chosen was given at Hyderabad in April 1991, a few weeks after the general elections for Parliament and many state assemblies were announced. The speech is a standard one which Rithambra has given, all over India to the enthusiastic response of hundreds of thousands of people. The political context of the speech is the bid by the BJP, the political arm of the *Sangh* family, to capture power in some north Indian states in the elections and to emerge as the single largest party in Parliament. In the preceding months, the BJP had determined the country's political agenda by its mobilization of Hindus on the issue of constructing a temple to the god Ram at Ayodhya, his reputed birthplace. The construction of this temple had become an explosive and divisive issue since the designated site was already occupied by Babri Masjid, a mosque built by Babar, the Muslim invader from Central Asia who was the founder of the Mughal dynasty which ruled over large parts of India for over 400 years. There had been much bloodshed five months earlier as many Hindus, the *kar sevaks*, lost their lives in police firing when they attempted to defy legal orders and begin the temple construction, a step which required a demolition or at least the relocation of the mosque. The killings of unarmed Ram *bhaktas* – devotees of Ram – in Ayodhya had led to a spate of riots between Hindus and Muslims in other parts of the country, including Hyderabad, a city with an almost equal proportion of the two communities where the tension between them had over the years regularly erupted in communal violence.

The political context of the speech – temple versus mosque, the abundance of imagery and allusions to the narratives of the epics *Ramayana* and the *Mahabharata* in its text – and the person of the speaker herself, are all replete with symbolic resonances, evocations and associations. They literally reek with a surfeit of meaning that burrows deep in the psychic recesses of the audience, going well beyond the words used as its carriers. Listening to her speak, the earlier question is once again raised: Is she an elite manipulator of Hindu cultural symbols (instrumental theory) or is she an articulator of what many Hindus feel but cannot express (primordialist viewpoint)? The answer is again not in terms of either/or but of the simultaneity of both the processes. Rithambra appeals to a group identity while creating it. She both mirrors her listeners' sentiments and gives them birth. My impression is that the images, metaphors, and mythological allusions of her speech have a resonance for the audience because they also have a resonance for her. This does not imply that the speech is a spontaneous pouring out of her heart. Like an actor she has honed this particular speech through successive deliveries and knows what 'works'. It is not raw feeling but carefully crafted emotion; an epic poem rather than a scream or a shout. Rithambra's power lies less in her persuasiveness on an intellectual, cognitive plane than on the *poetic* (Gr. *poiesis* — a making, shaping) that permeates her speech. It is this poetic which gives a first form to what are for her audience only vaguely or partially ordered feelings and perceptions, makes a shared sense out of already shared circumstances.[17]

As a renouncer of worldly life, a sannyasin, Rithambra conjures up the image of selflessness. Associatively, she is not a politician stirred by narrow electoral considerations or identified with partisan interest groups but someone who is moved by the plight of the whole country, even concerned with the welfare of all mankind. As an ascetic who has renounced all sexual activity, she evokes the image of the virgin goddess, powerful because virgin, a power which is of another, 'purer' world. There is also a subtle sexual challenge to the men in her audience to prove their virility (vis-a-vis the Muslims) in order to deserve her.

The key passages in the text of her speech are delivered as rhyming verses, in the tradition of bardic narration of stories from the Hindu epics. Perhaps people tend to believe verse more than prose, especially in Hindu India where the transmission of sacred knowledge has traditionally been oral and through the medium of rhymed verse. In any event, implicit in her speech is the claim to be less tainted with the corruption of language, a corruption which is widely laid at the door of the politician and which has led people to lose faith in what they hear from public platforms. If Rithambra is a politician, it is the politics of magic where she summons forces from the deep, engaging through coded ideas and ideals the deeper fears and wishes of her Hindu audiences whom she and the *Sangh parivar* are determined to make 'more' Hindu. As I listened to her I was once again reminded of Milan Kundera's statement that 'political movements rest not so much on rational attitudes as on fantasies, images, words and archetypes that come together to make up this or that political kitsch'.

. 'Hail Mother Sita! Hail brave Hanuman! Hail Mother India! Hail the birthplace of Ram! Hail Lord Vishwanath (Shiva) of Kashi (Benares)! Hail Lord Krishna! Hail the eternal religion (*dharma*)! Hail the religion of the Vedas! Hail Lord Mahavira! Hail Lord Buddha! Hail Banda Bairagi! Hail Guru Gobind Singh! Hail the great sage Dayananda! Hail the great sage Valmiki! Hail the martyred *kar sevak*! Hail Mother India!'

In ringing tones Rithambra invokes the various gods and revered figures from Indian history, ancient and modern. The gods and heroes are not randomly chosen. In their careful selection, they are markers of the boundary of the Hindu community she and the *Sangh parivar* would wish to constitute today and believe existed in the past. Such a commemoration is necessarily selective since it must silence contrary interpretations of the past and seek to conserve only certain of its aspects. The gods and heroes are offered up as ego ideals, to be shared by members of the community in order to bring about and maintain group cohesion. Identity implies definition rather than blurring, solidity rather than flux or fluidity and therefore the question of boundaries of a group becomes paramount. Rithambra begins the construction of Hindu identity by demarcating this boundary.

In the context of the preceding year's agitation around the construction of the Ram temple, the god Ram occupies the highest watchtower on the border between Hindu and non-Hindu. Rithambra starts by praising Ram's wife, the goddess Sita, and his greatest devotee, the monkey god Hanuman, who are then linked to contemporary concerns as she hails Ram's birthplace where the *Sangh parivar* wishes to construct the controversial temple and around which issue it has sought a mobilization of the Hindus.

A five-thousand-year-old religion, however, with a traditional lack of central authority structures such as a church and with a diffused essence, has over the centuries thrown up a variety of sects with diverse beliefs. It is Rithambra's purpose to include all the Hinduisms spawned by Hinduism. The presiding deity of the Shaivite sects, Shiva, is hailed, as is Krishna, the most popular god of the Vaishnavas.

The overarching Hindu community is then sought to be further enlarged by including the followers of other religions whose birthplace is India. These are the Jains, the Buddhists, and the Sikhs and Rithambra devoutly hails Mahavira, Buddha and the militant last guru of the Sikhs, Guru Gobind Singh, who, together with Banda Bairagi, has the added distinction of a lifetime of armed struggle against the Mughals. Nineteenth century reformist movements such as the Arya Samaj are welcomed by including its founder Dayananda Saraswati in the Hindu pantheon. The Harijans or the 'scheduled castes', the former 'untouchables' of Hindu society, are expressly acknowledged as a part of the Hindu community by hailing Valmiki, the legendary author of the *Ramayana* who has been recently elevated to the position of the patron saint of the Harijans.

From gods and heroes of the past, a link is established to the collective heroism of the *kar sevaks*, men and women who in their bid to build the temple died in the police firing at Ayodhya. The immortal gods and the mortal heroes from past and present are all the children of Mother India, the subject of the final invocation, making the boundaries of Hindu community coterminous with that of Indian nationalism.

'I have come to the Hindus of Bhagyanagar (Hyderabad) with a message. The saints who met in Allahabad directed Hindu society to either bend the government to its will or to remove it. The government has been removed. On the 4th of April, more than two and a half million Hindus displayed their power at the lawns of Delhi's Boat Club. We went to the Parliament but it lay empty.

The saints said, fill the Parliament with the devotees of Ram. This is the next task of Hindu society.

'As far as the construction of the Ram temple is concerned, some people say Hindus should not fight over a structure of brick and stone. They should not quarrel over a small piece of land. I want to ask these people, "If someone burns the national flag, will you say, 'Oh, it doesn't matter. It is only two metres of cloth which is not a great national loss.'" The question is not of two metres of cloth but of an insult to the nation. Ram's birthplace is not a quarrel about a small piece of land. It is a question of national integrity. The Hindu is not fighting for a temple of brick and stone. He is fighting for the preservation of a civilization, for his Indianness, for national consciousness, for the recognition of his true nature. We shall build the temple!

'It is not the building of the temple but the building of India's national consciousness. You, the wielders of state power, you do not know that the Ram temple is not a mere building. It is not a construction of brick and stone. It is not only the birthplace of Ram. The Ram temple is our honour. It is our self-esteem. It is the image of Hindu unity. We shall raise its flag. We shall build the temple!'

Hindi is a relatively passionate language. Its brilliant, loud colours are impossible to reproduce in the muted palette of English. As the Ram temple takes shape in Rithambra's cascading flow of language, as she builds it, phrase by phrase, in the mind of her listeners, it evokes acute feelings of a shared social loss. The Ram temple then, is a response to the mourning of Hindu society: a mourning for lost honour, lost self-esteem, lost civilization, lost Hindu-ness. It is the material and social counterpart of the individual experience of mourning. In a more encompassing formulation, the Ram birthplace temple is like other monuments which, as Peter Homans perceptively observes, 'engage the immediate conscious experience of an aggregate of egos by representing and mediating to them the lost cultural experiences of the past; the experiences of individuals, groups, their ideas and ideals, which coalesce into what can be called a collective memory. In this the monument is a symbol of union because it brings together the particular psychological circumstances of many individuals' life courses and the universals of their otherwise lost historical past within the context of their current or contemporary social processes and structure'.[18] The temple is the body in which Hindu identity is sought to be, well, embodied.

'Some people became afraid of Ram's devotees. They brought up Mandal.* They thought the Hindu will get divided. He will be fragmented by the reservations issue. His attention will be diverted from the temple. But your thought was wrong. Your thought was despicable. We shall build the temple!

'I have come to tell our Hindu youth, do not take the candy of reservations and divide yourself into castes. If Hindus get divided, the sun of Hindu unity will set. How will the sage Valmiki look after Sita? How will Ram eat Shabri's berries (ber)?** Those who wish that our bonds with the backward castes and the Harijans are cut will bite dust. We shall build the temple!

'Listen, Ram is the representation of mass consciousness. He is the god of the poor and the oppressed. He is the life of fishermen, cobblers, and washermen. If anyone is not a devotee of such a god, he does not have Hindu blood in his veins. We shall build the temple!'

Marking its boundary, making it aware of a collective cultural loss, giving it a body, is not enough to protect and maintain the emerging Hindu identity. For identity is not an achievement but a process constantly threatened with rupture by forces from within and without.

Constant vigil is needed to guard it from that evil inside the group which seeks to divide what has been recently united, to disrupt and fragment what has been freshly integrated. Rithambra addresses the feeling of threat and singles out the political forces representing this threat which must be defeated at the coming battle of the ballot box.

'My Hindu brothers! Stop shouting that slogan, "Give one

---

* Mandal refers to the reservation policy announced by the government of V.P. Singh at the height of the temple agitation. The policy sought to increase reservations in federal and state employment and admission to educational institutions for the backward castes at the expense of the upper castes.
** The sage Valmiki, reputedly a hunter belonging to a low caste, gave asylum to Sita in his forest abode after she was banished by Ram. Shabri was a poor untouchable who fed berries to Ram during his exile.

more push and break the Babri mosque! The mosque is broken, the mosque is broken!!" What mosque are you talking about? We are going to build our temple there, not break anyone's mosque. Our civilization has never been one of destruction. Intellectuals and scholars of the world, wherever you find ruins, wherever you come upon broken monuments, you will find the signature of Islam. Wherever you find creation, you discover the signature of the Hindu. We have never believed in breaking but in constructing. We have always been ruled by the maxim "the world is one family" (*vasudhe kuttumbkam*). We are not pulling down a monument, we are building one.

'Scholars, turn the pages of history and tell us whether the Hindu, riding a horse and swinging a bloody sword, has ever trampled on anyone's human dignity? We cannot respect those who have trod upon humanity. Our civilization has given us great insights. We see god in a stone, we see god in trees and plants. We see god in a dog and run behind him with a cup of butter. Hindus, have you forgotten that the saint Namdev had only one piece of bread to eat which was snatched by a dog. Namdev ran after the dog with a cup of butter crying, "Lord, don't eat dry bread. Take some butter too!!" Can the Hindu who sees god even in a dog ever harbour resentment towards a Muslim?

'Wherever I go, I say, Muslims, live and prosper among us. Live like milk and sugar. If two kilos of sugar are dissolved in a quintal of milk, the milk becomes sweet! But what can be done if our Muslim brother is not behaving like sugar in the milk? Is it our fault if he seems bent upon being a lemon in the milk? He wants the milk to curdle. He is behaving like a lemon in the milk by following people like Shahabuddin and Abdullah Bukhari.* I say to him, "Come to your senses. The value of the milk increases after it becomes sour. It becomes cheese. But the world knows the fate of the lemon. It is cut, squeezed dry and then thrown on the garbage heap. Now you have to decide whether you will act like sugar or like a lemon in the milk. Live among us like the son of a human being and we will respectfully call you 'uncle'. But if you want to behave like the son of Babar then the Hindu youth

---

* Widely regarded as two of the leaders of Muslim fundamentalism in India.

will deal with you as Rana Pratap and Chatrapati Shivaji** dealt with your forefathers." Those who say we are against the Muslims, lie. We are talking of the birthplace of Ram, not constructing at Mecca or Medina. It is our birthright to build a temple to our Lord at the spot he was born.

'We have religious tolerance in our very bones. Together with our three hundred and thirty million gods, we have worshipped the dead lying in their graves. Along with Ram and Krishna, we have saluted Mohammed and Jesus. With *vasudhe kuttumbkam* as our motto, we pray for the salvation of the world and for increase in fellow feeling in all human beings. We have never said, "O world! Believe in our Upanishads, believe in our Gita. Otherwise you are an infidel and by cutting off the head of an infidel one gains paradise." Our sentiments are not so low. They are not narrow-minded. They are not dirty. We see the world as our family.'

Here in the construction of the Hindu identity, we see the necessary splitting that enhances group cohesion. The process involves idealizing on the one hand and scapegoating and persecutory processes on the other. What is being idealized is the Hindu tolerance, compassion, depth of insight and width of social concern. These are the contents of a grandiose Hindu group self which makes the individual member feel righteous and pure. It raises his sense of worth for belonging to this group.

The increase in self-esteem can be maintained only by projecting the bad, the dirty and the impure to another group, the Muslim, with which one's own group is then constantly compared. This process is at the root of scapegoating and as Rafael Moses reminds us, this indeed is how the original scapegoat was conceived of in religion — the sacrificial animal being killed and thrown away with all the badness inside it so that the community of believers could remain pure and clean (like milk, I am tempted to add).[19] Of course, as a good vegetarian Hindu, Sadhvi Rithambra conceives the Muslim scapegoat not as an animal but as a lemon. As we shall see below, the Muslim is not only the object of scapegoating but also the subject of persecutory fantasies in the collective Hindu imagination.

** Popular embodiments of Hindu resistance to Mughal rule.

'Today, the Hindu is being insulted in his own home. The Hindu is not sectarian. How could he be if he worships trees and plants! Once (the Mughal emperor) Akbar and (his Hindu minister) Birbal were going somewhere. On the way they saw a plant. Birbal dismounted and prostrated himself before the plant saying, "Hail mother *tulsi!*"* Akbar said, "Birbal, you Hindus are out of your minds, making parents out of trees and plants. Let's see how strong is your mother!" He got off his horse, pulled the *tulsi* plant out by its roots and threw it on the road. Birbal swallowed this humiliation and kept quiet. What could he do? It was the reign of the Mughals. They rode farther and saw another plant. Birbal again prostrated himself, saying, "Hail father! Hail, honoured father!" Akbar said, "Birbal I have dealt with your mother. Now, let me deal with your father too." He again pulled out the plant and threw it away. The plant was a nettle. Akbar's hands started itching and soon the painful itch spread all over his body. He began rolling on the ground like a donkey, with tears in his eyes and his nose watering. All the while he was scratching himself like a dog. When Birbal saw this condition of his king, he said, "O Protector of the World, pardon my saying that our Hindu mothers may be innocent but our fathers are hard-bitten." Akbar asked, "Birbal, how do I get rid of your father?" Birbal said, "Go and ask forgiveness of my mother *tulsi*. Then rub the paste made out of her leaves on your body and my father will pardon you."

'I mean to say that the long-suffering Hindu is being called a religious zealot today only because he wants to build the temple. The Muslims got their Pakistan. Even in a mutilated India, they have special rights. They have no use for family planning. They have their own religious schools. What do we have? An India with its arms cut off.* An India where restrictions are placed on our festivals, where our processions are always in danger of attack, where the expression of our opinion is prohibited, where our religious beliefs are cruelly derided. We cannot speak of our pain, express our hurt. I say to the politician, "Do not go on trampling upon our deepest feelings as you have been doing for so long."

---

* The reference is to a comparison between the maps of India before and after the partition.

225

'In Kashmir, the Hindu was a minority and was hounded out of the valley. Slogans of "Long live Pakistan" were carved with red hot iron rods on the thighs of our Hindu daughters. Try to feel the unhappiness and the pain of the Hindu who became a refugee in his own country.

'The Hindu was dishonoured in Kashmir because he was in a minority. But there is a conspiracy to make him a minority in the whole country. The state tells us Hindus to have only two or three children. After a while, they will say do not have even one. But what about those who have six wives, have 30-35 children and breed like mosquitoes and flies?

'Why should there be two sets of laws in this country? Why should we be treated like stepchildren? I submit to you that when the Hindu of Kashmir became a minority he came to Jammu. From Jammu he came to Delhi. But if you Hindus are on the run all over India, where will you go? Drown in the Indian Ocean or jump from the peaks of the Himalayas?

'What is this impartiality toward all religions where the mullahs get the moneybags and Hindus the bullets? We also want religious impartiality, but not of the kind where only Hindus are oppressed. People say there should be Hindu-Muslim unity. Leave the structure of the Babri mosque undisturbed. I say, "Then let's have this unity in case of the Jama Masjid** too. Break half of it and construct a temple. Hindus and Muslims will then come together."

'You know the doctors who carry out their medical experiments by cutting open frogs, rabbits, cats? All these experiments in Hindu-Muslim unity are being carried out on the Hindu chest as if he is a frog, rabbit or cat. No one has ever heard of a lion's chest being cut open for a medical experiment. They teach the lesson of religious unity and amity only to the Hindus.

'In Lucknow there was a Muslim procession which suddenly stopped when passing a temple where a saffron flag was flying. The mullahs said, "This is the flag of infidels. We cannot pass even under its shadow. Take down the flag!" Some of your liberal Hindu leaders and followers of Gandhi started persuading the Hindus, "Your ancestors have endured a great deal. You also

---

** The best known mosque located in Delhi.

tolerate a little. You have been born to suffer. Take down the flag. Luckily, I was also there. I said to the leader who was trying to cajole the Hindus into taking down the flag, "If I took off your cap, gave four blows to your head with my shoe and then replaced the cap, will you protest?" This is not just our flag, it is our honour, our pride. Religious impartiality does not mean that to appease one you insult the other. Hindu children were riddled with bullets in the alleys of Ayodhya to please the Muslims. The Saryu river became red with the blood of slaughtered *kar sevaks*. We shall not forget.'

It is true that for the strengthening of cultural identity, a belief of the group members in an existing or anticipated oppression is helpful, if not necessary. Yet for the eight hundred million Hindus who are relatively more advanced on almost every economic and social criteria, to feel oppressed by Muslims who are one-eighth their number, demands an explanation other than one given by the theory of relative deprivation. This theory, as we know, argues that a group feels oppressed if it perceives inequality in the distribution of resources and believes it is entitled to more than the share it receives. There is a considerable denial of reality involved to maintain that the Hindus are relatively deprived or in danger of oppression by the Muslims. Such a denial of reality is only possible through the activation of the group's persecutory fantasy where the Muslim changes from a stereotype to an archetype; he becomes the 'arch' tyrant. As in individuals, where persecution anxiety often manifests itself in threats to the integrity of the body, especially during psychotic episodes, Rithambra's speech becomes rich in the imagery of a mutilated body. Eloquently, she conjures up an India the motherland with its arms cut off, Hindu chests cut open like those of frogs, rabbits and cats, the thighs of young Hindu women burnt with red-hot iron rods; in short, the body amputated, slashed, raped.

'They said, "Let's postpone the mid-term elections till the Hindu's anger cools down." I say, "Is the Hindu a bottle of mineral water? Keep the bottle open for a while and the water will stop bubbling?" It is nine hundred thousand years since Ravana kidnapped Sita and challenged god Ram. But to this day we have not forgotten. Every year we burn his effigy and yet the fire of our revenge burns bright. We will not forget mullah Mulayam* and his supporter Rajiv Gandhi. I have come to tell the young men and mothers of Bhagyanagar, listen to the wailing of the Saryu river, listen to the story told by Ayodhya, listen to the sacrifice of the *kar sevaks*. If you are a Hindu, do not turn your face away from the Ram temple, do not spare the traitors to Ram.

'After the incident on 9th November, many Hindu young men came to me. "Sister," they said, "Give us weapons to deal with mullah Mulayam." I said, "Why waste a bullet to deal with a eunuch?" Ram had become tired shooting his arrows. Ravana's one head would fall to be immediately replaced by another. Vibhishnu (Ravana's brother) said, "Lord, you will not kill this sinner by cutting off his heads. His life is in his navel." My brother Hindus, these leaders have their lives in their chairs (or power). Take away their power and they'll die by themselves. They are only impotent eunuchs. When Ram was banished from Ayodhya many citizens accompanied him to the forest and stayed there overnight. In the morning, Ram said, "Men and women of Ayodhya, go back to your homes." The men and women went back but a group of hermaphrodites, who are neither men nor women, stayed and asked, "Lord you have not given us any instructions." Ram is kind. He said, "In the future Kaliyuga you will rule for a little while." These, neither men nor women, are your rulers today. They will not be able to protect India's unity and integrity.

'Make the next government one of Ram's devotees. Hindus, you must unite in the coming elections if you want the temple built. Hindus, if you do not awaken, cows will be slaughtered everywhere. In the retreats of our sages you will hear the chants of "Allah is Great". You will be responsible for these catastrophes for history will say Hindus were cowards. Accept the challenge, change the history of our era.

'Many say, Rithambra, you are a sannyasin. You should meditate in some retreat. I tell them raising Hindu consciousness is my meditation now and it will go on till the saffron flag flies from the ramparts of the Red Fort.'**

---

* The Chief Minister of Uttar Pradesh where Ayodhya is located and who ordered the firing on the *kar sevaks* on 7 November 1990.
** The symbol of political power in India.

The feeling of helplessness which persecution anxiety engenders reverses the process of idealization, reveals the fragility of the group's grandoise self. The positive self-image of the Hindu – tolerant, compassionate, with special insight into the relationship between the divine and the natural worlds, between man and god — exposes another, negative side: the specific Hindu shame and fear of being cowardly and impotent to change the material or social conditions of his life. Indeed, we should always look closely at a group's specific form of self-idealization to find clues to its particular moment of self-doubt and self-hatred. What a group most idealizes about itself is intimately related to its greatest fear. For the Hindu, the positive self-image of tolerance has the shadow of weakness cleaving to it. Are we tolerant or are we merely weak? Or tolerant *because* weak?

The crumbling self, with its unbearable state of helplessness, demands restoration through forceful action. Rithambra channels this need for *agens* into a call for collective and united action in the political arena. She holds out the possibility of some kind of self-assertion through the coming electoral process where all the persecutory anti-Hindu forces, from within and without the Hindu fold, can be engaged and defeated. With this prospect, the negative self-image begins to fade, the group self becomes more cohesive. The Muslim, too, though remaining alien, becomes less demonic and more human, although still a cussed adversary.

'They ask what would happen to the Muslims in a Hindu India? I tell them the Muslims will not be dishonoured in a Hindu state nor will they be rewarded to get their votes. No umbrella will open in Indian streets because it is raining in Pakistan. If there is war in the Gulf then slogans of "Long live Saddam Hussein" won't be shouted on Indian streets. And as for unity with our Muslim brothers, we say, "Brother, we are willing to eat *sevian* (sweet noodles) at your house to celebrate Eid but you do not want to play with colours with us on Holi. We hear your calls to prayer along with our temple bells, but you object to our bells. How can unity ever come about? The Hindu faces this way, the Muslim the other. The Hindu writes from left to right, the Muslim from right to left. The Hindu prays to the rising sun, the Muslim faces the setting sun when praying. If the Hindu eats with the right hand, the Muslim with the left. If the Hindu calls India 'Mother', she becomes a witch for the Muslim. The Hindu worships the cow, the Muslim attains paradise by eating beef. The Hindu keeps a moustache, the Muslim always shaves the upper lip. Whatever the Hindu does, it is the Muslim's religion to do its opposite." I said, "If you want to do everything contrary to the Hindu, then the Hindu eats with his mouth: you should do the opposite in this matter too".'

After the laughter subsides, Rithambra ends by asking the audience to raise their fists and repeat after her, 'Say with pride, we are Hindus! Hindustan (India) is ours!'

The conclusion of Rithambra's speech complements its beginning. Both the beginning and the end are concerned with the issue of drawing boundaries of the group of 'us' Hindus. Whereas Rithambra began with a self-definition of the Hindu by including certain kind of Hinduisms — as personified by heroes, gods and historical figures — she ends with trying to achieve this self-definition through contrasting with what a Hindu is decidedly not — the Muslim. At the start, the boundary was drawn from inside out; at the end, its contours are being marked off by reference to the 'them', the Muslims, who lie outside the psycho-geographical space inhabited by 'us'. It is, of course, understood that 'their' space is not only separate and different but also devalued. In her enumeration of differences Rithambra cleverly contrives to end at a note which associates the Muslim with certain denigrated, specifically anal, bodily parts and functions.

I have suggested here that the construction/revival of the new Hindu identity in the text of Rithambra's speech follows certain well-marked turnings of the plot which is motivated, energized and animated by fantasy. To recapitulate, these are marking afresh the boundaries of the community, making the community conscious of a collective cultural loss, countering internal forces which seek to disrupt the unity of the freshly demarcated community, idealizing the community, maintaining its sense of grandiosity by comparing it to a bad 'other' who, at times, becomes a persecutor and, finally, dealing with the persecutory fantasies, which bring up to the surface the community's particular sense of inferiority, by resort to some kind of forceful action.

In describing these psychological processes, I am aware that my own feelings towards the subject could have coloured some of my interpretations. This is unavoidable, especially since I am a Hindu myself, exposed to all the cross-currents of feelings generated by contemporary events. My own brand of Hinduism, liberal-rationalist (with a streak of agnostic mysticism) can be expected to be critical of the new Hindu identity envisaged by the *Sangh parivar*. Thus, to be fair (the liberal failing *par excellence*), one should add that the Hindu is no different from any other ethnic community or even a nation which feels special and superior to other collectivities, especially their neighbours and rivals. This sense of superiority, the group's narcissism, its self-aggrandizement, serves the purpose of increasing group cohesion and thus the enhancement of self-esteem of its members. Rafael Moses, reflecting on the group selves of the Israelis and the Arabs, asks: 'And is perhaps a little grandiosity the right glue for such a cohesion? Is that perhaps the same measure of grandiosity which is seen in the family and does it serve the same purpose, thereby strengthening the feeling of specialness and of some grandiosity which all of us harbour in ourselves?'[20]

The *Sangh parivar* cannot be faulted for fostering a Hindu pride or even trying to claim a sense of superiority vis-à-vis the Muslim. These are the normal aims of any group's narcissistic economy. Perhaps we recoil from such aims because narcissism, both in individuals and groups, is regarded with much misgiving. A person who is a victim of his passions, sexual and aggressive, may be pitied and even seen by some as tragically heroic. An individual propelled by narcissism, on the other hand, is invariably scorned as mean and contemptible. Whereas the perversions of sex may evoke sympathy, the miscarriages of narcissism, such as a smug superiority or an arrogant self-righteousness, provoke distaste even among the most tolerant. The question is not of the *Sangh parivar*'s fostering of Hindu narcissism (which, we know, serves individual self-possession), but of when does this narcissism become deviant or abnormal. The answer is not easy for I do not know of any universal, absolute standards which can help us in charting narcissistic deviance or pathology in a group. One would imagine that the promotion of persecutory fantasies in a group to an extent that it resorts to violence against the persecuting 'other' would be deviant. Yet we all know that a stoking of persecutory fantasies is the stock-in-trade of all nations on the eve of any war and well into the duration of hostilities.

One could say that a group wherein all individual judgement is suspended and reality-testing severely disturbed, may legitimately be regarded as pathological. This, however, is an individualistic viewpoint which looks askance at any kind of self-transcendence through immersion in a group. In this view, spiritual uplift in a religious assembly, where the person feels an upsurge of love enveloping the community and the world outside, would be regarded with the same grave suspicion as the murkier purposes of a violent mob. It is certainly true that transcending individuality by merging into a group can generate heroic self-sacrifice but also unimaginable brutality. To get out of one's skin in a devotional assembly is also at the same time to have less regard for saving it in a mob. Yet to equate and thus condemn both is to deny the human aspiration towards self-transcendence, a promise held out by our cultural identity and redeemed, if occasionally, by vital participation in the flow of the community's cultural life.

It is, however, evident that it is this group pride and narcissism which has made it possible for the *Hindutva* forces to offer another alternative vision of India's future to the ones offered by the modernists and the traditionalists. The modernists are enthusiastic votaries of the modernization project although their left and right may argue over which economic form is the most suitable. Both, however, are neither interested in nor consider the question of cultural authenticity as important. The traditionalists, on the other hand, including the neo-Gandhians, totally reject modernity solely on the issue of cultural authenticity. The *Hindutva* forces have tried to offer yet another alternative by reformulating the project of modernity in a way where its instrumentalities are adopted but its norms and values are contested. The pivotal issue for them is not the acceptance of global techno-science and the economic institutions and forms of modernity but their impact on and a salvaging of Hindu culture and identity — as defined by them. It is apparent that such an approach to modernity will have great appeal to the emerging middle classes and sections of the intelligentsia which are neither committed to what I can only call universal modernism nor to a post-modern traditionalism.

The danger of stoking group narcissism, Hindu *garv* in our example, is that when this group grandiosity, expressed in a belief in its unique history and/or destiny, its moral, aesthetic, technological or any other kind of superiority vis-a-vis other groups, is brought into serious doubt, when it feels humiliated, when higher forms of grandiosity such as its ambitions are blocked, then there is a regression in the group akin to the one in the individual. The negative part of the grandiose self which normally remains hidden, the group's specific feelings of worthlessness and its singular sense of inferiority now come to the fore. If all possibilities of self-assertion are closed, there is a feeling of absolute helplessness. The group self feels paralysed while agitated to the extreme, a self-state which must be changed through assertive action. Such a regression, with its accompanying feelings of vulnerability and helplessness, is most clearly manifested in the sphere of group aggression which takes on, overtly and covertly, the flavour of narcissistic rage. As in the individual who seeks to alter such an unbreakable self-state through acts as extreme as suicide or homicide, the group's need for undoing the damage to the collective self by whatever means, and a deeply anchored, unrelenting compulsion in the pursuit of this aim, give it no rest. Narcissistic rage does not vanish when the offending object disappears. The painful memory can linger on, making of the hot rage a chronic, cold resentment till it explodes in all its violent manifestations whenever historical circumstances sanction such eruptions. I am afraid Ayodhya is not an end but only a beginning since the forces buffeting Hindu (or for that matter Muslim) grandiosity do not lie within the country but are global in their scope — they are the forces of modernization itself, of the wonderful attractions and the terrible distortions of the mentality of Enlightenment.

It would also be easy to dismiss Rithambra's — and the *Sangh parivar*'s — evocation of the Hindu past from a post-modern perspective which considers every past a social construction that is shaped by the concerns of the present. In other words, there is no such thing as *the* past since the past is transformable and manipulable according to the needs of the present. Yet as the

French sociologist Emile Durkheim pointed out long ago, every society displays and even requires a minimal sense of continuity with its past.[21] Its memories cannot be relevant to its present unless it secures this continuity. In a society in the throes of modernization, the need for continuity with the past, a sense of heritage, essential for maintaining a sense of individual and collective identity, becomes even more pressing, sharply reducing the subversive attractions of a viewpoint which emphasizes the plasticity and discontinuities of the past. It is this need for a continuity of collective memory, or more accurately of a collective representation of the past in times of rapid change, even turbulence, which the *Sangh parivar* addresses with considerable social resonance and political success.

References

1. Sudhir Kakar, *The Inner World: A Psychoanalytic Study of Childhood and Society in India* (Delhi: Oxford University Press, 1978).
2. Anthony Smith, *The Ethnic Origins of Nations* (Oxford: Basil Blackwell, 1986)
3. For a similarity in the Islamic world see Bassam Tibi, *The Crisis of Modern Islam* (Salt Lake City: Utah University Press, 1988).
4. For brief biographies of the first and second RSS 'supremos' see Walter V. Andersen and S. Damle, *The Brotherhood in Saffron* (Delhi: Vistaar Publications, 1987)
5. The social-psychological effects of modernization have been discussed in E. James Anthony and C. Chiland, eds. *The Child in His Family: Children and their parents in a changing world* (New York: John Wiley, 1978).
6. Quoted from a *Sangh parivar* journal in an article 'Women of Saffron' in *The Times of India*, Feb. 1993.
7. See Tu Wei-Ming, 'Beyond the Enlightenment Mentality', unpublished paper given at the Second International Conference on Global History at Technical University, Darmstadt, July, 1992, 4.
8. Erik H. Erikson, *Insight and Responsibility* (New York: W.W. Norton, 1964).
9. S. Freud (1921), 'Group psychology and the analysis of the ego', *Standard Edition of the Works of Sigmund Freud*, 18, (London: Hogarth Press, 1950).
10. Ernest Wolf, *Treating the Self* (New York: Guilford Press, 1988), 48.
11. Asghar Ali Engineer, ed., *Communal Riots in Post-Independence India* (New Delhi: Sangam Books, 1985), 238-71.
12. Paul Brass, *Ethnicity and Nationalism* (New Delhi: Sage Publications, 1991), 15.
13. See Peter Homans, *The Ability to Mourn* (Chicago: University of Chicago Press, 1991), 309.
14. The clearest description of the concept of complementarity is by Klaus Meyer-Habich; see his "Komplementaritaet", in J. Ritter and K. Gruender (eds.), *Historisches Woerterbuch der Philosophie*, Basel: Schwaber, 1967, IV, 933-34.

15. Don Miller, *The Reason of Metaphor* (Delhi: Sage Publications, 1991), 169.
16. For Rithambra's biographical details see 'Virtuous Virago'. *The Times of India* July 19, 1992 and 'Hindutava by the blood of her words', *The Daily*, July 9, 1991.
17. On the poetic function of rhetoric see, John Shotter, 'The social construction of remembering and forgetting', in D. Middleton and D. Edwards (eds.), *Collective Remembering*, London: Sage, 1990, 124.
18. Homans, *op.cit.*, 277.
19. Rafael Moses, 'The group self and the Arab-Israeli conflict', *International Review of Psychoanalysis*, 9, 1982, 56.
20. Moses, *op.cit.*, 63.
21. Emile Durkheim, *The Elementary Forms of Religious Life* (1912), New York: Free Press, 1965.

INDEX